COMMERCIAL
CATFISH FARMING

Second Edition

COMMERCIAL
CATFISH FARMING

JASPER S. LEE

Professor of Agricultural and Extension Education
Mississippi State University

THE INTERSTATE
Printers & Publishers, Inc.

Danville, Illinois

Library of Congress Catalog Card No. 80-82562

ISBN 0-8134-2156-X

The revised edition of *Commercial Catfish Farming* is dedicated to Lloyd J. Phipps. As the most prolific writer the field of agricultural education has ever had, Dr. Phipps had a tremendous impact on me. He taught me how to discipline myself for writing. He taught me the ground rules for success in my profession. He meant much to me as my graduate advisor and teacher at the University of Illinois. He now stands as a model for professional emulation. Every profession needs individuals who have the capacity of Lloyd J. Phipps—the capacity to be a clear thinker, a productive scholar, and an impeccable leader.

Foreword

This revised edition of *Commercial Catfish Farming* was prepared to incorporate the findings of recent research and new cultural practices in catfish farming. Some aspects have undergone little change since the book was first published. Other areas of catfish culture have changed considerably in recent years. These changes are due to more efficient cultural practices.

The changes in this book are based largely on the findings of research. The research carried out by agricultural experiment stations, other government agencies, private corporations, and individuals is very important in the catfish industry. These research efforts must be continued if the catfish industry is to continue to expand. Without such efforts, the industry will begin to wither and, ultimately, will fail due to a lack of increased efficiency.

The stress in this book is on developing a basic understanding of catfish farming. Sound management principles have been emphasized. The enterprising catfish farmer would do well to keep informed about the industry. He must be a "student" of the industry and must continually strive to learn more in order to be a better manager.

This comprehensive reference on catfish farming can be used by the catfish producer, educator, or interested novice. It is hoped that the revised edition will be as useful as was the original version.

Acknowledgments

Many persons are due appreciation for the assistance provided me over the past decade in writing, developing curriculum materials, and assisting educators in implementing instructional programs in the area of catfish culture. Special appreciation for assistance in preparing the revised edition of *Commercial Catfish Farming* is extended to Thomas L. Wellborn and Mayo Martin. Dr. Wellborn is Leader of the Wildlife and Fisheries Department, Cooperative Extension Service, Mississippi State University. Mr. Martin is Extension Biologist with the Fish Farming Experimental Station, Stuttgart, Arkansas.

Appreciation is expressed to Lynn Holleman for her assistance in typing and arranging the manuscript. Jeanette Evans, my secretary, is acknowledged for her assistance in all of my professional activities.

The revised edition of *Commercial Catfish Farming* would not have been possible without the encouragement and consideration given by my wife, Delene. My son and daughter—Stephen and Susan—have supported my work and have sacrificed family outings while I worked on the manuscript. I thank them for their understanding.

J.S.L.

Contents

1

The Catfish Industry

The commercial production of catfish has emerged in recent years to become a significant new agricultural industry in the United States. One reason for the enormous growth of the industry is the nature of the catfish.

- Catfish meat is high in protein and has an excellent flavor.
- Catfish are very efficient in converting feed to meat. (Producers frequently get 1 pound of gain for 1.5 pounds, or less, of feed.)
- Catfish are well suited for intensive culture. (One acre of pond may produce 3,000 pounds or more of catfish each year.)
- Catfish may be grown on land that will produce few, if any, other crops.
- Catfish farming can produce a high rate of return on investment. (Good management is essential!)

As the number of people on the earth increases, the demand for food likewise increases. And the demand is for economical food that can be efficiently produced!

In recent years attempts have been made to make more efficient use of all available resources. These resources include both freshwater and saltwater. Out of this effort to more effectively utilize freshwater has arisen the catfish industry.

The first significant efforts in catfish culture occurred in the early 1960's. Many of the early catfish farmers were hobbyists and started fish farming because of the novelty involved. Methods of culture have drastically changed. In the 1980's, the successful catfish farmer will have to use scientific management and cultural practices. Many of the larger farmers are hiring persons with master's and doctor's degrees in biology to help manage the farms.

1

Figure 1-1. A Channel Catfish. (Courtesy, Ralston Purina Company)

The catfish industry is larger than just fish farming. Much as grain or cattle farmers are supported by agribusinesses, catfish culture is supported by many nonfarm activities. Feed, chemicals, and equipment must be obtained from off the farm. The harvested catfish are processed in clean, automated plants and marketed through efficient, modern facilities. The industry has become sophisticated and far removed from the back-yard hobby operations of a decade or so ago.

Catfish Farming

The use of catfish for food is not new. Many streams and lakes have served as sources of this food in past years and have offered good sport and enjoyment to many fishermen. The commercial culture of catfish is new and is what this book is all about.

Catfish farming refers to the raising of catfish under conditions which are controlled by man. Fish grown under these conditions should be distinguished from those which grow naturally in streams and lakes and which are known as "wild catfish." In nature, the only association man has with wild fish is at the time of harvest. Such harvest may be by sport fishermen or commercial fishermen and usually involves ordinary hooks, lines, poles, trotlines, or seines.

Catfish farming is much more than merely catching fish. It is a highly technical industry requiring considerable knowledge of how catfish live, reproduce, and grow. It involves careful management of the conditions in which catfish grow from egg to adult. It has introduced a new element into agriculture—that of "fishery biology," which is the science that deals with the origin, traits, habits, and other characteristics of fish. Most agriculturists are not familiar with the peculiar traits of catfish. Their experience has often been limited to cattle, hogs, or row crops. The objective of catfish farming is similar to that of growing livestock; namely, to increase the production of food per unit of land area above the level that would be produced under natural conditions.

Catfish farmers—those who raise catfish—must be aware of the scientific practices that apply to the culture of catfish. They must be able to select the most desirable fish, supply the proper feed, control diseases and parasites, manage the water, harvest and market the fish, and cope with other managerial problems. Catfish grown under these conditions are said to be produced under "intensive culture," which involves obtaining the most favorable production from a body of water through the use of scientific management practices. Catfish produced under conditions of intensive culture also are usually superior in quality to those which grow naturally in streams and lakes.

The terms *commercial catfish production, catfish culture, intensive catfish culture,* and *catfish farming* are often used synonymously. The specific distinction between them, if any, is slight and would center around the word "commercial." In normal usage, commercial means that something is done for profit or sale. In the culture of catfish, there are those who grow them as a hobby and not for profit. In a strict sense, this would not be referred to as

Figure 1-2. Aerial View of a Catfish Farm. (Courtesy, Ralston Purina Company)

commercial catfish culture, but simply as catfish culture. The most commonly used of these terms is *catfish farming* which, as used in this book, refers primarily to a commercial situation but does not exclude the hobby fish farmer. In actuality, catfish have the same cultural needs for growth regardless of why they are grown.

Aquaculture and Catfish Farming

In any discussion of catfish farming the term *aquaculture* is likely to be mentioned. This term can be easily explained. It is derived from the Latin word "aqua," which means water, and "culture," which means to till, to cultivate, and to grow. Simply, aquaculture is to cultivate in water, or to water farm. It involves the cultivation of water so that a marketable crop of fish or other commodity can be produced.

Through aquaculture many different fish and fish-related products are being grown. In freshwater these include, in addition to catfish, trout, minnows, Israeli carp, bass, tilapia, buffalo fish, goldfish, mosquito fish, bluegills, and crayfish. The most important of these are catfish, trout, and minnows. Some efforts have been made to culture water so that a crop of fish is produced in it and another crop, such as Chinese water chestnuts, is produced on it. Considerable research is needed in order to perfect such aquacultural techniques, however.

Early Efforts in Fish Culture

The first efforts in fish culture were probably with species of fish other than catfish. Fish culture began in China around 2000 B.C. Increases in fish culture by the Chinese occurred parallel with increases in silkworms and the manufacture of silk. The excrement of silkworms was important in supplementing the food available to the fish.

Fish culture was introduced into Europe during the Middle Ages when "stewponds" became important. A stewpond was a pond in which living fish were stored. Fish were caught out of streams in the summer and autumn and stored until needed for

Figure 1-3. A Typical Catfish Farm Scene. (Courtesy, Otterbine Aeration)

food in the winter. Occasionally fish would remain in the stew-ponds through the winter and lay eggs in the spring. Thus, the fish reproduced and fish farming was underway. The death penalty could be imposed upon anyone who stole fish from the stewponds.

Catfish farming has become important only in the last few years in the United States. In 1960, less than 600 acres were de-voted to catfish farming. The early settlers from Europe probably introduced some forms of fish culture, primarily with trout. The culture of other fish, primarily minnows to be used for bait, was begun in the 1920's. In the 1950's attention was given to the cul-ture of buffalo fish, bass, crappie, and trout, but these did not al-ways prove satisfactory. Also, at about the same time, minnow production greatly increased. The catfish industry has been able to use some of the knowledge acquired in the culture of other fish. However, the climatic, nutritional, and growth characteristics of fish vary, thereby limiting the amount of transfer of cultural prac-tices from one species of fish to another.

The major commercially produced food and bait fish in the United States now are catfish, trout, crayfish, and bait fish (min-nows). Catfish tend to be produced in ponds in the areas with warmer climates and longer growing seasons. Trout prefer areas with cooler climates and flowing water. Crayfish are almost exclu-sively raised in ponds in areas with warm climates. Bait fish are raised in nearly all areas of the country. All together, about 160,000 acres of land is in commercial freshwater fish ponds in the United States.

Questions and Problems for Discussion

1. What are some reasons for the growth of the catfish industry?
2. What is "catfish farming"? What is its objective?
3. How do wild catfish differ from cultured catfish?
4. Why is catfish farming different from traditional farming, such as rais-ing livestock and row-crop farming?
5. What is aquaculture?
6. Why were stewponds important in Europe during the Middle Ages?
7. In addition to catfish, what other fish are commercially produced in the United States?

2

Determining the Nature
of Catfish Farming

The nature of catfish farming should be thoroughly studied before a catfish production program is initiated. An individual desiring to begin such a program should seek answers to a number of questions, some of which are:

- What are the types of catfish farming programs?
- What are the trends in the catfish industry?
- How can catfish farming fit into an existing farming program?
- What are the risks in catfish farming?
- What legal regulations must be met?
- What education is needed?

Once these questions have been satisfactorily answered, an individual is then ready to seriously study commercial catfish farming. In the past, many people have not realized that catfish farming is a complicated, demanding undertaking. The risks in catfish farming can be high. A good understanding is needed in order to reduce the possibility of significant financial losses. The following areas are discussed in this chapter:

Types of catfish farming programs
Trends in the catfish industry
Fitting catfish culture into an existing farm program
Risks in catfish farming
Legal regulations
Education needs

Types of Catfish Farming Programs

Catfish are produced and used for different purposes. There are five types of catfish farming programs based on use and size of fish grown. These include the production of food fish, fingerlings, broodfish, stockers, and fish for fee-lakes.

Food Fish Production. Catfish grown for human consumption are known as food fish. Most catfish used for this purpose weigh between 1 and 3 pounds. The fish, known as fingerlings, are stocked in the growing facility when they are 5 to 10 inches long. A marketable size can be attained in one growing season after stocking, provided proper feeding and management practices are followed. The growing of food fish is the most important type of fish farming program.

Food fish may be marketed in several ways. Many are sold in bulk quantities to processing plants. Others are sold live or dressed directly to consumers by the grower. The volume sold per consumer in this manner is usually small; however, in terms of the total volume of food fish, direct producer-to-consumer sales have accounted for a sizeable portion of the catfish produced. Food fish may be sold to "live haulers." A live hauler is a person with a hauling truck who buys fish on the farm and functions as a middleman. He may sell the fish to a processor or, as is more often the case, sell them to a fee-lake operator.

Fingerling Production. Fingerlings are small fish ranging from 1 to 10 inches in length. They are used primarily to stock growing facilities for food fish. However, some are grown into broodfish, stockers, and fish for fee-lakes. The successful production of fingerlings requires considerable knowledge of fishery biology. Special knowledge is needed in the areas of (1) managing broodfish so that eggs are produced and fertilized, (2) incubating and hatching eggs (spawn), (3) caring for fry (newly hatched fish), and (4) growing fingerlings to a suitable size for stocking in food fish growing facilities.

Broodfish Production. Broodfish are sexually mature fish kept for the purpose of reproduction. Sexual maturity is reached at various ages, depending upon size and available food. Normally, broodfish are about 36 months of age and weigh at least 3 pounds when first used for reproduction. The number of broodfish necessary so that the required number of fingerlings will be available is estimated on the basis of the weight of female broodfish. Many fingerling producers estimate the number of eggs spawned at 2,000 per pound of female fish weight, even though some spawn many more. Therefore, a 3-pound fish would spawn approximately 6,000 eggs. Broodfish are usually produced in conjunction with fingerlings or food fish. The quantity of broodfish needed as the catfish industry currently operates is not sufficient to merit special broodfish farms.

Stocker Production. The size of a stocker catfish is between that of a fingerling and a food fish. In other words, it is usually between 10 and 14 inches long and weighs less than ¾ pound. This is the least common type of catfish farming program. It is sometimes included with fingerling production. In some areas the demand for stockers is great because they will reach a marketable food fish size earlier in the growing season than will a fingerling.

Fish for Fee-Lakes. A fee-lake is a pond stocked with fish which is open to the public for fishing. Some fee-lakes charge a flat rate per day, others charge a fee based on the number of pounds of fish caught, and still others charge a fee which is a com-

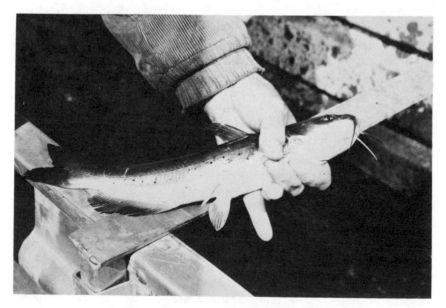

Figure 2-1. A Stocker-Size Channel Catfish.

bination of the two. Operators of fee-lakes may grow their own fish or purchase them from other growers. Frequently, the fish for fee-lakes located near large cities are purchased from other growers rather than raised on the site. Fee-lakes are also known by other names, such as "catch-out ponds" and "pay-lakes." Fish used in such a way may be known as "catch-out fish."

Trends in the Catfish Industry

The catfish industry began in the early 1960's. Since then there has been considerable expansion in acreage, yield, and scientific knowledge about catfish culture. Quality and uniformity of the dressed product have greatly improved. Research has been made into various innovative production systems, such as tanks with circulating water, raceways with flowing water, and multi-storied facilities with elaborate water management and control systems. These production systems were found to have certain advantages and disadvantages. The use of ponds continues to be the predominant production system. In fact, the acreage in ponds increases each year.

Increased Culture of Catfish. The acreage devoted to catfish farming increased from 400 acres in 1960 to nearly 40,000 acres in 1969. By 1976, there were 57,000 acres in catfish ponds. The predictions are that there may be 100,000 acres in catfish ponds by 1990.

Not only has the number of acres increased, but also the yield per acre and quality of the catfish produced have increased. In the early 1960's a yield of 1,000 pounds per acre was considered to be good, but there were no production standards then. By 1969, the average yield was 1,700 pounds per acre. In 1979, the per acre yield had reached 3,000 pounds with the better farmers achieving yields of over 5,000 pounds per acre.

The area with the greatest concentration of production has centered around the region along the Mississippi River, especially in the delta sections of the states of Mississippi and Arkansas. From there, catfish farming has spread east and west and also north to some extent. Catfish are cultured across the southern tier of states from the Atlantic to the Pacific. The movement of catfish culture into the northern and northwestern states has not been so rapid because of the shorter growing season—a result of the colder climate. However, some catfish culture has begun in these states in tanks and raceways where warm water is available from natural springs or industrial heating. Figure 2-2 shows the rank of states by geographical location in catfish culture.

Figure 2-2. Geographical Location of Catfish Culture by Rank of States.

The acreage in catfish culture for some of the major producing states is shown in Table 2-1. The quantity of raceways by length in feet is shown in Table 2-2.

Decline in Wild Fish. Through the years, the primary source of catfish has been wild fish which grew naturally in streams and lakes. The current annual catch of wild catfish has been in the range of 45 to 50 million pounds (whole fish weight) a year for the last decade. In recent years, there has been a slight decline to the lower limit of this range (around 45 million pounds). Wild fish will continue to be a factor in the catfish industry, but the proportion of such fish consumed will decline. Also, it is often felt that the quality of wild fish is inferior to that of cultured fish. Wild catfish make up about one-third of the catfish consumed in the United States.

Importation of Catfish. An important factor affecting the future of catfish farming may be the importation of cultured and wild fish from foreign countries. Currently, around 15 million pounds

Table 2-1

Pond Acreage Devoted to Catfish Farming by States

Rank	State	Estimated Acres in Ponds
1	Mississippi	27,370
2	Arkansas	10,175
3	Alabama	10,000
4	Texas	6,191
5	Louisiana	1,565
6	California	1,200
7	Kansas	988
8	Oklahoma	940
9	Missouri	772
10	Georgia	335
11	Ohio	330
12	Florida	235
13	Kentucky	180
14	North Carolina	75
15	Tennessee	59
16	South Carolina	19
17	Michigan	15
18	Nebraska	14
	Other states combined	69
	Total	60,532

Sources: "National Ecological Science and Technical Bulletin No. 38-9-16," Soil Conservation Service, Washington, D. C., March, 1979, and Thomas L. Wellborn, Jr. "Status of Fish Farming," Mississippi Cooperative Extension Service, March, 1980.

of catfish are being imported each year, primarily from Brazil and Mexico. Some persons feel that the greatest competition for the American fish farmer will come from Brazil, which produces close to 85 percent of all catfish imported into the United States. Frequently the imported fish do not measure up to the quality of domestically produced catfish. Perhaps a brief description of the method used to secure some of the Brazilian fish would be helpful in understanding why it is difficult to maintain quality.

The catfish imported from Brazil are primarily wild fish. They come from the region surrouding the first 50 miles or so of the mouth of the Amazon River and its tributaries. Natives of the area catch catfish from the streams and sell them to buyers who travel up and down the river with ice boats. Frequently several days may pass between the time the fish are caught and the ice boat arrives, thus creating a problem of the fish beginning to deteriorate before they are put on ice.

Table 2-2

Raceway Catfish Culture by States

Rank	State	Estimated Length of Raceways in Feet
1	Georgia	17,440
2	California	1,100
3	Idaho	1,000
4	Tennessee	600
5	New Jersey	100
	Total	20,240

Source: "National Ecological Science and Technical Bulletin No. 38-9-16," Soil Conservation Service, Washington, D. C., March, 1979.

Consumption of Catfish. Farmers must produce a catfish commodity that will be consumed. Production without consumption or with only partial consumption of that which is produced will result in the accumulation of a surplus. Surpluses cause prices to be low, sometimes so low that the farmer cannot make a profit. Many farmers have turned to catfish farming to replace or supplement less profitable crops.

Catfish are ultimately consumed as food by man, but to the fish farmer consumption may come about in several ways. One of these ways is to sell bulk quantities of fish to processors who in turn prepare them for sale as an edible product and market them through various retail outlets. Another way in which consumption occurs to the fish farmer is through fee-lakes. Regardless of the way in which fish leave the farm, consumption has occurred.

Catfish serve as a part of the meat portion of the diet of man. They must compete with beef, veal, pork, lamb, poultry, and other fish. The amount of meat consumed per person in the United States each year is close to 240 pounds. Of this amount, nearly 14 pounds, or about 5 percent, is composed of fish, including seafood. The per person consumption of catfish is about ⅓ pound per year. Some authorities have suggested that in the next few years the consumption will increase considerably.

As a food, catfish are highly nutritious. They contain high amounts of vitamins, proteins, and minerals and little or no saturated fat. They are low in carbohydrates and cholesterol. Catfish have excellent flavor and can be prepared in a variety of ways.

One of the problems facing the catfish farming industry is that of increasing the consumption of its product. Studies have been made to determine the characteristics of consumers and potential consumers. The greatest consumption occurs in the southeastern part of the United States where, in some local areas, several pounds of catfish may be consumed per person annually. The lowest level is in the New England states where lobsters, clams, and other fish products are readily available. The major market for catfish is along the river system of the Midwest and South.

Future consumption of catfish may well rest on the success the industry has in improving the efficiency of production and in creating acceptance of its product. The retail-price level of catfish has often placed them in the luxury category. Yet, they do not have a luxury reputation. Reducing the retail price of catfish will require more efficient production by the farmer and a reduction of the processing, wholesaling, and retailing costs. If costs are reduced the consumption of catfish will likely soar.

The catfish industry has a promotional program aimed at creating acceptance of catfish. Several significant points are currently being promoted. One of these involves establishing catfish as a gourmet food. The problem here is one of prestige. Many persons consider catfish to be scavengers and food for people with low financial means. Catfish have had difficulty competing with shrimp, lobster, and clams which are thought of as being more prestigious. At this stage, the industry's efforts have been somewhat successful in overcoming part of this image.

Another promotional effort that may well increase consumption is the publicity given to the fact that catfish can be prepared in a variety of ways. In the past, practically all catfish were fried with little thought being given to other methods of preparation. Various agencies promoting the consumption of this fish have developed and published new recipes which involve such things as broiling, boiling, baking, barbecuing, and flaking catfish or the making of gumbo.

Other areas in which the industry is working to promote the consumption of catfish include preparing the fish in a convenient form. This may result in a considerable volume being marketed as boneless fillets or catfish blocks, much as haddock or codfish blocks are prepared. Uniformity in quality and portion size is a must for restaurant trade, especially with "name" and fast-food restaurants. Housewives may also prefer the convenience of precooked and ready-to-cook forms of catfish.

Figure 2-3. Attractive Signs are Helpful in Promoting the Consumption of Catfish. (Courtesy, Cajun Catfish Restaurant)

Repeated demand for catfish by restaurant patrons will be based on their receiving a well-prepared product. Seventy percent of all fish sales are made in restaurants. Cooking procedures for catfish need to be given additional consideration. Even in the better restaurants the chefs frequently do not know how to prepare catfish in the most palatable way. Some fast-food restaurants may be more concerned with volume of food sold rather than quality of preparation. Catfish-specialty restaurants have greatly improved in recent years. Formerly, they were almost exclusively second-rate eating establishments, often located in a deteriorating part of town. Today, catfish-specialty restaurants tend to have modern and attractive appearances and are appealing to the general public.

Price Stabilization. Persons contemplating entry into catfish farming should be concerned about the price they will receive for the catfish produced. Prices received will ultimately depend on supply, demand, and general price level as related to the income of consumers. Prices paid for catfish in the past generally have been good. However, there have been times when producers did not receive a price adequate to cover production expenses. Of course, in such a situation it must be recognized that good management of the fish farm is essential.

The number of processors and producers has grown sufficiently for the price received for catfish to begin to stabilize. Future prices will be affected considerably by the image that consumers have of catfish and by the ability of the industry to produce a uniform, quality product.

The demand for catfish for fee-lakes appears to be good. Such outlets for catfish are seasonal in nature and need to be accessible to the general public. This means that locations close to population centers will be in greatest demand. In the past, fish for fee-lakes have often sold for a higher price than those for processing.

The trend in retail prices of all foods has generally been upward. Increased retail prices should indicate increased prices to farmers. However, it should be noted that the prices housewives pay are not necessarily a reflection of what the farmer receives. Food processors, wholesalers, and retailers all receive a share of what consumers pay. With elaborately packaged and prepared products, a greater share of the consumer's dollar goes to the packager and a smaller share to the catfish farmer.

Based on the current trend, the price outlook for catfish is favorable. Prices for catfish must increase if the costs of inputs of production increase. Otherwise, the profitability of catfish will decline. Future prices will ultimately depend on the demand for cultured catfish, the volume of imported and wild catfish available, and the ability of producers and processors to become more efficient. Producers who follow good management practices will likely make greater profits, and those who do not will likely lose money and go out of production.

Fitting Catfish Culture into an Existing Farm Program

Many persons who establish catfish farming operations are already engaged in one or more kinds of farming. Based on past fish-farm failures, farm experience is almost essential. In a recent year, 95 percent of those who entered fish farming dropped out for financial reasons. Nearly all of those who stayed had farmed before. The problem is to determine how the culture of catfish will fit into current farming operations. The desired farm is one which fits together all possible enterprises for the most efficient utilization of resources and produces the largest profit. Several factors should be examined in determining how catfish culture may fit into an existing farming operation. These include capital, labor, land, machinery and equipment, available market, and personal preference.

Capital. The amount of capital needed varies with the size and type of catfish farming operation. There must be provisions for the cost of feed, labor, fingerlings, land, equipment, water facilities, and other essentials. Farms usually have limited capital. Establishing a catfish farming operation will divert money required for the production of other crops. Farmers considering the initiation of a catfish farming program must make a careful analysis of their financial situation and determine the most productive use of their capital.

Labor. The amount of labor required varies with the type of fish farming program. Fingerling production requires considerably more labor than food fish production. Generally, the amount of labor required for food fish production is small, but at certain periods a sizeable amount may be needed. Harvesting requires that sufficient manpower be available to operate equipment and man the seines. Farmers who have fish harvested on a custom basis would not experience great increases in labor requirements at the time of harvest, however. Feeding fish normally requires only a few minutes per acre each day. Fingerling production requires labor to care for broodstock, manage spawning, and tend hatching troughs and fry. Mechanization reduces the amount of labor necessary for many aspects of catfish culture.

Land. The amount of land required for a catfish farm will depend on the size, type, and system of production used. Fingerling farms usually require fewer acres than do food fish farms. Raceway and tank systems of production require less land than do ponds. Also, land is required for roads, service areas, buildings, and, in the case of ponds, levees.

Alternative uses of land should be investigated to determine if a greater profit could be obtained from agricultural enterprises other than catfish. A catfish operation should be of sufficient size to reduce the fixed per-unit costs of production for such things as water wells, pumps, and motors. However, wells may also be used as sources of water for livestock or crop irrigation. Small acreages in catfish ponds may prove to be unprofitable.

Figure 2-4. Labor Is Required to Harvest Fingerlings.

Machinery and Equipment. Some of the machinery and equipment needed for catfish culture can be used with other crops, but most of it cannot. Self-feeders, seines, hauling tanks, and similar equipment are limited to use with fish crops. However, tractors, grass clippers, utility buildings, and some other items may be quite versatile in use. Most of the equipment needed for catfish must be purchased specifically for this crop and is not readily usable with other crops.

Available Market. The location of a suitable market for catfish is probably more of a problem than it is with other crops that have been established a long time. Farmers should have access to a market before going into catfish farming. Distance from a market will enter into the profitability of catfish. Transporting fish long distances can eat away at profits. Also, a large number of growers in an area may flood the market so that the demand and price for catfish will be low. However, the location of several growers in an area may attract a market outlet to the area.

Personal Preference. Personal preference is important. Successful fish growers must have a willingness to learn and to try new ideas. They must be willing to perform work not previously part of agriculture. Some farmers have gone into catfish raising as a novelty or hobby. In the past, others went in with the unfortunate hope of "getting rich quickly." Fish farmers must be willing to let catfish receive a high priority on the farm. Also, because it is a rather new agricultural industry, they must be willing to accept the risks involved.

Risks in Catfish Farming

Catfish farming involves risks, as do other areas of agriculture. However, some of these risks may be a little greater with catfish. Careful management can minimize the possibility of loss. A discussion of several of the main risks with catfish follows.

Loss of Fish. Fish are most often lost from either disease or oxygen depletion in the water. An entire population of catfish can die rather quickly from these two causes. Dead fish are readily observable floating on the surface of the water. Proper management can reduce the likelihood of losses. In a year's time, less than 5 percent of all farmers are likely to have critical problems with diseased fish. (Oxygen depletion and diseases are discussed in other sections of this book.)

Poor Quality Fingerlings. In most agricultural crops, the crop can be no better than the seed planted. With catfish, the fish crop can be no better than the fingerlings stocked. Only healthy, disease- and parasite-free fingerlings should be used. Also, fingerlings should be of uniform size and free of foreign fish.

Water Supply Failure. A dependable supply of good water is essential, especially in raceway and tank systems of culture. Wells need to be constructed so as to minimize the possibility of failure of the water supply. Standby pumps should be on hand in case of pump failure. Electrical generators are needed if the power supply is interrupted. Catfish in high-population culture situations cannot live long without sufficient water.

Pesticide Contamination. The problem of pesticide contamination is very real with catfish. Fish containing excessive amounts of pesticides should not be used for human food. In fact, the Food and Drug Administration may condemn fish containing pesticide amounts above the tolerance level. This risk can be eliminated by using water that is free of pesticides and placing ponds on land that has not been used for crops which were treated with pesticides. The feed of catfish may be a source of pesticide residues from the ingredients and should undergo analysis to determine if pesticides are present. Most commercial feed manufacturers attempt to avoid using ingredients which might contain excessive pesticides.

Harvest Losses. The procedures used in harvesting catfish should result in a minimum of loss. Seines usually harvest a high percentage of the fish crop in good condition. Injured and bruised catfish are usually rejected by processors. Care should be used in harvesting and transporting to insure that a high percentage of the fish crop reaches the market in good condition.

Market and Price Instability. Marketing is a vital segment of catfish farming. Without good markets it is likely that prices will be unstable. The marketing situation is more stable than in previous years, but it is not so well established as it is for other agricultural crops, such as beef cattle and wheat. Prices may suddenly change, and if the change is downward, catfish may become unprofitable, resulting in financial losses. In the past, some processors have had difficulty in making profits and have ceased operations, thus leaving farmers with no available market.

Legal Regulations

Catfish farming is being affected by more and more legal regulations. It is likely that new regulations will be developed in the years ahead. The regulations tend to vary among the states except for those regulations of the Federal government.

The regulations are divided into six areas: worker health and safety, environmental concerns, licensing, transporting fish, fish theft, and provisions for cooperatives.

Most of the regulations on worker health and safety are under the Occupational Safety and Health Administration (OSHA), an agency of the United States Department of Labor. The regulations are designed to promote safe and healthful working conditions. The rules set by OSHA establish maximum levels of exposure for employees to hazards in the work setting. The regulations of greatest impact on the catfish industry deal with noise, eye protection, respiratory protection, protective garments, and safety features in buildings and on equipment. About half of the states have developed programs of their own which are approved by OSHA.

The Environmental Protection Agency (EPA) of the Federal government has regulations to protect the environment from pollution. Air, water, soil, and noise pollution can be produced by the catfish industry. Further, water and soil pollution can have effects upon the productivity and wholesomeness of catfish. The greatest area of concern is water—both its source and its disposal. Water for catfish ponds cannot be obtained from sources which are contaminated with harmful pollutants. Catfish farmers may be required to register their use of water from streams.

Water from catfish ponds, processing plants, and other sources cannot be dumped into streams and lakes if it would upset the natural processes. Water from catfish operations often contains feed particles, fish wastes, and other pollutants. In most cases, some type of treatment of waste water is needed by holding it in lagoons, by removing harmful elements, or by other means. A catfish farmer should consult with the local health department, pollution control board, or other agency on water pollution problems. The disposal of untreated waste water into streams is usually prohibited.

Licenses are required in some states to grow catfish. In other states catfish farming has been defined as an agricultural enterprise, and as such, no licenses are required. Before beginning the culture of catfish, the proper authorities should be consulted to determine if a license is required. Farmers operating retail fish markets may also be required to have a permit, such as that from a health department.

A few states have regulations against the importation of certain undesirable species of fish. Most notable of these is the "walking catfish" which can be a very undesirable pest and is of no economic value to catfish farmers. Persons transporting fish across state lines may be subject to inspection and should attempt to keep trash fish out of the catfish. At least one state, California, has banned the importation of live catfish.

Laws have been passed in some states making it a crime to take or carry away catfish which are grown, managed, harvested, and/or marketed as a cultivated crop. Penalties for conviction may carry stiff fines, imprisonment, or both. Clearly posted "no trespassing" signs erected at designated intervals on catfish ponds may be required.

Catfish farmers in some locations have formed cooperatives to provide feed and other supplies as well as to process and market the fish. State, federal, and local regulations may be involved. Such arrangements have proven very beneficial to some farmers. The services of a competent attorney are needed to assist with such business arrangements.

Education Needs

Catfish farming is a business venture which requires a knowledge of fish culture. The successful catfish farmer will be one who is well educated in how to raise catfish. Some farmers have learned it on their own in the past. Persons having formal education with some specific training in catfish culture will likely be the most successful in the future. Some persons will have college degrees in an area closely related to catfish culture.

Education is needed because of the economic and scientific principles involved. Sufficient education and experience is essential for a good manager. Efficient catfish farmers will understand fishery biology, nutrition, reproduction, diseases and parasites, water management, harvesting, and marketing. They will also understand the economic principles involved. Most catfish farmers cannot stay in business very long without returning a profit.

Since there are many new developments each year, a catfish farmer must strive to keep up-to-date. Workshops, field days, short courses, magazines, and brochures are helpful in keeping aware of the latest developments. Assistance can be secured by contacting the local county agent, vocational agriculture teacher, or land-grant university.

Questions and Problems for Discussion

1. What questions should be answered in determining whether or not to go into catfish farming?
2. Name and identify the five types of catfish farming programs.
3. What have been some trends in the catfish industry?
4. Which area of the United States has the greatest production of catfish?
5. How nutritious is the meat of catfish as a food?
6. What factors are important in determining how catfish farming may fit into an existing farm?
7. What are the main risks involved in catfish farming?
8. What legal regulations may apply to catfish farming?
9. What are some factors on which the future consumption of catfish may depend?
10. Why is education important in catfish farming?

3

Establishing a Catfish Farm

Getting started in catfish farming requires careful planning. The financial needs for establishing a catfish farm are high, and the needed capital must be obtained in order to finance the operation. Unlike the yield of traditional crop and livestock farms which can be predicted early, the yield of catfish is difficult to measure except at the time of harvest. Since they are grown in water, it is almost impossible to determine accurately the number and weight of the fish in a pond. This means that individuals considering fish farming need reliable information in the decision-making process. It has been very difficult to obtain this information; however, recent research efforts have produced findings which are helpful.

To help individuals who might be interested in establishing catfish farms, this chapter presents a discussion of the following:

> Selection of a site for a catfish farm
> Necessary equipment and facilities
> Investment required for catfish production
> Expected returns from catfish farming
> Costs and returns from fingerling production
> Financing catfish farms

Selection of a Site for a Catfish Farm

Many areas of the United States are suited to some type or system of catfish farming. Important factors to consider when determining the suitability of an area for the culture of catfish include soil characteristics, topography, temperature fluctuations, availability of water, and geographic location.

Soil Characteristics. The soil in many areas has the ideal physical characteristics for catfish farming. Ponds must be con-

23

structed in areas where the soil will hold water. Soils, especially subsoils, that are high in clay are preferred. The presence of sand strata, rock fissures, and layers of gravel indicates that the soil may not hold water.

The past history of the use of land in an area should be investigated. Areas with a large percentage of the land in row crops may have high residues of pesticides in the soil if pesticides were used on the crops. The soil should be tested to determine if excessive amounts of pesticides are present. Land with pesticide residues may not be suitable for catfish farming. However, former cropland is usually not covered with trees; thus pond construction costs are less.

The characteristics of the soil in an area may not need to be considered if fish are grown in tanks and vats.

Topography. Topography refers to the features of the surface of the earth, or "lay of the land." Some land is hilly, whereas land in other areas may be nearly level. Pond construction may be simplified by placing a dam across a small valley between hills, but harvesting may be more difficult. It is usually best to locate ponds where the topography is flat or nearly level. Money will be saved by using level land because construction costs are less.

Temperature Fluctuations. Locations with long periods of warm temperatures are best suited for catfish culture. When the temperature of water gets below 45°F, catfish usually cease to eat. Fish that do not eat do not grow. Under normal pond conditions the southern part of the United States is best suited for catfish because longer periods of the year have suitable temperatures for catfish culture; hence the growing season for catfish is longer. In locations in northern areas where heated water is available, the disadvantage of cooler temperatures is largely overcome.

Availability of Water. An adequate supply of good water must be available for catfish farming. Good water is free of pesticides, has a suitable pH of 6.5 to 8.5, and is free of other harmful elements, such as pollution or excessive mineral content. Many farmers rely on water from springs and wells, especially deep wells. Water obtained from streams may introduce trash fish, parasites, diseases, pesticides, and industrial wastes into a fish pond.

Geographic Location. As used here, geographic location refers to the proximity of fish farms to markets. Farms located near markets are most desirable. Fish can be transported long distances in tank trucks with aeration equipment, but the expense of hauling reduces profit. Cost of land and other investments may be less at greater distances from markets, thus offsetting increased transportation charges. Fee-lakes should always be conveniently located for sport fishermen.

Necessary Equipment and Facilities

The culture of catfish, as does the culture of all other agricultural commodities, requires certain equipment and facilities. Some of the equipment used with other agricultural enterprises can be adapted for use with catfish farming. However, most of the needed equipment is limited to use with fish. The equipment required is new and somewhat different from that with which the traditional row-crop or livestock farmer is familiar. However, farmers who have produced minnows and other fish crops may find the necessary equipment to be similar.

The equipment and facilities should be especially suited for fish culture. These needs will vary with the type of fish farming program. For example, the needs of fingerling producers vary from

Figure 3-1. Vats Equipped with Aerators May Be Needed on Some Catfish Farms.

the needs of food fish producers. A summary of the equipment and facilities needed for the different types of programs follows.

Equipment and Facilities for Producing Food Fish. The basic facility needed for the production of food fish is a structure to hold or manage water. Ponds have been most common; however, raceways, vats, and tanks are being used to some extent and will likely increase in use. The size, arrangement, and cost of ponds may vary considerably. Water in ponds is relatively free of movement except for that caused by wind, incoming water, and artificial agitation. Raceways are constructed so that the water flows through them. The flow may be caused by the natural movement of streams or by the use of pumps which add water at one end and remove it at the other. Vats are most often used as temporary holding facilities for food fish, but some are used as fish growing structures. They are usually constructed of concrete and contain water which is made to flow or which is agitated. Tanks are usually round or rectangular and utilize considerable water flow. They may be stocked at high population densities. The amount of fish grown per volume of water is less in ponds than in the other water structures. This is because water in ponds is not so easily controlled. However, the cost of constructing and maintaining ponds is usually less per volume of water.

Many fish farmers use deep wells as sources of water. Others attempt to secure water from streams or rely on excess water from rainfall which runs into ponds. The best source of water is a deep well. Securing water from other sources results in risking the presence of pesticide residues. Water should be tested to determine if pesticide residues are present.

Drainage systems are needed to carry away excess water and to aid in draining ponds. These may consist of ditches or large pipes. They should be constructed to permit the movement of tractors for mowing and spraying to control weeds.

Many fish farmers find that they need small storage or utility buildings, feed storage bins, and related facilities. Such facilities are usually constructed as needed, depending upon the size of the fish farm.

Various equipment for hauling, feeding, and harvesting is needed. Hauling equipment usually includes trucks with tanks and attached aeration equipment. Feeding equipment may include automatic self-feeders, power blowers that blow feed out into the water, and other equipment for handling and hauling feed. Harvesting equipment may include seines, seine haulers, fish graders, seine barges, and truck- or tractor-mounted power booms. Farmers who have their fish harvested on a custom basis do not need harvesting equipment.

Some farmers produce fish in cages placed in ponds or streams. Cages are large wire baskets which float in the water. Their use has not always proved satisfactory.

Other equipment that food fish producers may need includes boats, motors, boat trailers, water-testing kits, tractors, mowers, and trucks. Farmers who operate retail fish markets will need holding vats, cleaning equipment, refrigeration facilities, scales, and other equipment necessary for operating a market.

Equipment and Facilities for Producing Fingerlings. Fingerling producers need equipment that is especially suited for handling broodfish and fingerlings. Normally, fingerling production will require some of the same equipment as food fish. Farmers involved with two or more types of programs can use some of the same equipment with each type.

A major factor affecting equipment needs is the system of spawning used. Most fingerling producers use pond spawning and artificial hatching. Holding ponds are needed for broodfish. Spawning ponds are needed during the spawning season. Spawning pens may be used in the ponds. Spawning nests are a must. Hatching facilities will vary, but generally include troughs with paddle agitation. Rearing ponds are required for growing fry into fingerlings. Dip nets, seines, hauling tanks, aerators, scales, and water-test kits are needed. Vats may be needed for holding fingerlings. Graders are necessary to insure that fingerlings are sold or stocked in lots of uniform size.

Equipment and Facilities for Producing Broodfish. Most of the equipment and facilities needed in broodfish production may also be used with the other types of catfish farming. Broodfish operations are usually not so large as fingerling and food fish operations. Producers of fingerlings often raise their own broodfish. Ponds, seines, dip nets, hauling tanks with aerators, feeding equipment, and miscellaneous other equipment may be required.

Equipment and Facilities for Producing Stockers. Stocker catfish are little more than overgrown fingerlings. Therefore, the equipment and facilities needed are similar to those needed for producing fingerlings, with the exception of hatching and spawning facilities.

Equipment and Facilities for Operating Fee-Lakes. In addition to some of the normal equipment and facilities required for handling fish, fee-lakes require some different equipment. Fee-lakes must be made convenient and comfortable for the fishing public. Attractiveness is important. Picnic tables, rest rooms, drinking water, rental boats, bait and tackle shops, fish-cleaning facilities, and water safety equipment are but a few of the items needed.

Ponds should be constructed to cater to the sport fisherman. Shade should be available near the water. Boat ramps with ready access by automobiles should be provided (if boats are permitted in the pond). Fishing piers and platforms that extend out into the water may be desirable.

Investment Required for Catfish Production

The financial investment required to go into catfish farming varies with the type of fish to be produced and the system of production to be used. Every farm presents a different situation. Catfish farms may be large or small and they may produce combinations of other crops and livestock. All of the characteristics of a particular farm must be considered to determine the financial requirements for catfish farming.

Initial Costs. The purchase of land and the establishment of the water facility are the major initial costs. Land includes more than the solid portion of the earth or soil. It includes streams and lakes, natural forest, minerals, sunshine, temperature, rainfall, wild fruits, and wildlife, including wild fish. The amount of financial investment required for land will depend on the presence of these features and on improvements that have been made. Locations relative to towns, major highways, and other desirable features will also influence the outlay required. Land for catfish farming may be obtained by lease or purchase.

The most common water facilities are ponds and raceways. Some farms also have vats, tanks, and troughs, depending upon the production system used. Also included as initial costs are water wells, pumps, and pipe systems.

The cost of ponds is affected by several factors including size, shape, lay of the land, and amount of timber that must be removed prior to construction. Small ponds cost more per acre to build than do large ponds. A square pond is more economical to build than is a rectangular pond. However, fish are more easily harvested in a rectangular pond. Lay of the land influences the amount of work which must be done to smooth the bottom of the pond. Construction costs of ponds may range from $400 to $1,500, or more, per acre.

Raceways usually cost considerably more to construct than ponds per volume of water. However, the level at which fish are stocked is greater in raceways, which means that less water area is needed to produce the same amount of fish.

Another initial cost that requires a sizeable investment is the establishment of a water supply. This usually means drilling a deep well and purchasing a pump and motor. Cost of water wells varies with depth and size. Using shallow wells is questioned because of the presence of traces of pesticide residues in water from such wells. Cost of a well, pump, and motor may range from $4,000 to $30,000.

Initial costs also include storage buildings, hauling trucks and tanks, vats, feed bins, self-feeders, roadside markets, dressing equipment (if used), and other equipment that will last indefinitely. Facilities of this nature will add considerably to the initial cost of catfish farming. Farmers raising fingerlings must also include the costs of broodfish, spawning equipment, and hatchery facilities.

Table 3-1

Amount of Financial Investment Required
to Establish a Small Catfish Farm

(Two 5-Acre Watershed Ponds on
Rolling Land in a Rural Area)

Cost of land	$2,400.00
Cost of pond construction	9,785.00
Equipment	2,270.49
Trucking costs	468.75
Total	$14,924.24

Source: "Budgeting for Selected Aquacultural Enterprises," Bulletin 495. Auburn, Alabama: Agricultural Experiment Station, 1977.

Table 3-2

Amount of Financial Investment Required
to Establish Larger Catfish Farms

(Land in Mississippi River Delta)

	Farm Size		
Item	160 Acres (Eight 20-Acre Ponds)	320 Acres (Sixteen 20-Acre Ponds)	640 Acres (Thirty-two 20-Acre Ponds)
Land	$ 85,086	$168,606	$335,646
Pond construction	68,316	129,778	259,043
Water wells and drainage pipes	32,150	64,300	128,600
Feeding and feed storage equipment	6,020	7,920	13,940
Miscellaneous equipment	85,130	104,765	150,935
Total	$276,702	$475,369	$888,164

Source: "An Economic Analysis of Producing Pond-Raised Catfish for Food in Mississippi," Bulletin 870. Mississippi State: Mississippi Agricultural and Forestry Experiment Station, 1978.

A portion of the amount for initial costs should be figured as a part of the annual fixed costs so that a realistic financial summary may be prepared.

Annual Fixed Costs. Annual fixed costs include costs which are sometimes overlooked by persons contemplating fish farming. Interest, amortization payments (amounts for repayment of borrowed money), property taxes, insurance, and depreciation are the major annual fixed costs. Initial expenditures for ponds, wells, and other facilities are usually amortized for 10 to 30 years. A loan is amortized by repaying a portion of it at regular intervals, such as once each year. Loan payments for catfish farmers are usually arranged to be due shortly after harvest, often in the late fall or winter.

Variable Production Costs. Costs that vary with the number of catfish produced are known as variable production costs. These include items such as fingerlings, feed, chemicals, and fuel to operate equipment; these are sometimes known as "out-of-pocket" costs. The most significant production costs are feed, fingerlings, and harvesting. Cost of fingerlings varies with size and quality and may fluctuate from year to year. Fingerlings often sell for ½ to 1 cent per inch of length. When supply is short fingerlings may sell for 1 cent or more per inch.

Another major item of cost is feed. The price of commercially prepared feed for catfish has been considerably more than the cost of feed for other farm animals. A big advantage is that catfish have good feed conversion ratios. Many farmers are able to get a pound of growth from slightly less than 2 pounds of feed. It is anticipated that the cost of feed will decline and become a smaller cost item in catfish culture. Persons considering going into catfish farming should determine the cost of feed from local feed mills.

Table 3-3

Amount of Financial Investment to Establish
a Ten-Segment[1] Raceway System

Land	$ 3,000
Construction	20,520
Equipment	800
Trucking costs	625
Total	$24,945

[1]A segment is 100 feet long and 24 feet wide.

Source: "Budgeting for Selected Aquacultural Enterprises," Bulletin 495. Auburn, Alabama: Agricultural Experiment Station, 1977.

Harvesting may be done by the fish farmer himself or by a custom operator. Larger farms can more nearly justify the expense of harvesting equipment than can smaller farms. In many communities one or two men may own the harvesting equipment and harvest the fish of all farmers. Charges for custom harvesting may vary, depending upon how the labor is obtained and paid. Many fish farmers estimate that it costs 3 cents per pound to harvest fish.

Expected Returns from Catfish Farming

Returns from the pond production of food catfish are related to a number of factors, including the production system that is used. The two basic systems are single cropping and multiple cropping. Single cropping means that the pond is stocked and harvested one time a year. The usual procedure is for fingerlings to be put in the pond in the early spring and harvested that fall.

Figure 3-2. Food Fish Being Harvested. (Courtesy, Ralston Purina Company)

Multiple cropping involves year-round production. The ponds are stocked, selectively harvested, and restocked, with harvesting and stocking occurring at intervals for several years. The time of a partial harvest depends on the size of the fish. The number of fish restocked depends upon the number removed during partial harvest. Multiple cropping tends to make better use of facilities and labor throughout the year.

The returns from catfish farming may be given as "gross return" or "net return." It is important that distinction be made between them. Gross return refers to the amount received for catfish when sold. It is simply the number of pounds of catfish sold multiplied by the price received per pound. For example, the gross return from 2,000 pounds of catfish when sold for 50 cents per pound would be $1,000. Costs of feed, wages, and other items are not considered in computing gross returns.

Net return, commonly called profit, refers to the amount of money remaining after all costs of production have been paid. It is determined by subtracting all of the costs of growing and harvesting fish from the gross return. Costs that should be included in computing net return are those for land, machinery and equipment, fingerlings, interest on borrowed money, feed, chemicals, labor, harvesting, and hauling.

Table 3-4

Costs and Returns from a Small Catfish Farm

(Two 5-Acre Watershed Ponds on Rolling Land
with Single Cropping—One Year)

Variable Costs

Fingerlings (8 in. @ 8¢/each, 2,525 per acre)	$ 2,020.00
Feed	4,993.75
Trucking	150.00
Disease control	100.00
Algae/weed control	6.00
Parasite control	16.00
Maintenance	19.20
Aeration	10.00
Seasonal labor	79.20
Miscellaneous expenses	15.00
Interest on operating capital (9% on $7,409.15)	333.41
Operator's labor (170.75 hrs.)	375.65
Total variable costs	$ 8,118.21

Fixed Costs

Land tax	13.50
Depreciation	391.50
Loan (interest)	1,319.19
Total fixed costs	$ 1,724.19
Total Variable and Fixed Costs	$ 9,842.40
Receipts (25,000 lb. marketable fish)	$11,250.00
Net Returns	$ 1,407.60

Source: "Budgeting for Selected Aquacultural Enterprises," Bulletin 495. Auburn, Alabama: Agricultural Experiment Station, 1977.

Data on returns from catfish farming should be carefully studied to determine if the amounts given refer to gross return or to net return. Also, the costs used in determining net return should include both fixed costs and variable costs.

Studies of the returns from catfish have shown that considerable variation exists from one farm to another. The most crucial return is the net return since it is the profit or the amount received for the fish after the costs of production have been deducted. Net return varies with the pounds of fish produced per acre. Farmers producing 1,000 pounds of fish per acre probably would not show

Table 3-5

Costs and Returns from a Small Catfish Farm

(Two 5-Acre Watershed Ponds on Rolling Land
with Multiple Cropping—One Year)

Variable Costs	
Fingerlings (8 in. @ 8¢/each, 75,750)	$ 6,060.00
Feed	13,733.40
Trucking	450.00
Disease control	300.00
Algae/weed control	12.00
Parasite control	48.00
Maintenance	38.40
Aeration/pumping	116.80
Seasonal labor	237.60
Miscellaneous expenses	45.00
Interest on operating capital	999.46
Operator's labor	1,054.90
Total variable costs	$23,095.56
Fixed Costs	
Land tax	$ 27.00
Depreciation	1,115.00
Loan (interest)	3,351.97
Total fixed costs	$ 4,493.97
Total Variable and Fixed Costs	$27,589.53
Receipts (68,750 lb. marketable fish)	$31,875.00
Net Returns	$ 4,285.47

Source: "Budgeting for Selected Aquacultural Enterprises," Bulletin 495. Auburn, Alabama: Agricultural Experiment Station, 1977.

a profit. Farmers producing above this level, for example, 1,500 or 2,000 pounds, would be more likely to show a profit.

The greatest returns will be to farmers who have a greater number of acres in catfish farming, provided sound management practices are followed. Likewise, in the case of a decline in price, the larger farmers stand to lose more money. Also, farmers with large acreages and low yield per acre stand to lose more money than do farmers with smaller acreages in catfish.

The price of catfish is closely related to the returns that can be expected. Prices vary with season and location of farm. Many catfish have sold for 60 to 75 cents per pound, live weight. Prices paid by processors usually range between 50 to 60 cents per pound. Prices may be less in some locations in the future.

Table 3-6

Estimated Production and Returns from Larger Catfish Farms

Farm Size					
160 Acres (Eight 20-Acre Ponds)		320 Acres (Sixteen 20-Acre Ponds)		640 Acres (Thirty-Two 20-Acre Ponds)	
Pounds Produced	Gross Returns (@ 60¢/lb.)	Pounds Produced	Gross Returns (@ 60¢/lb.)	Pounds Produced	Gross Returns (@ 60¢/lb.)
655,785	$393,471	1,323,611	$794,166	2,653,243	$1,591,945

Source: Adapted from "An Economic Analysis of Producing Pond-Raised Catfish for Food in Mississippi," Bulletin 870. Mississippi State: Mississippi Agricultural and Forestry Experiment Station, 1978.

Farmers contemplating entry into catfish culture need to determine how to use land for the greatest profit. Much of the land used for catfish culture is suited for other crops. Alternate uses of land need to be considered. Some farmers have received greater returns from catfish than from agronomic crops, such as rice and soybeans. Other farmers are rotating rice, catfish, and soybeans on the same land. Such a rotation yields greater returns from the agronomic crop because the fish excrement and unconsumed feed increases the nutrient level of the soil. Examples of returns from different sizes and types of fish farms are shown in Tables 3-4, 3-5, and 3-6.

Costs and Returns from Fingerling Production

The quality of food catfish is closely related to the quality of the fingerlings used to stock growing ponds. Some catfish farmers raise their own fingerlings. Others purchase them from fingerling farmers. Whether fingerlings are purchased or raised, catfish farmers need information about the costs and returns in raising fingerlings.

To get started producing fingerlings requires considerable investment. Ponds, pumps, vats, hatchery equipment, broodfish, harvesting equipment, and other items are needed. Table 3-7 summarizes the costs for establishing 66-acre and 134-acre fingerling farms.

Table 3-7

Estimated Costs in Establishing Fingerling Farms

Item	66-Acre Farm[1]	134-Acre Farm[1]
Land	$ 80,000	$160,000
Levee construction	48,946	93,006
Gravel	13,371	25,770
Vegetative cover	352	624
Plumbing	18,910	32,660
Wells and pumps	25,055	50,110
Vathouse	9,219	9,219
Hatchery/storage building	15,000	15,000
Broodfish	2,208	4,800
Hatchery equipment	3,500	4,600
Feeding equipment	2,410	2,410
Harvesting equipment	1,798	1,798
Hauling tank	1,150	1,150
Truck	7,650	7,650
Pickup	4,500	4,500
Tractor	7,300	7,300
Mower	1,000	1,000
Miscellaneous	1,846	1,846
Total	$244,215	$423,443

[1]These are acres of surface water in ponds.

Source: "Costs and Returns of Producing Catfish Fingerlings," Bulletin 831. Fayetteville: University of Arkansas, November, 1978.

Once a fingerling farm is established, there are certain operating costs. These include feed, labor, maintenance of facilities, transportation, chemicals, electricity, and other items. Table 3-8 presents a summary of the annual operating costs for 66-acre and 134-acre fingerling farms.

Returns from fingerlings can vary considerably. On a 66-acre farm that produces 1,500,000 fingerlings a year, the estimated gross returns would be $150,000 at 10 cents per fingerling. This represents a net return of $25,198. On a 134-acre farm that produces 3,024,000 fingerlings a year, the estimated gross returns would be $302,400, or a net return of about $93,757. These returns would be made under ideal conditions, and each fingerling farmer would need to carefully assess the potential of the particular farm.

Table 3-8

Estimated Annual Operating Costs for Fingerling Farms

Item	66-Acre Farm[1]	134-Acre Farm[1]
Feed	$59,878	$106,220
Electricity	2,586	5,529
Labor (for harvest)	710	1,419
Maintenance		
Reservoir	157	298
Feed equipment	60	60
Vathouse/hatchery	72	72
Well-pump-motor	188	376
Transportation	1,305	1,800
Tractor and operation	980	1,960
Chemicals and drugs	1,630	3,475
Other	300	600
Interest	3,366	5,344
Total	$71,232	$127,153

[1]These are acres of surface water.

Source: "Costs and Returns of Producing Catfish Fingerlings," Bulletin 831. Fayetteville: University of Arkansas, November, 1978.

Financing Catfish Farms

Adequate financing must be available for the initial outlay to establish a catfish farm and for the operational costs of production. A few farmers may have the necessary capital in reserve, but most of them depend upon outside sources for financial assistance.

Table 3-9

Estimated Annual Operating Costs for Larger Catfish Farms

	Farm Size		
Item	160 Acres (Eight 20-Acre Ponds)	320 Acres (Sixteen 20-Acre Ponds)	640 Acres (Thirty-two 20-Acre Ponds)
Repairs and maintenance	$ 7,427	$ 10,983	$ 16,193
Vegetative cover	712	1,235	2,464
Water wells and pipes	964	1,929	3,858
Feeding equipment	404	499	903
Disease, parasite, and			
weed control	123	123	123
Harvesting equipment	703	703	703
Miscellaneous equipment	4,521	6,494	8,142
Fuel	13,635	25,475	50,657
Pumping	9,196	18,116	36,305
Power, transportation,			
feeding, harvest, etc.	4,439	7,359	14,352
Chemicals	2,093	4,135	7,475
Fingerlings	33,984	68,592	137,495
Feed	142,419	287,479	575,303
Labor			
Management	20,000	20,000	32,000
Hired (full-time)	20,000	26,000	32,000
Hired (for harvest)	1,818	3,622	7,333
Interest on operating capital	8,045	14,869	28,616
Total	$270,483	$497,613	$953,922

Source: "An Economic Analysis of Producing Pond-Raised Catfish in Mississippi," Bulletin 870. Mississippi State: Mississippi Agricultural and Forestry Experiment Station, 1978.

Sources of Financing. An improved capital-lending structure for catfish farming has become established in recent years. Most of the regular agricultural lending agencies are used by catfish farmers. However, the receptivity of such agencies to requests for capital may vary widely, depending on the local situation. Sources of credit have included private individuals, local commercial banks, life insurance companies, the Farmers Home Administration, and agencies operating under the supervision of the Farm Credit Administration. The Farm Credit Administration includes the federal land-bank system, federal intermediate credit banks, production credit associations (PCA), and banks for cooperatives. In some locations, the production credit associations have been the most active agencies in providing assistance for catfish farming.

A few lending agencies have aquaculture loans. Such loans may be used to feed, tend, harvest, and perform other activities associated with catfish farming.

The Farmers Home Administration (FmHA) provides a variety of loans. These include farm-ownership loans, operating loans, emergency loans, economic-emergency loans, soil and water loans, recreational loans, business and industrial loans, resource conservation and development loans, and farm labor housing loans. Each of these has some special application to catfish farming. Information on the loans may be obtained from the local office of the FmHA, and there are 1,800 local offices in the United States.

Types of Credit. Three types of credit are available for catfish farming: short-term, intermediate, and long-term. Short-term loans provide operating capital to cover production costs. The duration of short-term loans is usually one year or less. Such loans are used to purchase feed, chemicals, and other production inputs. Repayment is usually scheduled to coincide with the marketing of the fish crop.

Intermediate loans are for periods of time longer than one year and usually not exceeding seven years. These loans are for developing water facilities and for purchasing equipment. They are usually arranged so that the annual payments come due about the time the fish are harvested. Collateral may include equipment, fish, and first mortgages on improved real estate.

Long-term loans run for a number of years and are most often used to purchase land. Collateral may include first mortgages on other real estate as well as on the land being purchased.

Factors Considered in Making Loans. Lending agencies have criteria for screening applications for loans. All agencies do not use the same measures; however, most utilize some of the following types of information:

1. Character.—This includes the moral character, dedication, reputation, honesty, and health of the person seeking the loan.
2. Management ability.—This refers to a satisfactory record of earnings and profits during previous years. Often, the

available supply of labor on a farm is a consideration in making a loan.

3. Financial ability.—This includes the net worth of a person as well as whether or not progress is being made toward a sound financial position.

4. Repayment ability.—This refers to the ability of a farmer to repay borrowed capital. All lending agencies look at a farmer's previous record to determine if loans have been repaid as scheduled.

5. Purpose of loan.—A request for credit must be justifiable. Loans should be secured only when needed.

6. Collateral.—Lending agencies usually take a lien, or legal claim, on a farmer's property as security in the repayment of a loan. Catfish farmers have two kinds of collateral: primary and secondary. Primary collateral includes fish or any other income-producing asset. The sale of primary collateral is to be the source of the money for repaying the loan. Secondary collateral includes items which are not a source of money for repayment of the loan. It includes equipment, land, trucks, and anything else to back up the fish.

Tables 3-4, 3-5, and 3-9 contain information about the annual financial operating costs for various sizes and systems of catfish farms.

Questions and Problems for Discussion

1. What four areas should be studied in deciding whether or not to establish a catfish farm?
2. What factors should be considered in selecting a site for a catfish farm?
3. What facilities and equipment are required for producing food fish? Fingerlings?
4. What are the major initial costs for catfish farming?
5. What are some annual fixed costs in catfish farming?
6. What are the major variable production costs in catfish farming?
7. What are the basic pond production systems?
8. Distinguish between gross return and net return from catfish farming.
9. What types of credit may be needed in catfish farming?
10. What factors do lending agencies consider in making catfish production loans?

4

Determining the Biology of Catfish

A knowledge of the biology of catfish can be of value to farmers. It helps them to understand the importance of water quality, nutrition, and disease control, among other things. Many similarities exist between catfish and other animals, such as livestock, and yet there are great differences. There are even differences among species of catfish.

Some catfish grow to be large fish weighing 100 pounds or more. Others may never grow larger than 5 pounds. Some catfish are colorful and have spots. Others are drab and have no spots. In the identification of catfish, it is helpful to remember that all of them are covered with a thick, leathery skin and that all of them have barbels about the mouth. This is in contrast with most other fish which have scales and no barbels.

This chapter presents the following areas of catfish biology:

> External parts of catfish
> Body functions of catfish
> Stages of growth of catfish
> Locomotion
> Classification of catfish
> Identification of common species
> Species used for fish farming

External Parts of Catfish

All catfish, regardless of species, have essentially the same major external parts. The shape, size, and location of these parts may vary somewhat from one species to another. The body of all catfish can be divided into three sections: head, trunk, and tail. The head extends to the hindmost part of the operculum (gill cover) where it joins the trunk. The trunk is the middle section of the body and extends from the operculum to the anus. The portion behind the anus is the tail. Figure 4-1 shows the locations of these sections.

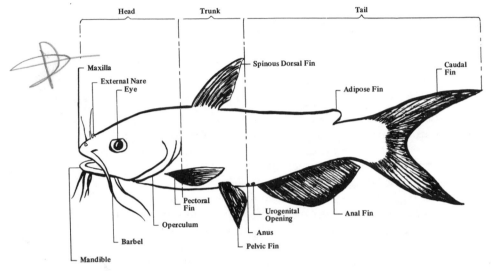

Figure 4-1. Major External Parts of a Catfish.

The head of the catfish is usually distinguished as being large and relatively broad. Well-developed jaws are a part of the mouth. The lower jaw is known as the "mandible" and the upper jaw is the "maxilla." Small teeth for holding food are present in each jaw. A pair of eyes is present on the head. The eyes are located on the side of the head so that a fish can see behind as well as in front. An external nare is in front of each eye. These are used for smelling and not for respiration. Several "dermal barbels," or feelers, are located around the mouth and serve as sensory organs. The gills are covered by the "operculum."

Scales, as found on bass and other common fish, are not present on catfish. Instead, catfish are covered with a skin that tends to have a leathery feeling. Mucous glands are present in the skin to produce the "slime," or mucus, which makes catfish slippery. Not only does the mucus aid in movement through the water, but it also serves as protection against organisms which cause disease.

Catfish have several fins. Two dorsal fins are located along the top of the back. The dorsal fin closest to the front of the fish is known as the spinous dorsal fin. The first ray of this fin is a strong, stiff, serrated spine with a sharp point. The first rays of the pectoral fins, located on each side of the fish just behind and below the gills, also form sharp pointed spines. These spines, especially in the spinous dorsal fin, can inflict painful wounds when fish are handled. The adipose dorsal fin does not contain rays as do the other fins. Also found on catfish are two pelvic fins, one anal fin, and one caudal fin.

Body Functions of Catfish

Catfish are cold-blooded organisms. This means that the body temperature is regulated by the temperature of the water which surrounds them. Catfish also have special body features which allow them to live in water. Animals with body features allowing them to exist in water are known as "aquatic animals."

The bodies of catfish are composed of "systems." Each system performs a function which is essential to life and continued existence. A brief discussion of the body systems and the functions of each as related to catfish is presented in the following paragraphs.

Skeletal System. A skeletal system is the bony, rigid framework of the body of a catfish to which tissues and inner organs are attached. It is composed of bone and cartilage. The functions of the skeletal system are: (1) to support and give shape to the body, (2) to protect the delicate organs of the body from injury, and (3) to provide a place for the attachment of muscles.

Catfish are vertebrates; that is, an inner skeleton and vertebral column (backbone) are present. The inner skeleton of catfish should be distinguished from the hard outer skeleton of animals such as crayfish. The hard outer skeleton is known as an exoskeleton. Animals with exoskeletons are known as "invertebrates" because they do not have vertebral columns.

Muscular Systems. The function of the muscular system is to produce movement of and within the bodies of catfish. The most important muscles are those used in securing food, moving the body, obtaining oxygen, and eliminating carbon dioxide, known as respiration. Bands of strong muscles along the back produce the movement necessary for swimming. Weaker muscles provide other movements of the body.

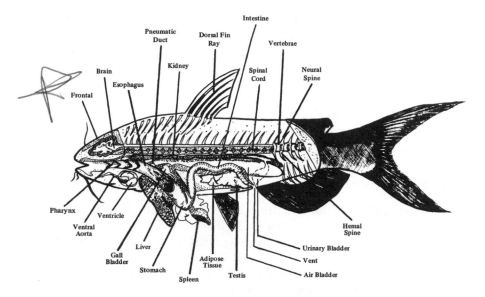

Figure 4-2. Major Internal Parts of a Catfish.

Digestive System. All of the parts of catfish that have to do with the intake and digestion of food compose the digestive system. Food is taken in through the mouth and passed through the pharynx and esophagus to the stomach. The stomach of a catfish tends to be tubular-shaped and is separated from the small intestine by a pyloric valve. Digestion of food occurs in the stomach and in the small and large intestines.

Excretory System. The excretory system is concerned with the elimination of waste materials from the body. It is composed of kidneys, urinary duct, urinary bladder, and urogenital opening. The main function of the kidneys is to extract wastes from the blood. The urinary duct carries excretory matter into the urinary bladder which stores excretory matter until it is expelled through the urogenital opening, or vent.

Respiratory System. In catfish, the gills are the organs of respiration. Many thread-like projections known as "gill filaments" are present on each gill. The gill filaments contain numerous tiny capillaries. By circulating through the gill filaments, the blood is brought into close contact with the water so that carbon dioxide can be discharged and oxygen can be absorbed. A continuous supply of water is required to flow over the gills. Water is taken in through the mouth and forced out between the operculum and the body. Figure 4-3 shows the arrangement of the gill and gill filaments.

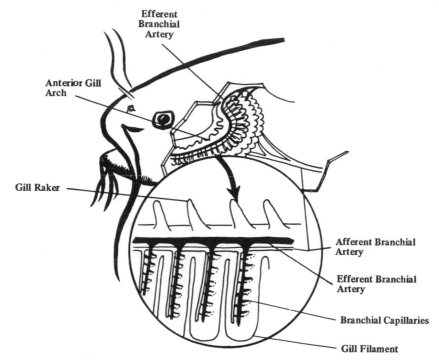

Figure 4-3. Arrangement of a Gill.

The "air bladder" assists in respiration but is more important in helping a catfish to maintain its balance. The air bladder contains a mixture of gaseous oxygen, nitrogen, and carbon dioxide. It serves as a float and attempts to adjust the weight of a fish so that it equals the weight of the water displaced. The amount of gas in the air bladder varies with the pressure applied by the surrounding water and varies as the depth in the water at which the fish is swimming varies. If a catfish is suddenly jerked from the bottom of a lake into the air, his stomach may be forced out of his mouth. This is because the air bladder was under considerable pressure in deep water and rapidly expanded after the fish was pulled from the water.

Circulatory System. The function of the circulatory system is to circulate blood throughout the body of a catfish. The blood of a catfish is similar to that of other fish and higher animals. Both red and white corpuscles are present. As in all animals, a pulsating motion of the heart causes the blood to flow. There are two main types of blood vessels: "arteries" and "veins." Blood is circulated through the arteries to the gills and then to all areas of the fish. Blood is returned to the heart through the veins and recirculated to the gills and body. In the gills the blood discharges carbon dioxide and picks up oxygen.

Nervous System. The nervous system includes the brain, spinal cord, and many nerves. The brain of the catfish is not highly developed when compared to that of other vertebrates. The nervous system of the catfish functions much as in other animals.

Sensory System. The sensory system has to do with sight, sound, touch, taste, and smell. The main sense organs of a catfish are eyes, ears, olfactory sac, and skin, especially the dermal barbels.

The eyes of catfish are smaller than the eyes of other fish. Catfish, unlike many other fish, do not rely solely upon sight for the location of food. Fish that find food mainly by its odor, as do catfish, usually have small eyes. The eyes of catfish do not have lids. Water keeps the eyeballs moist and free from foreign objects so that it is unnecessary for a lid to be present. Catfish have relatively good vision; however, sight is somewhat limited in water. Catfish are nearsighted and usually do not see objects more than a few feet from them.

Catfish, like most other fish, do not have external ear openings. Vibrations in the water are picked up through the ear bones in the skull. Vibrations in water travel faster and farther than in the air. Catfish do not hear fish farmers talking because these vibrations are in the air. But, noise made in the water or on the ground near the water is readily detected by fish. In addition to hearing, the ears serve as an organ of equilibrium.

The sense of smell of catfish is accomplished by the olfactory sacs located beneath the external nares. A pair of external nares is found on catfish, one on each side of the head between the mouth and eyes. The external nares are openings similar to nostrils and are concerned with smell. They have nothing to do with respiration which is accomplished through the gills.

The most distinguishing feature of catfish is the presence of dermal barbels, sometimes known as feelers. Barbels serve catfish in several ways. Their primary function is to create a sense of touch. However, barbels are also used by catfish to help maintain their position relative to the bottom of a stream or lake and to assist in locating food.

Reproductive System. The reproductive system of catfish is similar to that of other fish and animals. The female has two ovaries in which eggs develop. At the time the female lays the eggs, or "spawn," the male catfish swims over them and discharges sperms, or "milt." The sperms swim to the eggs and fertilization occurs. Sperms are produced in the testes of the male catfish. Both eggs and sperms are discharged through the urogenital opening of each sex.

Stages of Growth of Catfish

The growth of catfish, so far as the fish farmer is concerned, may be divided into six main stages: egg, fry, fingerling, stocker, food fish, and broodfish. Fertilized eggs hatch in seven to eight days, provided the temperature and other conditions of incubation are satisfactory. The stage from time of hatching until a length of 1 inch is reached is known as the "fry stage." A newly hatched fry has a yolk sac present for six to eight days. During this period of time the term *sac fry* is used. After the yolk sac is absorbed, the term *fry* or *advanced fry* is used. When a length of 1 inch is reached catfish are known as "fingerlings." The length of fingerlings ranges from 1 to 10 inches. Most catfish growing facilities are stocked with fingerling-sized catfish. Fish larger than 10 inches long but weighing less than ¾ pound (about 14 inches long) are known as stockers. Food fish usually weigh 1 to 2 pounds or more; however, some processors will accept them as small as ¾ pound. Broodfish are usually first used for spawning when they weigh 3 pounds or more and are about three years of age. Figure 4-4 illustrates the stages of catfish growth as a cycle.

Locomotion

The movement of fish is known as "locomotion" and is made possible by the "locomotor organs." Locomotion is facilitated by a streamlined body shape which offers very little resistance to the

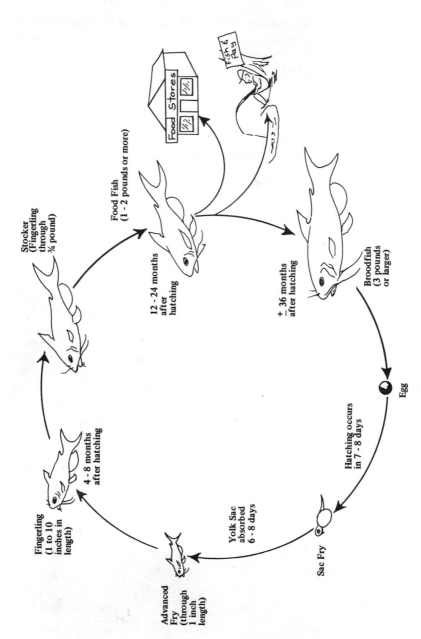

Figure 4-4. Stages of Catfish Growth.

water. The air bladder keeps a fish the same weight as the amount of water it displaces; thus, a catfish is able to remain stationary with very little use of muscles.

The tail is the main locomotor organ. Movement of a catfish through water is caused by alternating contractions of bands of muscles on the sides of the tail or trunk. These muscular contractions cause the caudal fin to be lashed from side to side enabling the fish to move forward. The pectoral and pelvic fins are used in swimming much as oars are used to provide movement of a boat. Direction of movement is regulated by the caudal, pectoral, and pelvic fins. Dorsal, anal, and caudal fins assist fish in keeping upright positions. Balance is maintained by the pelvic and pectoral fins.

Classification of Catfish

The study of any plant or animal is made easier if the various plants or animals are grouped together based on some common characteristics. Catfish can be classified in several ways. Possible ways of classification include habitat, that is, freshwater or saltwater, season in which spawning occurs, or scientific classification. Scientific classification is a system of classification which shows true genetic relationships of all animals, including fish. It is based on the principle of evolution.

Classification is simply grouping together animals with similar characteristics. It is used to systematize the study of all animals, including catfish. Relationships can be observed easily. Members in the same category have similar characteristics. Thus, it is possible to make general statements about all members of the same category in a classification scheme.

Fishery biologists (persons who scientifically study fish) use the scientific classification system. This system is based on the similarity of structure, function, and development of animals. The scientific classification system divides all living things into two groups, known as kingdoms. The kingdoms are plant and animal. The catfish is a member of the animal kingdom. The animal kingdom is divided into phyla, classes, orders, families, genera, and species. A phylum (singular form of phyla) is a wide group of animals with some common characteristics. A class is a narrower group under a phylum. Each phylum may have several classes. An order is a still smaller group in which members have the same phylum and class characteristics, and also characteristics common to the order. The family, genus, and species represent smaller and smaller groups of individuals which have characteristics of the larger groups, and in addition, each has its own special identifying characteristics.

All catfish have names which fit the scientific classification scheme. Scientific names are descriptive names used by people in all countries. Common names, such as "mudcat," are often used only in isolated regions and are not meaningful to people in other regions. Scientific names show a systematic relationship of one species of catfish to other catfish, other fish, and other animals without any two animals having the same name. The scientific name is obtained by putting the genus and species together. For example, the genus of the channel catfish is *Ictalurus* and the species is *punctatus;* therefore, the scientific name is *Ictalurus punctatus.* All members of a species possess certain common characteristics but differ slightly among themselves. However, they resemble one another more than they resemble other species. Figure 4-5 shows the scientific classification of a channel catfish.

Kingdom	Animal
Phylum	*Chordata* (with spinal cord)
Subphylum	*Craniata* (with cranium)
Superclass	*Gnathostomata* (with jaws)
Class	*Osteichthyes* (bony fish)
Subclass	*Actinopterygii* (rayed fins)
Superorder	*Teleostei* (perfected bones)
Order	*Siluriformes* (catfish)
Family	*Ictaluridae* (freshwater catfish)
Genus	*Ictalurus* (catfish)
Species	*punctatus* (spotted)

Figure 4-5. Scientific Classification of a Channel Catfish. (Source: "Genetics and Breeding of Channel Catfish," Bulletin 223. Auburn, Alabama: Agricultural Experiment Station, 1978)

Identification of Common Species

The name "catfish" is said to have originated from the purring sound made by certain fish when taken from the water. The purr is a trait of the ordinary house cat, thus the name "catfish." Also, catfish have barbels which are said to resemble the "whiskers" on a cat. The name "catfish" is applied to many slightly different fish in practically all parts of the earth. Some catfish, notably a species found in the Nile River, are said to have the ability to deliver an electric shock. Catfish are found in freshwater and in saltwater. The kinds of catfish cultured by catfish farmers grow in freshwater.

There are around 1,250 species of catfish. Less than 50 species are found in North America. Of these, only a few are prominent as food or sport fish. The most common species of catfish are:

Channel Catfish *(Ictalurus punctatus)*
Blue Catfish *(Ictalurus furcatus)*
White Catfish *(Ictalurus catus)*
Flathead *(Pylodictis olivaris)*
Speckled Bullhead *(Ictalurus nebulosus marmoratus)*
Brown Bullhead *(Ictalurus nebulosus)*
Black Bullhead *(Ictalurus melas)*
Yellow Bullhead *(Ictalurus natalis)*

Bullhead catfish are commonly known as "mudcats." They are usually not cultured as a fish crop. In fact, bullheads are pests in most fish farming operations.

Distinction between the common species of catfish is usually made by observing the arrangement and color of the external features. The most prominent identification features are the fins. It is not always easy to identify catfish. However, if certain basic characteristics are kept in mind, identification may be made more easily. A summary of the major identifying characteristics of catfish species commonly grown on fish farms is listed below. (Bullheads are included so that they may be distinguished from the desired catfish.)

Deeply forked tail, or caudal fin	Channel Catfish Blue Catfish
Blunt tail, or caudal fin	White Catfish Bullhead Catfish
Rounded anal fin	Channel Catfish White Catfish Bullhead Catfish
Straight anal fin	Blue Catfish
Spots on body	Channel Catfish (commonly) Blue Catfish (rarely)

Figure 4-6. Channel Catfish. (The blue catfish and the channel catfish are often confused. The most distinct difference is the shape and structure of the anal fins. In the channel catfish the anal fin is rounded and has 25 to 35 rays. The upper part of the body is bluish or olive, fading to silver on the sides and white on the belly. Young fish are spotted. The spots usually disappear by the time the fish weighs 5 pounds. Channel catfish weighing 2 or 3 pounds are most desirable for food fish. Five pounds is considered large but a channel catfish may reach a weight of 75 pounds.)

Figure 4-7. Blue Catfish. (Blue catfish average 3 to 20 pounds but may reach a weight of as much as 150 pounds. Their color is dull-blue or bluish olive on the upper part of the body, fading to silver on the sides and white on the belly. The anal fin is straight and has 30 to 35 rays. The tail, like that of the channel catfish, is deeply forked. Spots are not usually present on blue catfish; however, a few blue catfish have been observed to have spots.)

Figure 4-8. White Catfish. (The major distinction between the white catfish and the channel catfish is that the tail of the white catfish is not deeply forked. The white catfish is without spots and has a larger head and a somewhat lighter color.)

Figure 4-9. Bullhead Catfish. (Bullhead catfish are a nuisance in catfish farming and are often known as "mudcats." Several species of bullheads are common: black, brown, yellow, and speckled. The speckled bullhead is actually a southern variety of the brown bullhead. The black bullhead outnumbers the other species. Muddy, sluggish water is preferred by the black and yellow bullheads, whereas the brown bullhead prefers a clearer water.

The *black bullhead* has gray or black barbels. Its back is black to greenish or gold. The underside is greenish-yellow or bright yellow. It may reach a length of 16 inches and a weight of 1 to 2 pounds.

The *brown bullhead* is a slender fish whose anal fin is about half the length of the body. Its barbels are black or gray. Color of the brown bullhead is dark yellowish-brown on the back with dark green mottling. Maximum length is 12 inches.

The *yellow bullhead* is a thick, chunky catfish that reaches somewhat larger sizes than the brown or black bullhead. It may weigh 2 pounds and reach a length of 16 inches. Color varies from light olive brown to black with yellow, sometimes streaked with darker-colored sides and a yellow or milky white belly.)

Species Used for Fish Farming

The predominant species of catfish grown on fish farms is the channel catfish.

It is commonly agreed that the channel catfish has the greatest potential for fish farming. In fact, this species comprises all but a very small percentage of the commercially produced catfish. Other species which have potential are the blue catfish and the white catfish. Most persons in the catfish industry recommend that beginning fish farmers produce channel catfish and, if successful, experiment on a small scale with growing the blue or white species.

There are advantages and disadvantages for each species. White catfish are more tolerant to crowding, high water temperatures, and low oxygen levels than either channel or blue catfish. However, white catfish do not dress-out so well. Blue catfish grow more uniformly and dress-out better than either channel or white catfish. The blue catfish is more difficult to transport and culture than the other two common species.

It is possible that in the future some type of hybrid or crossbred catfish will be predominantly cultured. Research projects are currently underway attempting to determine the feasibility of such breeding practices in catfish farming.

Questions and Problems for Discussion

1. List and describe the three sections of a catfish.
2. What are the major characteristics that distinguish catfish from other fish?
3. How is the body temperature of a cold-blooded animal, such as a catfish, regulated?
4. What are the body systems and their functions in catfish?
5. What role does the air bladder play?
6. List and briefly describe the stages of growth of a catfish.
7. What is locomotion? How do catfish accomplish locomotion?
8. What is the importance of a scientific classification system and the use of scientific names?
9. What characteristics are commonly used to identify channel catfish, blue catfish, and white catfish?
10. What species of catfish is commonly grown on fish farms?

5

Constructing Water Facilities

Farmers usually select facilities to match the crop to be produced. With catfish, the kind of water facilities determines how fish are to be raised. Likewise, the method of raising fish has considerable bearing on the planning and construction of facilities. And once a facility is established, it is usually not practical to quickly change to another facility!

A catfish farm may have a combination of facilities unique to that particular farm. Economy, usefulness, and productivity are important. Before construction is started, it is important to know the kinds of facilities that will be needed. In recent years, farmers experimented with many different facilities—tanks, ponds, raceways, vats, and the like—with the result that ponds are increasingly emerging as the predominant water facility for catfish farming.

This chapter contains the following information:

> Kinds of water facilities
> Selecting pond sites
> Designing pond layouts
> Constructing ponds
> Constructing raceways
> Constructing vats

The major factor in selecting water facilities is the nature of the production system to be used. Those farms that will produce fingerlings and food fish will need different facilities from those which will only produce food fish. The nature of the available land will also have considerable influence on facility construction. Land that is of little use otherwise can often be used for catfish farming; however, some of the best cropland has been converted to catfish farms.

Kinds of Water Facilities

Good water facilities make it easy for the catfish farmer to maintain an environment that is conducive to the health and growth of fish. The kind of facility constructed will depend on the size of the farm and type of fish farming program to be followed. Some of the facilities commonly used include ponds, raceways, tanks, vats, and aquariums.

Ponds. The most common water facilities, or impoundments, used in catfish farming are ponds. Several different kinds of ponds may be used, depending on the type of catfish farming operation.

1. Growing pond.—A pond in which catfish are grown to the size of food fish. The arrangement and size of growing ponds are determined by the topography of the land, size of farm, and pond design as related to the economics of production. It is more economical to construct large ponds, but the cost of harvesting may offset any savings in construction costs.

2. Fee-lake.—A pond in which catfish are grown or held until caught by sport fishermen. A site which is unsuitable for a growing pond may be satisfactory for a fee-lake. Size and arrangement may vary considerably, especially since such ponds are usually not seined often. Fee-lakes are sometimes known as catch-out ponds.

3. Holding pond.—A small pond in which broodfish are maintained between spawning seasons. These ponds are needed on farms producing fingerlings and are often built in conjunction with spawning and rearing ponds. Holding ponds are often 1 acre or less in size. A farm may need more than one holding pond, depending on the number of broodfish kept. Several small ponds of about ¼ acre each are often preferred so that a disease outbreak among the fish can be confined and kept from infecting all broodfish. A holding pond that is ¼ acre in size can be stocked with 100 broodfish weighing 4 pounds each. Also, the smaller-sized ponds are needed if more than one species of broodfish is maintained and the species are kept separate.

4. Spawning pond.—A small pond of 1 to 5 acres in which broodfish are placed for spawning. The broodfish are placed in pens in the pond or in the open pond.

5. Rearing pond.—A small pond in which fry are placed for growing into fingerlings. The size of a rearing pond depends upon the number and size of fingerlings to be produced. One acre of rearing pond will usually produce sufficient fingerlings 7 inches long to stock 15 acres of growing ponds.

Raceways. A raceway makes use of flowing water. It may be a long narrow structure or a series of structures, sometimes ponds, through which water flows. The water may flow naturally, or it may be forced to flow by being pumped. Some structures in which the water flows slowly are known as semi-raceways. The main advantage of raceways is that catfish may be stocked in them in higher populations per area of land than in ponds.

Two kinds of raceways are used, based on how the water is circulated. Raceways in which the water enters at one end and is disposed of at the other end are known as "open," or "flow-through" raceways. The water is not used again. Raceways in which the water enters at one end and is removed at the other end, filtered, aerated, and used again are "closed" raceways. Most closed raceways are not completely closed but are "modified closed." The techniques of filtering and aerating water have not been highly perfected for large scale fish production; therefore, water cannot be reused indefinitely without the addition of new water.

Raceway fish culture requires more energy than pond culture due to the need to operate pumps to circulate the water. This has caused the use of raceways to become less profitable as the costs for fuel and electricity have increased.

Tanks. The use of tanks in the culture of catfish has received considerable attention in recent years. Tanks utilize flowing water and are round (circular) or rectangular (linear). Tank systems may be open or closed, the same as with raceways. Closed systems require water-circulating, cleaning, and aerating equipment. Catfish are stocked at high rates, meaning that tanks are used for very intensive culture.

Round tanks may range up to 20 feet in diameter and 30 inches in depth. The water flows in a circular pattern and drains out through a center drain. Round tanks are constructed so that there is a fall of approximately 2 inches from the outer circumference to the center drain. In other words, the bottom slopes toward

Figure 5-1. Round Tanks Used for Catfish Culture.

Figure 5-2. Rectangular Tanks Used for Catfish Culture. (Note the water jets for aerating incoming water.)

the center and, by doing so, makes cleaning easier. In fact, round tanks designed in this manner tend to be more self-cleaning than rectangular tanks.

Rectangular tanks vary in size, but are often 25 feet long, 3 feet wide, and 30 inches deep. The bottom may slope toward one end or toward the middle to facilitate cleaning and draining. With tanks that drain at one end, the water usually enters at the opposite end and flows the length of the tank. With tanks that drain in the middle, water usually enters at each end and flows toward the middle. Fish are more easily harvested from rectangular tanks than from round tanks.

Figure 5-3. A Super Intensive System of Culture. (Note that the metal tanks are stacked five high and are supported by steel frames. This is a controlled environment system in which the temperature remains constant the entire year. The water is filtered, aerated, and recirculated through the system.) (Courtesy, Aqua Systems)

Rectangular tanks may be designed so that they are arranged in stacks four or five high. In this type of system the tanks are 16 to 18 inches deep, 5 or 6 feet wide, and 15 to 20 feet long. Some systems of this type have been constructed in buildings with special equipment, making it possible to control the temperature of the water and have year-round production.

Tanks are available from commercial manufacturers or are custom-made on the farm. When tanks are constructed, durable materials that are free of toxic paints or chemicals should be used. Aluminum and painted galvanized steel are often used. Since tanks often hold a large amount of water, a good foundation, braced to prevent collapse, is essential.

The culture of fish in tanks lacks long-time use and research. Many of the requirements and problems of tank culture are still being investigated. Except for small operations or for use as temporary holding areas, tanks are not widely used. Ponds have been considered more likely to be profitable and better suited to large-scale catfish farming. No large catfish farms use tanks as their main method of culture.

Vats. Vats are usually considered to be temporary holding

Figure 5-4. Holding Vats with Suspended Aerators.

facilities for fingerlings, broodfish, and food fish. These containers are constructed of concrete or concrete block on a slab of concrete and covered with a metal shed. Vats are most often needed on farms that frequently handle fish, such as those producing broodfish or operating retail markets.

Aquariums. An aquarium is a glass, or partially glass, rectangular tank with a capacity of from 5 to 50 gallons. For catfish, aquariums are designed so that water is constantly flowing through them rather than just being "bubbled" (aerated). In pet fish aquariums the water is aerated rather than made to flow. Aquariums are used for spawning purposes, especially in research activities where various crosses are being investigated. Fry and fingerlings may also be grown in aquariums. This facility, however, is not commonly used by fish farmers.

Selecting Pond Sites

Considerable care should be taken in selecting pond sites. Economy of construction, ease of operation, and productivity are dependent upon location. No two farms are exactly alike; however, several factors in selecting pond sites apply to nearly all farms.

Ease of Drainage. Every pond should be located and constructed so that it can be drained individually and completely. In selecting pond sites, consideration should be given to the elevation of the drainage area in relation to the elevation of the bottom of the ponds. Gravity-flow drainage may be used in draining ponds with bottom elevations higher than drainage ditch elevations. Ponds with bottom elevations below that of the drainage ditch must be drained by being pumped.

Freedom from Flooding. Sites for catfish ponds should be selected so that water from creeks or rivers will not overflow into the ponds. Such overflow will often contaminate the water in the pond and permit the introduction of trash fish from the overflow water. Also, overflowing water allows fish to swim out of the pond and be lost. Sometimes it is necessary to cut diversion ditches around ponds to prevent flooding.

Former Use of Site. The past use of land should be determined. Land that has been used for row crops may contain certain harmful pesticide residues. Most pesticides are toxic to catfish. Some are not readily broken down in the soil, and residues may have accumulated that will kill fish. The former use of a site may be determined by asking the previous landowner and by looking for the presence of crop stalks and other crop residues. A thorough test of the soil should be made if a fish operation is planned on cropland where chlorinated hydrocarbon pesticides have been used.

Proximity to Row Crops. Ponds located on sites adjacent to row crops may be contaminated by pesticides applied to the crops. Pesticides may drift into the pond and kill the fish or make them unsafe for consumption. Aerial pesticide applicators should not make turns over ponds because of the possibility of failure to cut off spraying equipment. Also, catfish ponds should not be planned where runoff water from row crops will enter the ponds if pesticides have been used.

Water-Holding Capacity of Soil. A thorough examination should be made to determine whether or not the soil is capable of holding water, especially during dry seasons. This involves boring or digging down into the soil several feet to determine the presence of gravel layers, soil structure, depth of water-holding material, rock fissures, indications of sand strata, and other soil characteristics which might interfere with good water-holding capability. Technicians from the Soil Conservation Service (SCS) can provide assistance in determining the water-holding capacity of soil.

Economics of Construction. A question which might be asked with reference to economics of construction is: "Should ponds be constructed on good, level land free of trees, which may be more expensive to purchase, or on rolling land with trees, which may be less expensive to purchase?" Although level land is often more expensive to purchase, it may be more profitable in the long run. It is usually easier to harvest fish in ponds on level land.

Designing Pond Layouts

Ponds for catfish farming should be designed for maximum efficiency of production. The designing of pond layouts includes determining the type, size, and arrangement of ponds. Some factors influencing design, such as natural boundaries, property lines, highways, and topography, are not easily controlled, however.

Types of Ponds. Three types of ponds have been used for catfish culture: ravine, excavated, and levee. The ravine pond is made by placing a dam across a gorge, gully, or hollow between hills. It is often used on hilly land but is not the best type for food fish production. However, it is likely to be satisfactory for fee-lake use.

An excavated pond is one which is constructed by removing the soil and using it for building a levee or embankment for the pond. This type of pond may be constructed on any fairly level land that is not subject to overflow or flooding from the surrounding area. One of the problems with this type of pond, since it tends to be "dug out," is that it is difficult to drain it by gravity. The water in excavated ponds with bottoms below the elevation of the bottoms of nearby drainage ditches must be pumped out. Pumping the water out of a pond at the time of harvest makes harvesting more expensive.

Levee ponds have been found to be very successful in areas with flat land. This type of pond is constructed without excavation and involves building a levee around the pond area. The levee pond is similar to an irrigated rice field, except that the pond is deeper. Wherever topography permits, the levee-type pond is preferred for catfish farming.

Size of Ponds. The size of a pond may be dictated by the size and other physical features of the site. If there is a choice of size, it is best to select a size that can be managed and harvested easily.

Ponds of less than 1 acre to more than 100 acres have been used for producing catfish. Large ponds cost less per acre to construct than small ones; however, large ponds have several disadvantages. Erosion of the levee is a more serious problem with large ponds. This is because the water area is greater; thus the wind is able to create larger waves. The control of disease outbreaks is more difficult in large ponds. Also, the harvesting of a large pond presents greater problems. A 50-acre pond stocked with 1,500 fish per acre contains 75,000 to 100,000 pounds of fish at harvest time. Locating a suitable market and getting the fish there can also present a considerable job. In contrast, small ponds provide more flexibility for management, harvesting, overcoming oxygen shortages, and treating for diseases and parasites. Also, small ponds can be drained and refilled quickly.

The size of ponds has a significant effect on the costs of production. It is often recommended that catfish ponds be 10 to 20 acres or larger. However, persons who are inexperienced would do well to begin with one or two small ponds of 1 to 5 acres for the first year. Larger ponds could be constructed after a year's experience. Ponds of 20 acres may be most profitable. Figure 5-5 shows

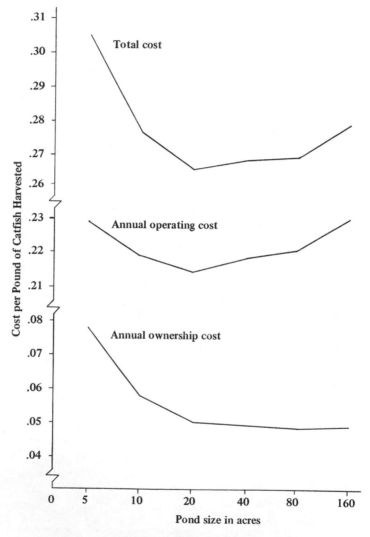

Figure 5-5. Cost per Pound of Catfish Harvested by Size of Pond. (Computations are based on 160 acres of land devoted to each size.) (Courtesy, Mississippi Agricultural and Forestry Experiment Station)

the cost per pound of catfish harvested for ponds of different sizes at varying price levels.

Arrangement of Ponds. Economics of construction and harvesting should be considered in planning the arrangement of ponds. One of the first steps in planning ponds is to determine the requirements for the type of fish farming program to be followed. In case the fish farm is limited to the culture of food fish, only growing ponds will be needed. If fingerlings are produced, holding, spawning, and rearing ponds will be needed. Ponds used as fee-lakes may also need some special consideration in planning.

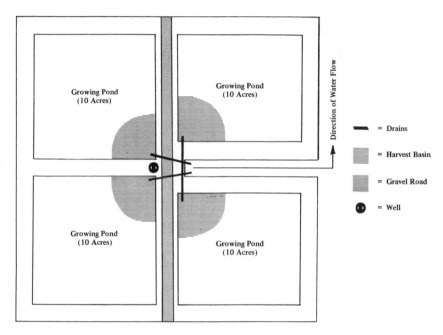

Figure 5-6. Possible Arrangement of Ponds for Food Fish Production.

Shape of ponds affects initial and harvesting costs. A square-shaped pond requires less levee than a rectangular pond for the same number of acres of water. The amount of levee required increases proportionately as the pond shape changes from square to rectangular. A square pond 1 acre in size requires 835 feet of levee; a 1-acre pond 100 feet wide by 435 feet long requires 1,070 feet of levee. Square ponds may be more economical to construct, but economy of harvesting favors ponds that are rectangular. Less seine is required for harvesting the fish from a rectangular pond as compared with a square pond of the same acreage. Also, feeding from the dam is easier with rectangular ponds.

It is a good practice on farms with several ponds to construct

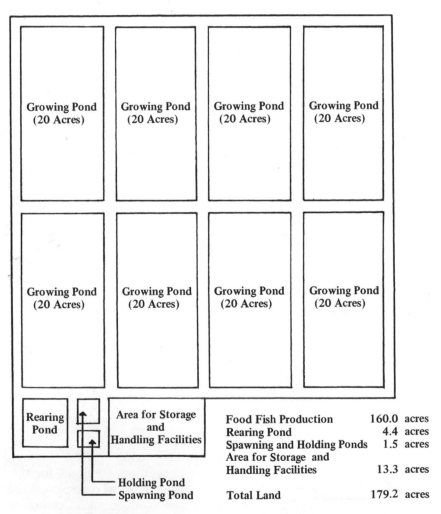

Figure 5-7. Possible Arrangement of Ponds on a Farm Producing Food Fish with Fingerling Facilities. (Note: a portion of the acreage in each pond is occupied by the levees; therefore, the acreage of water in each growing pond is somewhat less than 20 acres.)

all of them about the same width so that additional feet of seine will not be required for the larger ponds. The length of ponds may vary, but the width should be almost the same. In addition, by constructing ponds next to each other, both sides of the levee are used to hold water, thus reducing the cost of construction per acre of water.

Planning the arrangement of ponds involves considering the location of water wells, arrangement of drainage pipes and ditches, and accessibility with trucks and tractors. All plans should provide for the maximum utilization of water supplies and drainage facilities. It is often a good procedure to arrange small ponds so that the long axis is parallel with the prevailing winds. This will provide for maximum aeration. Large ponds should be constructed so that the long axis is at a right angle to the prevailing winds. This is because winds traveling a long distance over water may create large waves and cause severe erosion of the levee. It is often recommended that ponds be three times as long as wide if conditions permit.

Holding, spawning, and rearing ponds are often located separately from growing or fee-lake ponds. Sometimes the ponds for fingerling production are located on one side of the farm adjacent to growing ponds.

Ponds used for fee-fishing need to be conveniently located for sport fishermen. The arrangement of such ponds often involves making the surroundings comfortable and attractive. Shade, parking area, and other features should be a part of the planning.

Constructing Ponds

A number of factors should be considered in constructing ponds for catfish farming. The initial cost of construction needs to be kept down; however, sacrifices should not be made which will result in increased maintenance and production costs. A local office of the Soil Conservation Service will provide assistance in preliminary planning and designing before construction is begun.

Preparation of Site. Pond sites should be cleared of all trees, stumps, roots, and other obstacles before construction is initiated. Such obstacles and trash will interfere with harvesting operations and, if left in a pond, may give fish an undesirable flavor. Trees and brush should be cut back a distance of at least 15 feet from the water line to allow for the movement of feeding and harvesting equipment. Sometimes a preliminary survey is made to locate the area to be cleared. After clearing, the location and slope of the dam is surveyed and staked out.

Construction of Levees. A pond is no better than the levee, or dam, which surrounds it. A levee is no better than the foundation it has and the soil of which it is made. The foundation of a levee is prepared by removing the soil located where it will be constructed down to the parent material (a depth of about 3 feet on most soils). This procedure is an attempt to assure a good bond between the mineral soil and the soil in the levee. The top soil that is removed from the levee site should be piled to one side and, when the levee is completed, spread over the top of the levee in a layer 2 to 6 inches thick. It is not necessary to spread top soil below the water line on the front side of the levee.

Catfish ponds are often constructed during summer and fall. This allows time for the soil to settle during rainy seasons in late fall and winter before being stocked with catfish in early spring. A grass or other vegetative cover which grows during the winter may be seeded in the fall. A cover will reduce erosion and somewhat reduce the muddiness of the water in a new pond.

Figure 5-8. A Levee Under Construction.

Constructing the above-ground portion of the levee is the most expensive and important operation in building a pond. Soil with a high proportion of clay should go into the core of the levee. Soil with the second highest proportion of clay should go into the section of the dam on the water side. The soil lowest in clay content should be placed on the back of the dam. Construction procedure should involve applying 6-inch layers of soil with each layer being well-packed before another layer is added. Packing is often done by driving the heavy construction equipment over the dam during construction. A new levee will usually shrink about 15 percent due to settling. All roots, sod, vegetation, leaves, wood, and other decomposable matter should be removed from the soil used to build a levee.

Levees are often constructed with a 3-to-1 slope on each side. This means that for every 1 foot in height, there should be 3 feet of levee extending toward both the upstream and downstream sides. On ponds larger than 10 acres, a 4-to-1 slope on the upstream side and a 3-to-1 slope on the downstream side is often recommended. Smaller ponds may be constructed with a 2-to-1 slope on the downstream side.

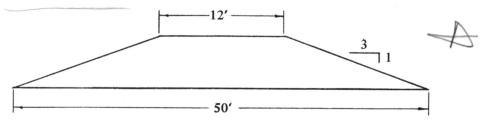

Center of levee

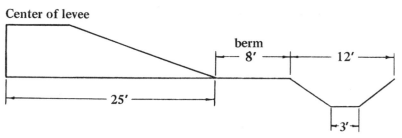

Figure 5-9. Pond Levee Specifications. (Courtesy, Mississippi Agricultural and Forestry Experiment Station)

Levees should have a minimum top width of 10 to 12 feet to permit the passage of trucks or tractors. The tops of main levees should be graveled to make travel possible in all kinds of weather. A freeboard of 2 feet is recommended. Freeboard is the distance from the normal water level to the top of the levee.

Construction of Pond Bottoms. Ponds should be constructed to facilitate harvesting. The bottom of ponds should be graded and sloped at about 0.2 foot for each 100 feet into a "harvest basin." All roots and stumps should be removed from ponds. The bottom should be smooth so that holes of water do not remain when the pond is drained. If harvesting is to involve water drawdown, a harvest basin is generally constructed. Harvest basins usually occupy about 10 percent of the total area of a pond. Basins are constructed 18 to 24 inches deeper than the normal level of the pond bottom. Basins should have sloping sides and extra smooth bottoms. With ponds built on land that slopes 2 to 3 feet per 100 feet, harvest basins may not be needed. Circular-shaped basins are most suitable for surrounding fish with seines; however, rectangular basins are satisfactory.

A harvest basin is, in effect, a small pond within a pond. As water in a pond is drained, fish move to the basin where water remains. Large ponds should be seined while full of water to yield a partial harvest. This reduces the volume of fish to be handled in the harvest basin.

A few farms have used harvest basins outside the levee. This involves the water and fish passing from the pond through a drainpipe into the basin. Outside harvest basins have the advantages of less mud and can often be more easily reached with equipment.

Construction of Pond Drainage Facilities. It is essential that all catfish ponds have adequate facilities for draining and regulating water. Such facilities often involve turn-down drainpipes, through-the-levee pipes with valves or plugs, and other water regulatory devices. Also it may be a good idea for some ponds to have spillways in case of heavy rainfall in the watershed area.

One of the most popular water regulatory and drainage devices is the turn-down pipe. Such a pipe is located at the lowest point of the base of the levee. A turn-down pipe serves both as an overflow and as a drainpipe. Water levels are established by pivoting the pipe, thereby increasing or decreasing the depth of water required to flow out of the pond.

The construction of a turn-down pipe involves placing a screen over the end of the pipe inside the pond to prevent the loss of fish and obstruction of water flow by turtles. A special anti-seep collar should be placed around the drainpipe inside the levee to prevent water from seeping along the pipe and causing leaks. Turn-down pipes need to be securely held in the desired position to prevent unplanned drainage. An upright post with a chain and

Figure 5-10. Turn-Down Pipe in "Up" Position. (Courtesy, Louisiana Wildlife and Fisheries Commission)

lock should be used to prevent the pipe from accidentally tilting downward, thus draining out the water and causing the loss of fish. The swivel joint should be heavily greased to assure easy operation. Sometimes swivel joints are made by placing an elbow on the end of the pipe coming through the levee and placing another "upright" pipe in the elbow. Swivel joints made with elbows alone tend to rust and become difficult to turn. Another type of turn-down pipe is specially made using a ring-joint technique.

A solid footing should support the turn-down pipe assembly and the drainpipe through the levee. Footings may extend 4 or

Figure 5-11. Turn-Down Pipe in "Down" Position. (Courtesy, USDA, Soil Conservation Service)

more feet into the bottom of the pond. The drainpipe through the levee should have a fall of about 1 foot per 100 feet.

Some turn-down pipes are constructed with a double-sleeve device that permits water to be drained from the bottom of the pond rather than from the surface. Since water at the bottom of the pond is lowest in oxygen, this technique tends to remove water low in oxygen. Sometimes the double-sleeve device is used when fresh water is added to the surface of a pond to reduce the possibility of oxygen depletion.

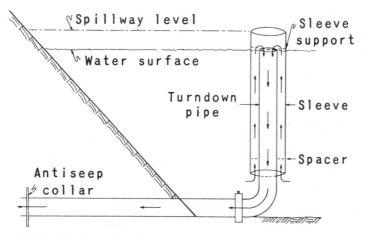

Figure 5-12. Double-Sleeve Turn-Down Pipe. (Courtesy, USDA, Soil Conservation Service)

The size of pipe used in drainage facilities needs to be carefully selected. The size to use depends on the size of the pond, the speed at which drainage is desired, and the rate that water enters a pond. As the diameter of a pipe is doubled, water-flow capacity increases more than four times. A 4-inch drain will empty an acre pond with an average depth of 3 to 4 feet in about 60 hours. This is assuming that no water is entering the pond. A 6-inch pipe will empty the same pond in half the time, or 30 hours. A 12-inch pipe will require $1/9$ as much time as a 4-inch pipe to drain a pond.

A 4-inch pipe will generally handle small ponds up to 3 acres in size. Pipes 6 to 12 inches in diameter are recommended for ponds of 15 to 20 acres.

A spillway may be needed, depending on whether or not a pond has sufficient drainage pipes and on whether there is a large watershed area. Spillways should be large enough to permit the outward flow of surplus water caused by rainfall and filling. A screen will be needed to prevent the loss of fish. For average-sized ponds with a watershed area of less than 50 acres, the spillway size may be found by dividing the total number of acres in the watershed area by 2 to obtain an estimated spillway width. It is usually a good procedure to add an additional 10 feet to the width as a safety precaution.

Figure 5-13. Water Regulatory Device Used by the Fish Farming Experimental Station.

The spillway may be located at one end of a dam, at both ends of a dam, or at a convenient point along the side of a pond. The spillway should be paved with rock or concrete or completely covered with a good sod. The type of construction to use will depend on the location of the spillway, the type of soil on which it is to be built, and the anticipated volume of water flow out of the pond.

Drainage facilities usually include ditches to carry off excess water and water drained from the ponds. Such ditches are often 12 feet wide at the top and 3 feet wide at the bottom. A berm (distance between levee and top edge of ditch) 8 feet wide is recommended.

Maintenance of Pond Levees. A vegetative cover to control erosion should be established on pond levees. Commonly used permanent grasses include centipede and Bermuda. These grasses tend to grow well in warm locations where the bulk of the catfish are grown. In areas where these grasses are not adapted, a hardy variety with good ground-covering ability should be selected. Centipede is a low-growing grass and requires little mowing. It will not grow runners into the water and can be destroyed by heavy cultivation or disking. Bermuda grass is hardy and spreads by runners. It does well on moist soils that are fairly fertile. The sod of Bermuda grass is not so thick or low growing as is the sod of centipede grass. Therefore, it requires more attention to keep out undesirable weeds and to maintain the sod. Bermuda grass will grow runners as far as 2 feet from the levee into the water, but usually this does not cause a problem. In some locations where a year-round green color is desired, tall fescue may be seeded on levees.

The first step in preparing a new levee for seeding is to apply 500 to 1,000 pounds of a complete fertilizer, such as 13-13-13, per acre of levee surface. This is followed by light disking. A permanent cover of either centipede or Bermuda grass is seeded at the rate of 15 to 30 pounds per acre. During the first growing season it should be fertilized three times at the rate of 2 pounds of actual nitrogen per acre. To speed the growth of a cover, the top soil that was removed for the levee site should be spread evenly over the levee before seeding. Occasionally, fertile soil from other sources is hauled in.

It is often impossible to get a permanent cover established before winter on levees constructed in late summer or fall. Winter weather, which may include considerable rain, is often hard on new levees and may cause considerable erosion. A temporary winter cover, such as ryegrass or wheat, should be established. Ryegrass should be seeded on levees at the rate of 60 pounds per acre. Wheat should be seeded at the rate of 2 to 4 bushels per acre. These temporary covers will offer some protection for the soil and prevent serious erosion problems during the winter. A permanent cover should be established in the spring.

An established sod also needs maintenance. This involves applying 3 pounds of actual nitrogen per acre once a year. If livestock graze on the levees (which is not desirable in catfish farming), a heavier rate of fertilization should be used. Weeds and seedlings should be controlled by mowing and clipping. The use of herbicides to control weeds around catfish ponds should be minimized because of the possibility of residues entering the water and being absorbed by the fish.

The levees on large ponds may need to be covered at the waterline with large stones or sacks in which concrete has been allowed to set. This will reduce the erosion damage caused by waves. On all newly constructed ponds it is a good idea to cover exposed areas, which are highly subject to erosion, with hay until a cover is established. Levees may need a gravel top if travel by motor vehicles is anticipated on a year-round basis.

Occasionally levees will suffer damage in the form of deep gully erosion or breaks. These should be repaired as soon as possible so that the damage will not become major. Special care should be used in sodding a waterway. Sometimes it may be necessary to construct concrete diversions.

Figure 5-14. A Levee Riprapped with Sacks of Concrete.

Construction of Diversion Ditches. Diversion ditches resemble terraces and are used to prevent unwanted water from entering ponds. Not all ponds need diversion ditches. However, those constructed on sites with large watershed areas often need diversion ditches to carry away excess rainfall. Ponds with large watershed areas may be flooded following heavy rains and remain muddy most of the year. A diversion ditch is laid out around one side of a pond and continues around and below the levee where the water may be safely released. The ditch should have a 0.2 foot of fall, or slightly more, per 100 feet. Vegetative covers should be established on ditches to reduce erosion.

Constructing Raceways

Since raceways are used for the intensive culture of catfish in flowing water, construction procedures should provide for optimum production with a minimum of maintenance. The number of fish produced per unit of area in raceways is considerably greater than in ordinary ponds. Raceways usually cover a small acreage. However, considerable land not actually in raceways may be required.

Sometimes distinction is made between raceways and semi-raceways. Raceways tend to be small, perhaps no more than 1/10 acre, and utilize "super-intensive" production. This requires a high volume and velocity of water flow. Semi-raceways require less water. Both the volume and the velocity of water are less. Semi-raceways are usually larger than raceways and produce a smaller number of fish per acre.

Raceways are usually in segments, known as "raceway units." Screen partitions or water-control structures form the segments. Raceways may be constructed of concrete, asphalt, concrete blocks, or earth. On occasion, earthen raceways have been lined with layers of polyethylene or similar material. The most commonly used raceways are of unlined earth and tend to have less than super-intensive culture.

The major disadvantage of raceways is the high initial cost of construction. Construction costs vary with size and number of raceway segments, materials used in construction, and availability of good water at an economical rate. Trout farmers have used raceways more extensively than have catfish farmers. Trout raceway facilities are more often constructed of concrete than of earth.

Figure 5-15. Earthen Raceway Units Showing Water-Control Structures.

Selection of Site. In selecting a site for a raceway, consideration should be given to topography, soil characteristics, erosion control, and water supply. The ideal site is one which requires a minimum of land grading. Land that is hilly and has slopes of 7 percent or more should be avoided because of the expense of construction. The soil should have good water-holding ability, much as that on which ponds are constructed. The desirability of a site may be affected by the possibility of overflow from nearby streams or flooding from a large watershed area. Diversion channels or dikes may be needed on some sites to keep out water.

The most significant factor in site selection is the water supply. Water may be obtained from streams, springs, deep wells, or reservoirs. The quantity of water available must be sufficient to maintain the desired flow at all times. The water should be free of pollution and other substances which may be toxic to fish. A water supply of 1,250 gallons per minute is needed for each acre of raceway. The requirement for semi-raceways is less. In channels 10 feet wide at the bottom and 4 feet deep with 1-to-1 side slopes, a flow of 530 gallons per minute is often recommended. At this rate, the water in a raceway segment 100 feet long would be completely exchanged in about one hour.

Design of Raceways. The design of raceways varies with the physical features of the construction site. Yet, there are certain fundamentals which apply to nearly all sites.

Raceways should be conveniently located in relation to the source of water. Likewise, design may include developing a dependable water-supply system. A water-supply reserve capable of meeting emergency needs is essential. An earthen storage reservoir located at the beginning of a raceway capable of gravity flow into the raceway may be used to supply water in case of pump failure. A reservoir may also be constructed at the end of a raceway to collect water for disposal or recirculation.

Raceway channels should be designed to insure uniform flow throughout the cross section of the channel. Each channel should be as straight as possible. Curves tend to create dead areas in the water. When it is necessary to put curves in a raceway, they should be gradual and flat. Sharp curves should be located in transition sections and should not be stocked with catfish.

Raceways are sometimes constructed to make use of the contour of the land. Flow of water in the channel should not depend upon grade but upon the addition of water at one end and its removal at the other end. A grade (slope) of 1 to 2 percent is preferred. The grade of a raceway is determined by dividing the channel length into the distance water falls over the baffle at the water-control structure.

Channels are constructed by a combination of excavating and building a levee along the sides. Segments of raceways are often 100 feet long, 10 feet wide at the bottom, and 3 to 4 feet deep. Raceways may consist of 15 to 20 segments, or more. One segment of the size described here will produce the equivalent of 1 acre in pond production. Side slopes of 1-to-1 or 2-to-1 are often used. Where possible a 1-to-1 slope should be used. A few raceways have been constructed with 3-to-1 slopes. To some extent, slope determines the top width and volume of water required. Raceways that are 10 feet wide at the bottom are 16 to 30 feet wide at the top. All areas along the edges of raceways exposed during construction should have a ground cover established to prevent erosion.

Semi-raceways are usually much larger than raceways and are

constructed of earth. Semi-raceways may be 50 feet wide and 800 to 1,200 feet long. The reduced water velocity of semi-raceways does not present some of the problems of erosion and excessively muddy water as with earthen raceways. Crushed stone may be used to line the banks of earthen semi-raceways to reduce erosion.

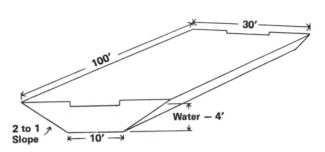

Figure 5-16. Dimensions of a Raceway Segment.

Establishment of Water-Control Structures. Water-control structures, or weirs, divide raceways into segments and regulate the flow and depth of water. They also serve to aerate the water as it flows through the weir opening and falls over the baffle into the next segment. In most raceways the distance of water fall is 1 to 2 feet.

Water-control structures must be constructed to prevent undermining, overturning, and other movement which might be caused by water. Soils high in clay tend to provide better foundations for water structures than other soils. Materials used in constructing water-control structures should be durable and economical. Commonly used materials include reinforced concrete, reinforced concrete blocks, wood, sheet metal, and culverts with flashboard risers.

The design of water-control structures should permit the removal of water from the bottom of raceways and include screens to prevent the loss of fish. Removing water from the bottom aids in carrying away metabolic wastes and in removing water with a low level of dissolved oxygen. A siphon arrangement may be adequate in some situations. Another more reliable method of removing water from the bottom involves constructing a vertically adjustable baffle on the upstream side of the weir. This baffle is rather wide and extends down into the water so that the water flows under it rather than over it, as with the baffle on the downstream side which regulates water depth. The rate at which water is pumped into a raceway and removed should be adjusted to prevent overflow and to keep the raceway from becoming empty. Overfilled raceways may place excessive pressure on the water-control structures, thus causing failure.

Figure 5-17. A Semi-Raceway.

Constructing Vats

Vats are used for temporarily holding fingerlings, food fish, and broodfish. Typically, vats are constructed of concrete blocks on a concrete slab. A roof supported by wood posts or steel pipes covers the vats. Vats constructed of concrete blocks should be lined with asphalt or epoxy paint for waterproofing. Only paints which will not pollute the water should be used. A common size for vats is 3 feet deep, 4 feet wide, and 30 feet long. Length may be varied to meet individual needs. Vats are frequently 50 feet or less in length. Several vats may be placed under a single shed. A dependable source of good water must be available. A typical arrangement is for water to be added to a vat at one end and re-

Figure 5-18. A Well-Constructed Vat System. (Courtesy, Master Mix Feeds)

moved at the other. Aerators must be installed to insure that the water contains sufficient oxygen. Each vat must be constructed so that drainage may be either partially or completely accomplished. It may be preferable to partition vats or to construct several small vats than to have one large vat.

Questions and Problems for Discussion

1. What are the common water facilities used in catfish farming? What are the distinguishing characteristics of each?
2. What is the distinction between open and closed raceways?
3. What factors should be considered in selecting a site for ponds?
4. Describe the ideal pond for the culture of food fish. Include type, size, and arrangement.
5. What is a harvest basin?
6. Why is a turn-down pipe with a double-sleeve device useful in regulating water depth?
7. How is the size of a drainage pipe related to the speed of draining a pond?
8. What is involved in maintaining pond levees?
9. How should a raceway be designed?
10. Why should raceways be designed so that water is removed from the bottom?

6

Securing and Managing Water

Water is the environment of catfish. Top catfish yields occur when the water provides favorable conditions for catfish growth. Water from the cheapest source is not always suitable, and even water from the best source may not be suitable without some alteration.

This chapter describes the following concerns in securing and managing water:

> Water quality
> Sources of water
> Volume of water needed
> Problems in water management
> Oxygenation of water
> Fertilization of water
> Filtering and recyling water
> Prevention of off-flavors

Water Quality

The terms *water quality* and *water chemistry* are often used in attempting to describe good water. "Water quality" refers to the suitability of water for catfish culture. It includes all of the physical, chemical, and biological factors that influence how water can be used. Any characteristic of water that affects the reproduction, survival, growth, production, or management of catfish is a part of water quality.

"Water chemistry" refers to the makeup of water. Hardness and quantity of oxygen are examples of water chemistry. Water chemistry can be determined through scientific procedures, while water quality is abstract and difficult to determine precisely.

A pond with "good" quality water will produce more and healthier fish than will a pond with "poor" water. Some of the important factors in water quality are temperature; salinity (saltiness); suspended particles, such as clay; plankton; pH; weeds; oxygen; and pollutants. Some sources of water are more likely to have quality problems than other sources are.

Sources of Water

Water for catfish culture can be obtained from several sources: surface runoff, wells, springs, and industrial effluent. The suitability of the water from these sources for catfish culture varies. Under the proper conditions, water from each may be suitable. This, of course, depends upon water quality. (Water obtained from city water supplies may contain chlorine. A level of 0.1-0.2 ppm is toxic to fish. City water should be de-chlorinated before using with fish. Chlorine is removed by filtering the water through charcoal, by adding sodium thiosulfate to the water, or by allowing the water to stand in an open container for at least 24 hours.)

Surface Runoff. Rainfall which does not soak into the earth is known as runoff. Surface runoff may include water taken from streams and reservoirs as well as the surplus rainfall from the area immediately surrounding a pond that may run into the pond. Runoff may be the most economical source of water for catfish culture.

One of the most serious problems in using runoff is that it may pick up harmful residues or aquatic pests. Runoff from cropland may carry pesticide residues which will build up in fish. Industrial operations dump pollutants that are harmful to catfish into streams. Water secured from streams may introduce diseases, parasites, and undesirable wild fish. Meshed screen or saran socks may be placed over the ends of pipes or other water inlets to prevent the entry of trash fish. Streams are often considered to be poor sources of water for catfish culture. Water from livestock feeding operations is unsanitary and should not be used in fish culture.

Wells. Two types of wells may be used: deep and shallow. Deep wells are generally preferred because traces of pesticide residues are occasionally found in water from shallow wells. Well water is usually free of parasites, diseases, and undesirable fish.

Figure 6-1. Good Water Is Essential in Catfish Farming.

Well water is usually more expensive than water from the other sources because of initial drilling and pumping costs.

Well water cannot always be pumped directly into a fish farming operation. Frequently, well water is 60°F or less in temperature. Catfish grow best in water that is 75 to 85°F. It may be necessary to temporarily pump water into reservoirs for warming before using in fish culture. Water from wells is usually low in oxygen and should be aerated before being placed in fish ponds.

In general, well water is the best water for catfish culture, because it is relatively free of harmful impurities. However, in the future it may be necessary to turn to other sources because of the gradual decline of ground water. The underground water level in some locations is declining fairly rapidly, one reason being the large quantity used for fish culture.

Figure 6-2. A Deep Well Equipped with Pump and Engine.

Springs. Springs may be used as sources of water for catfish culture. The water from springs resembles that of wells in that it may be low in oxygen and cold as it comes from the earth. Before a fish farm is established using spring water, the volume of water produced should be determined for all times of the year. Springs may have a tendency to produce less water in dry weather when the demand by a catfish farm may be the greatest. Such a decline in water volume could place a fish farm in serious trouble. In using spring water, precautions should be taken to prevent the entry of undesirable fish that may grow between ponds and the site of the spring. The use of spring water is limited to areas where springs are found.

Industrial Effluent. Some industrial and manufacturing plants may release waste water (effluent) which is safe for use in catfish farming. Electric power generating plants frequently release water which is chemically safe for use in growing fish. Such water has usually been warmed several degrees and may make possible the year-round production of catfish. Also, the use of warmed water may make it possible to produce catfish in colder climates not usually suitable for catfish. It is imperative that a chemical analysis of industrial waste water be made to determine its safety for use in catfish culture.

Volume of Water Needed

The volume of water needed for growing catfish depends on the size of the fish farm and the system of production used, that is, whether pond, raceway, or tank. Water is required for filling ponds and for replacing water lost by evaporation. Raceways require a continuous supply of flowing water.

Water requirements for ponds are usually stated in terms of acre-feet. One acre-foot is the amount of water required to cover 1 acre 1-foot deep. A pond of 3 surface acres with an average depth of 4 feet would require 12 acre-feet. One acre-foot contains ap-

Table 6-1

Approximate Amount of Time Required to Pump
1 Acre-Foot of Water at Different Pumping Rates

Pumping Rate	Time Required to Pump 1 Acre-Foot of Water (325,851 gallons)
(gpm)	*(hours)*
100	54.3
200	27.2
300	18.1
400	13.6
500	10.9
1,000	5.4
1,500	3.6
2,000	2.7

proximately 326,000 gallons. A well producing 1,000 gallons per minute (gpm) will produce 4.4 acre-feet in 24 hours. A 1,000-gpm well is generally considered adequate for a 40-acre fish farm.

The water in raceways is exchanged twice per hour. If a raceway holds 30,000 gallons of water, a well producing 1,000 gpm is required. Semi-raceways require less water in proportion to the volume of water held.

The volume of water needed with tanks and vats can be calculated by determining the volume of the tank or vat and the rate of exchange. The rate of water exchange varies with the rate at which fish are stocked. Higher rates of stocking require increased flow of water. In small round tanks of 400 to 425 gallons, capacity rates of flow used have ranged from 3.5 to 12.5 gpm. The rates of stocking for these flow rates have varied from 5 to 15 fish per cubic foot of water.

The size of wells or pumps needed is determined after the required volume of water has been calculated. It is often necessary to convert gallons to cubic feet and vice versa in the computation of water requirements. Several useful formulas are:

Cubic feet to gallons = number of cubic feet × 7.481
Gallons to cubic feet = number of gallons ÷ 7.481
(7.481 gallons = 1 cubic foot)

Gallons to cubic inches = number of gallons × 231
Cubic inches to gallons = number of cubic inches ÷ 231
(231 cubic inches = 1 gallon)

Problems in Water Management

Water may have problems which begin with its source or it may develop problems if improperly managed. A fish farmer must find a good source of water and follow practices which keep it good. The culture of fish involves some pollution of the water accompanied by efforts to reduce the extent of pollution. With any type of fish culture, the quantity that can be grown in a given amount of water is limited to the environment the water provides. Fish wastes, feed particles, and other factors in water quality need to be controlled, if possible.

Water management is primarily concerned with preventing or reducing problems which restrict production. These problems are related to temperature, oxygen depletion, water contamination, water chemistry, turbidity and color, weeds and algae, plankton bloom, and gas buildup. The effects of these problems on catfish range from mildly reducing the efficiency of growth to causing the death of the fish.

Temperature. The temperature of the water is related to feed intake and fish growth. With catfish, the best rate of growth and feed utilization is obtained when the water is 85°F. When water temperature is below 60°F and above 95°F, feeding and growth are markedly reduced.

The best water temperature for growth is not necessarily the best temperature for catfish eggs to hatch. Eggs hatch best in the high 70's, 6 to 8 degrees below the best growth temperature.

Sudden changes in water temperature can cause fish to suffer shock or even to die. Sudden changes rarely occur unless the fish are being hauled or a large amount of water is quickly being added to a pond, raceway, or other container. Fish should never be removed from water of one temperature and suddenly thrust into water which is considerably cooler or warmer. A change in temperature of from 10 to 15°F may cause stress or may even kill catfish. Most fish readily tolerate gradual temperature changes without harm.

The skillful catfish farmer will reduce feed and avoid fertilizing water in the winter. Likewise, the same farmer will supply oxygen to the water as the temperature increases. Chemical and biological reactions which require oxygen increase with higher water temperature.

Oxygen Depletion. Oxygen is required for catfish to carry on body functions and to remain alive. Oxygen depletion may cause the death of all the fish in a pond, raceway, or tank in a few hours. The larger fish will die first. Water in which fish are grown should contain at least 4 to 5 ppm of dissolved oxygen (DO) at 6 inches below the surface. Fish will die when the oxygen level is below 1.0 ppm. Oxygen depletion may be caused by one or more of the following:

1. Feeding activity of fish.—The body functions of fish require oxygen. As fish feed, they become more active and, hence, use more oxygen. The process of food digestion also uses oxygen.
2. Decay of organic matter.—Oxygen is tied up when weeds, leaves, feed, and other organic matter decompose. Over-

Figure 6-3. Oxygen Depletion May Result in Considerable Loss of Fish. (Courtesy, Bureau of Sport Fisheries and Wildlife, U.S. Department of the Interior)

feeding may contribute to problems of oxygen deficiency. No more than 35 pounds of feed should be fed per acre each day. A sudden die-off of plankton (small plants and animals that drift around in water) will tie up the oxygen.

3. Overstocking.—A heavy rate of stocking fish may result in oxygen being used from the water faster than it is being replaced.

4. Plant and animal life.—Wild fish and aquatic plants consume oxygen and compete with catfish.

5. Weather conditions.—Oxygen problems are often indirectly related to weather conditions. Several days of cloudy weather with very little wind may cause the supply of oxygen in the water to become low. With limited light the algae die, and decay occurs, tying up oxygen. Also, sunlight causes the phytoplankton (small plants) to produce oxygen through the process of photosynthesis.

6. Source of water.—Adding water low in oxygen reduces the amount of dissolved oxygen per volume of water. Water

from springs or wells that is pumped directly into fish-growing facilities may cause a decrease in oxygen supply.

7. Chemical reactions.—Chemical reactions occurring in the water may use oxygen.

8. Increased salinity.—Salty water does not hold as much dissolved oxygen as fresh water does. This is seldom a problem in catfish culture.

9. Water temperature.—Warm water will hold less oxygen than cold water will. At 41°F water will hold 12.8 ppm of dissolved oxygen, whereas at 86°F it will hold a maximum of 7.6 ppm.

The time of the day is related to the amount of dissolved oxygen in the water. The highest level of oxygen occurs in the afternoon and the lowest level occurs just before sunrise. Catfish are more likely to die from oxygen depletion at about sunrise than at any other time. Low oxygen may be revealed by the fish coming to the surface of the water and gasping for air. Less than 3.0 ppm of dissolved oxygen at a depth of 6 inches indicates that serious trouble may be ahead. When fish show signs of distress and the oxygen level drops below 2.0 ppm at a depth of 2 feet, measures should be taken immediately to restore oxygen to the water. Fish under stress from lack of oxygen will not eat and are more susceptible to diseases and parasites.

Sometimes the term *BOD (biological oxygen demand)* is used in describing oxygen uses. This includes the oxygen tied up by dead or dying plankton; decay of uneaten food, metabolic by-products, and vegetation; weeds, leaves, and moss; and other organic material.

Water Contamination. Water may become contaminated with pesticides, industrial wastes, and other substances. This problem, commonly known as pollution, is especially great in the cases of some natural streams and lakes where millions of wild fish have been killed. Such contaminated water is unfit for fish production. Residues of agricultural pesticides containing chlorinated hydrocarbon ingredients are problems in areas where such chemicals are commonly used on crops. Catfish containing traces of these chemicals are subject to condemnation and are unfit for consumption. Plasticizers, the softening agents in certain plastic and rubber products, may also cause considerable problems, the extent of

Figure 6-4. Freak Catfish Fry with Two Heads—Possibly the Result of Pollution. (Courtesy, Mayo Martin, Bureau of Sport Fisheries and Wildlife, U.S. Department of the Interior)

which are unknown. The problem of contaminated water is largely overcome by securing water from deep wells.

Water Chemistry. The makeup of water affects its suitability for use in catfish farming. The presence of traces of minerals and pH are a part of water chemistry. The term, *pH*, refers to whether the water is acidic or alkaline. A pH of 7.0 is neutral. Numbers less than 7.0, for example, 5.5, indicate that the water is acidic, and numbers greater than 7.0, for example 8.5, indicate that the water is alkaline, or basic. The pH of water may vary with the time of day at which pH tests are made. An average of a series of water tests taken periodically from just before sunrise until sunset may prove more reliable than a single pH test. When taken over a period of several days, the tests should be made at the same time each day. The desirable pH range is 6.3 to 7.5; however, 5.0 to 8.5 may be used satisfactorily for fish culture under certain conditions.

Traces of minerals, such as dissolved limestone, are present in most water. Some of these may be beneficial to fish culture. The presence of minerals (most often calcium or magnesium), when associated with pH, is known as "hardness." Agricultural limestone should be added to water with a pH less than 7.0 and a total hardness less than 20 ppm. This treatment will add more minerals and make the water harder. If the total water hardness is more than 200 ppm, the pond should be treated with ammonium sulfate to reduce the hardness.

Water in some locations may contain excessive iron or zinc. Iron is rapidly oxidized and may be harmful to fish when large quantities are present. Zinc may combine with other metals, such as copper, and be toxic. It is a good procedure to avoid using galvanized metals in fish culture.

Turbidity and Color. Turbidity refers to the suspended materials in water. The materials may be particles of clay (mud), tiny plants and animals (plankton), or other materials. The presence of certain plankton is desirable. The presence of some clay particles usually causes no problem. Ponds which receive runoff water may occasionally contain large amounts of clay and silt. These may settle to the bottom and smother fish eggs and fish food organisms.

Fish yields may be reduced by muddy water, and conditions which contribute to an undesirable flavor in fish may be caused by muddy water. The design and construction of ponds should minimize muddying conditions. Banks, slopes, and dams need to be covered with grass. Hay may be scattered on the water around the edges of ponds with muddy water. This treatment may be repeated in about 10 days; however, it should be used with discretion. Decaying hay will tie up oxygen and may cause an oxygen deficiency. Another treatment for muddy water is to scatter gypsum over the surface of ponds at the rate of 200 to 800 pounds per acre. An application of gypsum may be repeated at 7- to 10-day intervals until the water clears.

When ponds get runoff containing large amounts of plant leaves, stems, and wood, the water may become discolored. If water is the color of tea or weak coffee, extracts from plant materials may have altered its color. Abnormal water colors do not usually affect fish directly. Discolored water may restrict the passage of light through the water and, thereby, reduce plant growth. Sometimes agricultural limestone is added to water to correct this problem.

Weeds and Algae. Plants which grow in catfish ponds have different roles. Some are useful and desirable. Others are harmful and are considered to be weeds. Even the desirable plants can create unfavorable conditions if too many are present.

Aquatic weeds cause problems in several ways. They may

shade the water and prevent the growth of desirable plankton. Some of the weeds grow very rapidly and in massive amounts. They may tangle equipment and cause difficulties in harvesting catfish. The growth and decay of weeds may tie up oxygen and contribute to problems of oxygen depletion.

Most aquatic plants need to be controlled only when they cause problems. Four methods of control are available: mechanical, environmental manipulation, biological, and chemical.

Mechanical control involves cutting and removing the weeds from the water. This method is practical in small areas or when only a few weeds are present. For example, if a pond contains only a few willows, the best control is probably to cut them off and pull the tops out of the water. Since willows sprout readily, other methods of control will need to be used for more permanent control.

Controlling weeds by environmental manipulation involves creating conditions in ponds which are unfavorable to weed growth. It is possible to control weeds that grow in the shallow water around the edges of a pond by deepening the edges to a minimum of 18 inches. Some weeds are controlled by periodically lowering the water in a pond, especially in colder weather. Some weeds will die when they are out of water and exposed to below freezing temperatures.

To some extent, the design and construction of ponds relates to the water problems that may occur. The growth of weeds and algae is reduced in ponds with a minimum of water area less than 2½ feet deep.

Biological aquatic weed control is felt to have a lot of promise. It has not been developed where it is practical for widespread use in catfish farming. One application of biological control has been to add plant-eating fish, such as white amur, tilapia, grass carp, and Israeli carp to the catfish pond. With this method, there is the problem at harvest of sorting out these fish from the catfish. Also, large populations of the weed-eating fish may be required. Some of these fish are pests themselves. The importation and stocking of the grass carp, for example, has been banned in 35 states.

Chemical control of aquatic weeds involves the use of herbicides. Under most conditions, it is felt that chemical control is the most practical, economical, and safest method of controlling weeds. In using herbicides, it is essential to correctly identify the weeds and to apply the correct chemical. All herbicides should be used in accordance with regulations of the Environmental Protection Agency. Most herbicides are registered for specific uses, and these may change from time to time. The manufacturer's label on containers should be read and followed. Failure to follow proper procedures may result in damage to fish, the environment, nearby crops, and livestock. Some of the chemicals that are commonly used are copper sulfate, Diuron, 2,4,5-T, Aquazine, and Silvex.

The use of herbicides in ponds should be minimized because of possible residue contamination of the fish. Most herbicides should not be used within 60 days of fish harvest. In fact, only a few chemicals have been approved for use with food fish.

Figure 6-5. Water with an Algae Problem.

Four types of weeds are commonly found in catfish ponds: algae, submersed plants, emersed plants, and floating plants.

Algae are tiny, single-cell plants which do not have true leaves or flowers. Free-floating algae cells or groups of cells are commonly known as phytoplankton, the plant form of plankton as contrasted with the animal form, zooplankton. Phytoplankton produces oxygen and helps to reduce the chances of oxygen depletion. A certain level of phytoplankton is desired. A good phytoplankton bloom will tend to shade out weeds. If the water appears soupy green or brown, an excessive phytoplankton growth, or bloom, may have developed. Excessive phytoplankton is best eliminated by removing water from the pond and adding fresh water. This, in effect, dilutes the plankton concentration. Chemical controls for pond algae are shown in Table 6-2.

Filamentous algae may cause serious problems in ponds. The

Table 6-2
Possible Chemical Controls for Pond Algae

| | Algae/Weed to Be Controlled | | |
Control	Plankton Algae	Filamentous Algae	Muskgrass
Copper sulfate, also known as bluestone[1]	Yes	Yes	Yes
Karmex (Diuron) (Apply ¼ pound active ingredient per surface acre of pond. Dilute with water to insure even spray application.)	Yes	Yes	Yes
Simazine (Aquazine) (Apply 5-8 pounds active ingredient per surface acre of pond. Dilute with water to insure even spray application.)	No	Yes	Yes

Note: Read and follow instructions on label before using any chemical in water. The possible controls listed in this table have been satisfactorily used by some fish farmers. Their listing here does not imply a recommendation by the author.

[1]The toxicity of copper sulfate to fish depends on water hardness. Use copper sulfate as follows:
Do not use if total hardness of water is 0-49 ppm.
Use 0.5 to 1.0 ppm if total hardness of water is 50-99 ppm.
Use 1.0 to 1.5 ppm if total hardness of water is 100-149 ppm.
Use 1.5 to 2.0 ppm if total hardness of water is 149-200 ppm.

Source: "Aquatic Weed Identification and Control: Algae," Information Sheet 1035. Mississippi Cooperative Extension Service, 1979.

filamentous form consists of long, stringy, hairlike strands of algae. Filamentous algae are sometimes known as "pond scum" and compete with the desired plankton for light and nutrients.

Muskgrass is a form of algae that may resemble flowering plants. It has stems with wheel-like leaves or branches. There are two common kinds of muskgrass: *Chara* and *Nitella*. *Chara* tends to feel rough and gritty to the touch, while *Nitella* feels smooth.

Weeds that are rooted to the bottom of ponds and grow to the surface of the water are known as "submersed weeds." Common submersed weeds which may cause problems in catfish ponds are bladderwort, pondweed, watershield, hydrilla, parrotfeather, coontail, and fanwort. Some of these plants have floating leaves, while others have leaves that occur entirely below the surface of the water. Perhaps the weed which is most dreaded is hydrilla. This weed is not native to the United States. It was imported as an aquarium plant. Hydrilla is a serious threat to all freshwater because it is hardy, prolific, and almost impossible to stop once it is started. Table 6-3 summarizes chemical control measures for submersed weeds.

Weeds that grow in shallow areas and extend above the water are "emersed weeds." Emersed weeds which may cause problems in catfish ponds are water primrose, cattail, lotus, arrowhead, willow, water lily, smartweed, bulrush, and spikerush. Several chemicals have been used to control these weeds. Table 6-4 presents a summary of possible chemical control for emersed weeds.

Weeds that are not attached to the bottom and float about on the surface of the water are "floating weeds." Sometimes these weeds may form a green blanket on the surface of the water. Floating weeds include water hyacinth, duckweed, and alligator weed. It is possible to remove floating weeds from a pond by raking them out onto the bank or to control them by using certain chemicals. Table 6-5 presents possible chemical control measures for floating weeds.

Plankton Bloom. The tiny plants and animals which float and swim in pond water are known as plankton. Algae plankton (phytoplankton) produces oxygen and, when present in sufficient quantity, will aid in shading the bottom of the pond, thus reducing the growth of weeds. Pond fertilization, especially with phosphorus, encourages plankton growth. The animal form (zooplankton) is a natural food of catfish. Phytoplankton is not eaten by catfish.

Table 6-3

Possible Chemical Controls for Submersed Weeds

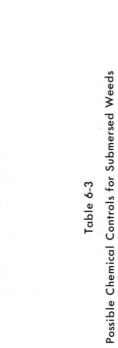

Control	Weed to Be Controlled						
	Bladderwort	Pondweed	Watershield	Hydrilla	Fanwort	Parrotfeather	Coontail
Simazine (Aquazine) (Apply 5 to 8 pounds per surface acre of pond. Dilute with water to insure even spray application.)	Yes	No	No	No	No	No	No
Aquathol Plus (Apply 1 gallon per surface acre of pond. In some cases, 1 gallon per acre-foot may be required.)	Yes	Yes	No	No	Yes	Yes	Yes
2,4,5-T (Apply 1 gallon of 4-pound acid per gallon 2,4,5-T; 8 ounces detergent; and 50 gallons of water per surface acre of pond.)	No	No	Yes	No	No	No	No

(Continued)

Table 6-3 (continued)

Control	Weed to Be Controlled						
	Bladderwort	Pondweed	Watershield	Hydrilla	Fanwort	Parrotfeather	Coontail
Silvex (Apply 1 gallon, 8 ounces of detergent, and 50 gallons of water per surface acre. Mix evenly, and spray plants.)	No	No	Yes	No	No	No	No
Mixture of 2 gallons Diquat and 3 gallons Cutrine per acre. (Dilute with water to insure even spray application.)	No	No	No	Yes	No	No	No
Aquathol (Endothall) (Apply 2 gallons per surface acre of pond.)	No	No	No	No	Yes	Yes	Yes

Note: Read and follow instructions on label before using any chemical in water. The possible controls listed in this table have been satisfactorily used by some fish farmers. Their listing here does not imply a recommendation by the author.

Source: "Aquatic Weed Identification and Control," Information Sheets 1028, 1029, 1030, and 1034. Mississippi Cooperative Extension Service, 1979.

Table 6-4

Possible Chemical Controls for Emersed Weeds

Control	Weed to Be Controlled							
	Bulrush	Cattail	Water Primrose	Smartweed	Lotus	Willow	Water Lily
Silvex (Apply 1 gallon, 8 ounces of detergent, and 50 gallons of water per surface acre of pond. Mix evenly, and spray on plants.)	Yes	No	No	No	Yes	No	Yes
2,4,5-T (Apply 1 gallon of 4-pound acid per gallon, 8 ounces of detergent, and 50 gallons of water per surface acre. Mix evenly, and spray on plants.)	Yes	No	Yes	No	Yes	Yes	Yes

(Continued)

Table 6-4 (continued)

Control	Weed to Be Controlled						
	Bulrush	Cattail	Water Primrose	Smartweed	Lotus	Willow	Water Lily
Dalapon (Apply 7½ pounds, 8 ounces of detergent, and 50 gallons of water per surface acre. Mix evenly, and spray on plants.)	No	Yes	No	No	No	No	No
Aquathol Plus (Apply 1 gallon per surface acre.)	No	No	No	Yes	No	No	No

Note: Read and follow instructions on label before using any chemical in water. The possible controls listed in this table have been satisfactorily used by some fish farmers. Their being listed here does not imply a recommendation by the author.

Source: "Aquatic Weed Identification and Control," Information Sheets 1026, 1032, 1037, 1027, and 1031. Mississippi Cooperative Extension Service, 1979.

Table 6-5

Possible Chemical Controls for Floating Weeds

| | Weed to Be Controlled | | |
Control	Water Hyacinth	Duckweed	Alligator Weed
Silvex (Apply 8 pounds of active ingredient, 8 ounces of detergent, and 50 gallons of water per surface acre. Mix evenly, and spray on plants.)	No	No	Yes
Diquat (Apply ¾ gallon, 8 ounces of surfactant, and 50 gallons of water per surface acre. Mix evenly, and spray on plants.)	Yes	Yes	No

Note: Read and follow instructions on label before using any chemical in water. The possible controls listed in this table have been satisfactorily used by some fish farmers. Their being listed here does not imply a recommendation by the author.

Source: "Aquatic Weed Identification and Control," Information Sheets 1033 and 1034. Mississippi Cooperative Extension Service, 1979.

Gas Buildup. Sometimes the water used for growing catfish will develop a high level of certain toxic gases, such as carbon dioxide, hydrogen sulfide, and ammonia. Carbon dioxide is a by-product of respiration and decomposition of organic matter. A level of 25 to 30 ppm will cause death. Aeration will reduce the amount of carbon dioxide in water. Hydrogen sulfide is associated with the decay of organic matter and is found in water near the bottom of ponds. It is toxic to fish at the level of 1 to 2 ppm. Ammonia in ponds is formed by certain bacteria in utilizing the protein in the excretory matter of fish. The level at which ammonia is toxic is related to the pH of the water. An ammonia level of ½ to 1 ppm can be toxic if the pH is high. Sudden increases in the number of fish in a pond or in rate of feeding may cause increases in ammonia level. Testing for the presence of ammonia is difficult. Tests have to be made on the spot, because water will lose it in a few minutes.

Oxygenation of Water

The presence of dissolved oxygen in water is probably the most important water quality factor in catfish farming. Numerous devices and water additives have been used in attempts to restore oxygen to water, since fish will die when the oxygen level is below 1.0 ppm. One common way of supplying oxygenated water is to remove water low in oxygen from the bottom of a pond and add fresh water high in oxygen to the surface. The amount of oxy-

Figure 6-6. Aerating Water by Using a Wooden Trough. (Courtesy, Bureau of Sport Fisheries and Wildlife, U.S. Department of the Interior)

Figure 6-7. Water Aerator Suspended in a Vat.

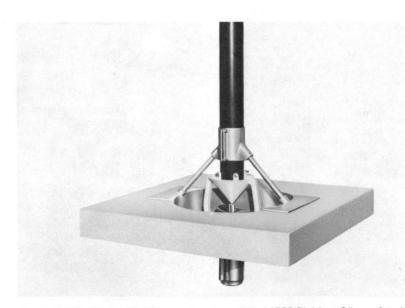

Figure 6-8. An Aerator That Floats. (Courtesy, AIR-o-LATOR Division of Roycraft Industries)

gen in the water at the bottom of a pond may be very low, espe-cially in the summer. This is normal and is not critical so long as sufficient oxygen is present to a depth of 24 to 36 inches.

Mechanical devices which aerate the water by spraying it through the air or by attempting to mix air with the water are used. Pumps may spray water into the air or splash it off boards or con-crete. When using pumps to aerate water, always pump water from the surface and not from the bottom of a pond. Devices which inject bottled oxygen into water are sometimes used.

Various chemicals have been used in attempts to restore oxy-gen. Potassium permanganate can be used at the rate of 1 to 3 pounds per acre. Fertilizers high in phosphate content can be used at the rate of 40 to 50 pounds of ordinary superphosphate per acre. Fertilizers containing nitrogen should not be used when oxygen is deficient.

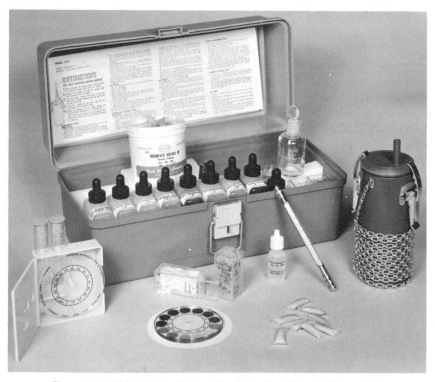

Figure 6-9. Kit for Testing Water. (Courtesy, Hach Chemical Company)

The amount of dissolved oxygen in water can be determined or estimated in several ways. Most common are commercial kits which simplify the process of water analysis. In fact, the available kits are used to test for other characteristics, especially pH and the presence of ammonia.

Fertilization of Water

The program of water management may include the fertilization of ponds, especially new ponds. Inorganic fertilizer may be added to stimulate the growth of plankton, a natural food for fish. The addition of fertilizer is a common practice with ponds constructed for sport fishing purposes and is sometimes practiced with ponds used for commercial catfish production. Once a good plankton bloom has been established, the conditions for maintaining the bloom must be regulated. A good bloom aids in keeping adequate oxygen in the water and usually develops without fertilization. Some authorities recommend that ponds for catfish culture not be fertilized, since overfertility is a problem with many established ponds. Overfertility may result in excessive plankton bloom and other problems.

It is essential that fertilizer be applied at the right time and in the proper amount. Pond fertilization should be started in the spring when the water temperature is around 65°F. The fish are usually stocked in the pond before fertilization. If adequate plankton bloom is present, it is not necessary to apply fertilizer. The adequacy of bloom can be determined by placing a bright object 12 to 18 inches below the surface of the water. If the object is not visible at this depth, a good plankton bloom is present and fertilization is not needed.

The growth of plankton requires nitrogen, phosphorus, and potassium. It is not necessary to have a high level of these nutrients in the water; however, a rather uniform level should be maintained. The amount of fertilizer to use will vary from pond to pond. A soil or water test should be made to get an indication of the nutrients present and those needed in fertilizer. Most soils contain adequate potassium for plankton growth. Nitrogen and phosphorus are most often added. It has been found that 50 pounds of 16-20-4 or 16-20-0 fertilizer per acre will produce good results. The latter fertilizer is used if soil or water tests reveal that adequate potassium is present. Applications of fertilizer are repeated at intervals of 10 days until a desirable plankton bloom is obtained. Three to five applications should produce the desired bloom. If not, the water should be checked for undesirable filamentous algae or aquatic weeds.

Fertilizer may be applied to ponds in several ways. The method of application should be one which will allow the nutrients in the fertilizer to be gradually dissolved and distributed throughout the pond. Methods include the following: (1) Fertilizer may be broadcast over the surface. (2) Whole bags of fertilizer may be placed in the water around the edge of the pond (small holes should be punched in the bags to allow wave action to dissolve and distribute the fertilizer). (3) A platform may be placed beneath the surface of the water with fertilizer placed on it. (4) Floating devices that move around a pond may be used.

The presence of aquatic weeds and other vegetation may reduce the effectiveness of pond fertilization. Increased plankton growth is not obtained if the nutrients in fertilizer are used by undesirable plants for growth. Aquatic plants should be destroyed before a fertilization program is initiated. New ponds frequently do not have the problems of excessive water vegetation as do older ponds. Good plankton bloom tends to shade out undesirable vegetation. Older ponds usually do not need fertilization, since uneaten food and fecal material from the fish tend to provide the nutrients needed for plankton growth.

As a precaution, it is well to remember that many commercial catfish ponds have problems of overfertility. The addition of commercial fertilizers would simply add to fertility and contribute to possible water-management problems.

Filtering and Recycling Water

Water in which catfish are grown becomes polluted with excess feed, feces, and other matter. If allowed to be carried to extreme, this type of pollution can greatly reduce the level of fish production. Part of the job of the fish farmer is to manage water so that the level of such pollution is minimized. This may involve using care in not overfeeding fish, replacing water in a system with fresh water, developing optimal conditions for biologically removing pollutants, and, perhaps, establishing a deliberate program of filtration. Of course, all factors in the management of water may be utilized to maintain a suitable environment for fish.

Interest in filtering and recycling water has increased in recent years. This may be due to a lowering of water tables in the earth and the expansion of catfish farming into areas without springs and where drilling dependable wells is risky. Filtering refers to the removal of certain materials from water. These are usually floating in the water and are often capable of being decomposed. Recycling refers to using the same water over and over in a fish-production system. Water laden with undesirable materials is made ready for recycling by filtering in some way so that it is relatively free of harmful materials.

The natural processes occurring in ponds tend to filter water and make it suitable for fish culture. The high levels of stocking and feeding used in fish culture may overbalance the water so that the natural processes are incapable of meeting the demand placed on them. This makes it necessary to turn to external filtration systems. In raceways, vats, tanks, and troughs, the problem is usually more critical because of increased rates of stocking and the lack of natural filtration processes. Especially is this true if the systems are closed.

Three types of filtration may be used: biological, mechanical, and chemical. Combinations of all three types may be needed in fish farming, especially with super-intensive systems of production such as in tanks and raceways.

Biological Filtration. Biological filtration is most common and involves activity by bacteria in the water in breaking down organic compounds, such as excess feed or feces. There are three stages in this process: mineralization, nitrification, and denitrification. Mineralization involves chemical breakdown of proteins and nucleic acids to form ammonia. Nitrification is the biological oxidation of ammonia into nitrites and nitrates. Denitrification involves the changing of nitrites and nitrates into free nitrogen or nitrous oxide. Various gaseous forms of nitrogen may escape from the water or be reused by life in the water. These processes occur naturally in ponds but must often be stimulated in closed systems.

In closed systems, special filter beds constructed of sand, gravel, and other materials are often used. Most often gravel is used because the surface area of the gravel makes a place available for the attachment of bacteria. It has been found that gravel covered with detritus particles is more effective in promoting the growth of nitrifying bacteria. (Detritus particles are loose materials on the surfaces of individual rocks and result from disintegration of the rock.) Crushed limestone rock is often used in making filter beds which may be 8 feet thick or more. The most rapid rate of biological filtration occurs at warmer temperatures, often 75 to 90°F.

Mechanical Filtration. The physical separation of particles suspended in water is mechanical filtration. It usually involves passing water through a screen or filter of some type. The filter media are most often sand and gravel. Sand and gravel of finer size usually do more effective jobs of cleaning water. The surface area of the mechanical filter bed is often equal to the surface area of the production system. However, the demand for water is a definite consideration. Mechanical filters occasionally need to be cleaned. Sometimes a backwash procedure is used where the flow of water is temporarily reversed through the filter bed.

Chemical Filtration. Biological filtration converts suspended organic matter to other forms which are usually less objectionable or which are released from the water. Mechanical filtration removes floating particles from water. Chemical filtration is used to remove substances not removed with biological or mechanical filtration. Chemical filtration may involve a number of procedures, such as removing dissolved substances by adsorption using charcoal filters, using ion exchange resins, and injecting air into water to form foam.

Prevention of Off-Flavors

Catfish occasionally develop off-flavors which reduce their desirability as food. Such off-flavors are generally attributed to conditions in the environment and are not well understood. Most problems with off-flavor are attributed to organisms in the water even though the exact relationship is unknown.

Before fish are harvested, a sample of several catfish should be taken from each pond, raceway, or tank system and cooked to check for off-flavors. If off-flavors are present in the cooked fish, harvesting should be delayed until the flavor problem is corrected. If fish are harvested before the presence of off-flavors is detected, it is suggested that they be held in vats a few days before processing. Catfish will lose their off-flavors in several days if they are held in vats with fresh running water and are fed rations known not to cause flavor problems.

Off-flavors may be attributed to several related conditions: (1) excessive plankton bloom, (2) the presence of muskgrass, (3) over-feeding, (4) decaying organic matter, (5) chemicals, (6) muddy water, and (7) feeds high in fish by-products.

Figure 6-10. Conditions Such as This May Contribute to Off-Flavor in Catfish.

Excessive Plankton Bloom. Excessive plankton is more likely to occur when the water contains a high level of fertility. Blue-green algae, when a considerable amount is present, will cause off-flavors in catfish. Dense concentration of blue-green algae may form on the surface of the water. Concentration of algae, or "scum," may mold and give off a foul, musty odor and cause the water to smell sour. Problems from plankton bloom are increased with heavy clay soils.

One of the simplest techniques of reducing plankton concentration, if ample water is available, is to flush the pond with water. Flushing with water in effect dilutes the concentration of plankton and washes much of it out of the pond. Algae should not be destroyed and should be allowed to remain in a pond because their decomposition ties up the oxygen in the water. This is very important, since large algae kills may result in a deficiency of oxygen and a loss of fish.

Muskgrass. Muskgrass, or *Chara,* is a kind of alga that grows from the bottom of a pond. It has a disagreeable musty odor which may be passed to fish. Muskgrass does not grow well in water with a high level of fertility. Construction of ponds according to recommendations (with a minimum of area with water less than 2½ feet deep) will also aid in preventing the growth of muskgrass.

Overfeeding. Feeding more than is consumed will result in accumulation of feed in the water and on the bottom of the pond. The accumulation of feed in a pond causes problems in two major ways: (1) The excess feed may sour. Catfish may absorb the flavor of sour feed. (2) The excess feed accumulation in the water will enhance the growth of blue-green algae, which sometimes cause off-flavor in fish, and may lead to oxygen depletion. If the water becomes sour from excessive feed accumulation, water should be removed from the bottom of the pond and added to the surface. The volume of feed should be reduced to the amount that will be consumed.

Figure 6-11. A Paddlewheel Aerator Is Effective in Water Management. (Courtesy, Otterbine Aeration)

Organic Matter. Decaying organic matter may cause off-flavors in catfish. Trees, stumps, and roots should be removed from pond sites during construction. Hay, leaves, manure, and other plant and animal matter should be kept out of growing ponds.

Chemicals. Off-flavors may be imparted by chemicals in addition to rendering fish unsafe for consumption. Agricultural and industrial dusts, sprays, and by-products may drift over ponds and cause off-flavors. The use of chemicals near fish ponds should be at times when the wind will not blow drifting dust toward the ponds. Operators of aerial application equipment should be cautioned not to spray catfish ponds.

Muddy Water. Fish grown or held in muddy water may acquire an unpleasant, muddy taste. The muddy water itself may not cause off-flavor but may contribute to other conditions which lead to off-flavor. All areas surrounding ponds should be covered with vegetation to prevent muddy runoff from entering the pond. Livestock entering a pond also tend to muddy the water.

Feed. The ingredients in feed may impart off-flavors to fish. Feeds with high amounts of various fish by-products such as fish oil may cause catfish to have an excessive fishy flavor. Most commerical feeds contain a balance of ingredients designed not to cause off-flavors. It is unlikely that the common brands of commercial feeds will cause off-flavor problems.

Questions and Problems for Discussion

1. Why is quality of water important in catfish farming?
2. Distinguish between the terms *water quality* and *water chemistry*.
3. What are the sources of water? Indicate which is best and why.
4. What are the main problems in water management?
5. What is water turbidity?
6. How do aquatic weeds cause problems?
7. What are four methods of aquatic weed control?
8. What precautions should be followed in using herbicides to control weeds?
9. What are the major causes of oxygen depletion?
10. What are some ways of restoring oxygen to water?
11. Why should caution be used in the fertilization of ponds?
12. What three types of filtration are used?
13. What is recycling?
14. How are food fish checked for off-flavors?
15. What are some possible causes of off-flavors in catfish?

7

Feeding Catfish

All living things—both plants and animals—require certain nutrients to carry on normal body functions and to grow. Catfish are not exceptions. Further, catfish are omnivorous; that is, they consume both plant and animal foods. Therefore, nutrients from both plant and animal sources should be included in the rations for catfish.

In the wild, catfish feed along the bottoms of ponds and streams. They consume what they can find—crayfish, fish, insects, other small animals, algae, and other plants. Usually, catfish are able to obtain a sufficient mixture of these foods in order to maintain reasonably balanced diets. With commercial catfish farming, the fish are often stocked too heavily for the natural foods in pond water. Catfish must receive a proper diet.

This chapter includes the following areas on feeding catfish:

> Types of rations
> Basic nutrient requirements
> Feed ingredients
> Forms of feed
> Feeding fry, fingerlings, and stockers
> Feeding for food fish production
> Ratio of feed to gain
> Methods of feeding
> Storing feed

Types of Rations

There are two basic types of rations, complete and supplemental. It is important to know and to be able to apply the differences in these rations.

A complete ration is one which supplies all of the nutrients needed by catfish. Fish grown in intensive culture where there is a large population of fish in a given amount of water must receive a complete ration. Fish in raceways, cages, tanks, and high-density ponds must be fed a complete ration.

A supplemental ration is one which supplies a portion of the nutrients needed by catfish. When catfish are stocked at low or moderate levels in ponds, they are able to obtain some natural food from the water. This means that some of their nutrient requirements can be met by the natural foods. Supplemental rations are usually deficient in certain vitamins and minerals. The natural food in a pond is sufficient to produce only from 50 to 400 pounds of catfish per acre each year. This is far below the level of production of successful fish farms.

Most ponds are stocked with 2,500 to 4,000 fingerlings per acre. Some farmers, using good management, may stock 5,000 or more. The per acre yield is 2,500 to 5,000 pounds or more each year, with the average being 3,000 pounds. It is obvious that the natural foods in a pond will not begin to support this level of production. Therefore, it is essential that supplemental or complete rations be fed. In most cases, complete rations are best.

Basic Nutrient Requirements

The basic nutrient requirements of catfish are similar to the basic requirements of many other animals; yet considerable differences in specific requirements exist. Most research into the nutritional needs of catfish has been primarily with those species which are commercially produced, especially channel catfish. The basic nutritive requirements of catfish are: (1) protein, (2) energy (carbohydrates and fats), (3) minerals, (4) vitamins, and (5) water.

The amounts and types of the nutrients needed by catfish vary with the age of the catfish, their production function, and their environmental conditions. Very young catfish grow rapidly and need higher levels of protein than larger fish need. During growth from fingerling to marketable food fish, one diet may be used with size of pellet being increased as the fish grow. Broodfish usually receive different feed, including raw flesh, prior to the spawning season.

Protein. Proteins are needed for growth and to replace tissues

Figure 7-1. A Modern Catfish Feed Manufacturing Plant.

which normally break down each day in the body of fish. Proteins are made of amino acids which, in turn, are primarily composed of carbon, hydrogen, oxygen, nitrogen, and sometimes other chemical elements. Catfish must receive sufficient protein for growth and body maintenance. Young catfish that are actively growing require somewhat higher levels of protein than do older, more mature fish. In nature, catfish eat food which usually has a rather high protein content. Natural foods high in protein include bacteria, plankton, insects, insect larvae, fish eggs, and fish.

Commercially produced catfish are grown at high-population densities, thus making the available supply of natural food inadequate to meet their needs. Sufficient protein must be supplied each day. A deficiency of protein in the diet of fish will cause a protein loss in the tissues of the body. Feeding protein in excess of the amount actually needed by fish will result in waste and increased feed costs. Since excess protein is excreted by the kidneys and gills it can cause water problems. It is important that catfish receive a balanced amount of protein containing the necessary amino acids.

Good growth is obtained when catfish are fed diets containing 25 to 40 percent crude protein. The best growth in ponds is obtained at the 25 to 30 percent level. Some of the commercially manufactured feeds for pond food fish culture contain 32 percent protein. Catfish grown under intensive conditions where little natural food is available, such as in raceways, tanks, and cages, need feeds with about 36 to 40 percent high-protein levels. Fingerlings respond best to feeds with 30 to 36 percent protein. Protein should be of both plant and animal origin. Common sources of protein in fish feeds are fish meal, corn gluten meal, soybean meal, feather meal, blood meal, and poultry by-product meal. A ration containing protein in excess of what fish need wastes protein and costs more. A ration for growing catfish should contain a minimum of protein in certain forms, as shown in Table 7-1.

Energy. Energy is required for activity, growth, and reproduction. It is obtained from carbohydrates, fats, and proteins. Rations should be designed so that the energy will be supplied by fats and carbohydrates rather than by proteins. The cost of ingredients con-

Table 7-1

Guidelines for Protein in Catfish Feeds

Ingredient	Minimum Percent in Food
Crude protein	30
Digestible protein	25
Animal protein	14
Fish meal protein	7

Source: "Report to the Fish Farmers." Washington: U.S. Department of the Interior, Bureau of Sport Fisheries and Wildlife, 1970, p. 32.

taining high amounts of protein is usually considerably greater than that of ingredients containing carbohydrates and fats. Energy in fish feeds is primarily supplied by cereals, cereal by-products, fish meal, and other meal by-products. The amount of carbohydrates in fish feeds is established by subtracting the sum of required protein, fat, ash, moisture, and fiber from 100 percent. The amount of fish meal used in feed should not exceed 20 percent because larger amounts may cause excessive accumulation of fat and result in off-flavor in fish. In terms of metabolizable energy, 1,200 calories are needed per pound of feed.

Carbohydrates are not essential in catfish rations if other sources of energy are available. However, carbohydrates are usually used because they are less expensive than other sources of energy. Feedstuffs containing plant matter, such as cereal by-products and grain, have carbohydrates. It is almost impossible to prepare a catfish feed that does not contain carbohydrates. Most floating catfish feed contains about 25 percent grain.

The major sources of fat in catfish rations are fish meal, fish oil, feather meal, soybean meal, cottonseed meal, and wheat. Fats contain essential fatty acids. The exact fatty acid requirement of catfish is unknown. Usually there are sufficient fatty acids in fish meal to meet basic dietary needs.

Excessive energy in a ration may cause "fatty" fish. The ratio of protein to energy is important. A ration with adequate energy will allow protein to be used for growth rather than for energy.

Minerals. The development of the catfish skeleton is dependent upon minerals. Calcium and phosphorus are primarily used for bone development. Magnesium, potassium, copper, iodine, and iron are needed in very small quantities. Rations should contain 1.4 to 1.5 percent calcium and 0.8 percent phosphorus. Salt should be added to rations at a rate of 0.5 to 1.0 percent.

Usually, feeds containing proteins derived from animal products contain most of the needed minerals. With rations containing ingredients of less than 15 percent animal products, a trace mineral supplement is recommended. This should be added during feed manufacturing. Catfish can obtain some minerals from water, but, except for calcium, most water tends to be low in essential minerals. It is known that animals require a number of minerals, but the exact mineral requirements of catfish have not yet been determined.

Table 7-2

Symptoms of Vitamin Deficiencies in Catfish
and Sources of Vitamins

Vitamin	Deficiency Symptoms	Sources of Vitamin
Thiamine	Reduced weight gain, lethargy, and difficulty maintaining balance	Soybeans, cereal bran, dried yeast, and fresh organ meats
Riboflavin	Opaque lens of one or both eyes and loss of weight	Fresh meats, cereal, grains, and oil seed
Pyridoxine	Erratic swimming, tetany, gyrations and muscular spasms, and reduced weight gain	Cereal grains and by-products, yeast, and fresh organ meats
Pantothenic acid	"Flabby" body tissues; excessive mucus on gills; eroded membranes on gills, lower jaw, fins, and barbels; lethargy; and weight loss	Cereal bran, yeast, organ tissues, and fish flesh
Niacin	Lethargy, reduced coordination, photophobia, and tetany from stress	Yeast, legumes, and organ meats
Folic acid	Lethargy and anorexia	Yeast, fish tissues, liver, and kidney
Vitamin B-12	Reduced weight gain	Meats, animal by-products, and fish meals
Choline	Reduced weight gain, bloody areas on kidneys, and enlarged liver	Wheat germ, soybean meal, and organ meats
Vitamin A	Fluid accumulation in body cavity, abnormal protrusion of eyes, and bleeding kidneys	Fish oils, fish meals, and all fish products with oil residues
Vitamin E	Protrusion of eyes, excessive fluid accumulation in body, and reduced growth	Wheat germ, soybeans, and corn
Vitamin K	Excessive hemorrhage resulting in death	Alfalfa leaves, soybeans, and animal livers
Vitamin D	No significant change in growth or mortality	Fish oils

Source: "Nutrition and Feeding of Channel Catfish," Bulletin 218. Auburn, Alabama: Agricultural Experiment Station, 1977, pp. 28-29.

Vitamins. Catfish need vitamins for health and grov̶ necessarily to build body tissues. Vitamin additives are important for catfish grown in intensive culture. Many ̶c̶ feeds contain a vitamin premix. A vitamin premix consists of a number of vitamins in varied amounts. Fish growth may be improved by as much as 15 percent by the addition of a vitamin premix to the regular feed. Currently, fish feed is being prepared with a vitamin premix similar to that used in poultry feed. The symptoms of certain vitamin deficiencies in catfish, along with sources of the vitamin, are presented in Table 7-2. The kinds and amounts of vitamins that should be used in a ton of catfish feed are shown in Table 7-3.

Water. Catfish, in addition to living in water, also need water for internal functions of the body. The amount necessary for this purpose is unknown. However, it is known that the water should be free of harmful impurities.

Table 7-3

Suggested Vitamin Premix for Supplemental and Complete Catfish Rations

| | Amount per Ton of Feed | |
Vitamin	Supplemental Feed	Complete Feed
Vitamin A	2,000,000 IU	5,000,000 IU
Vitamin D	200,000 IU	1,000,000 IU
Alpha tecopherol acetate (d or dl in beadlet form)	10 g	50 g
Menadione sodium bisulfite	5 g	10 g
Choline chloride	400 g	500 g
Niacin	15-25 g	90 g
Riboflavin	2-6 g	18 g
Pyridozine	10 g	20 g
Thiamine	0	20 g
D-calcium pantothenate	6-10 g	36 g
Folic acid	0	5 g
Vitamin B-12	2-8 mg	15 mg
BHT antioxidant	10 g	10 g
Ascorbic acid	0-100 g	100 g
Biotin	0	100 mg

Source: "Catfish Food Formulation for Hard Pellet (Sinking) Pond, Raceway and Cage Ration." Stuttgart, Arkansas: Fish Farming Experimental Station, 1977, p. 2.

Feed Ingredients

Commercially prepared feeds are often used in catfish farming. Such feeds should be properly formulated and labeled. The tags or labels on feed bags should be checked to determine if the feed contains sufficient nutrients and if these nutrients are supplied by the most efficient ingredients. The nutrients that should be contained in feed for growing channel catfish are shown in Table 7-4.

Table 7-4
Nutrient Levels in Feed for Channel Catfish in Growing Ponds

Purified Nutrient	Percent Level Producing Best Growth	Percent Range in Level for Acceptable Growth Rate
Protein	28	28-39
Carbohydrate	20	10-20
Fat	10	5-10
Fiber	10	10-20
Minerals	Not available	

Source: "Report to the Fish Farmers." Washington: U.S. Department of the Interior, Bureau of Sport Fisheries and Wildlife, 1970, p. 31.

Feed for catfish can be formulated with a variety of ingredients. The sources of these ingredients are important. Catfish feed should contain fish meal. Ingredients, such as cottonseed meal, containing pesticide residues, should not be used. The ingredients of a feed that have have been found to produce fast, economical growth are shown in Table 7-5.

Forms of Feed

Feed for catfish may be prepared in several forms and particle sizes. The most common form is the extruded, hard pellet. This form is economical to manufacture and, since all ingredients are pressed together, prevents fish from selecting certain ingredients and rejecting, or wasting, others. Hard pellets are easy to handle and can be fed with blowers or self-feeders. The hard pellet does not float but will quickly sink to the bottom of a pond. Pellet size may vary so that smaller pellets may be fed to smaller fish.

Table 7-5

Sample Formula for a Sinking-Pellet
Complete Catfish Feed[1]

Ingredient	Amount per Ton
	(pounds)
Fish meal, menhaden (60% protein)	240
Blood meal (80% protein)	100
Feather meal (80% digestibility)	100
Soybean meal, solvent, toasted, dehulled (44% protein)	450
Cottonseed meal, solvent, dehulled (41% protein)	250
Dried distillers' solubles	160
Rice bran	400
Wheat shorts	200
Dehydrated alfalfa (17% protein)	70
Salt, iodized	20
Vitamin premix	10
	2,000

[1]This formula will yield a complete feed with the following guaranteed analysis:

Crude protein, more than 36%
Animal protein, more than 15%
Crude fiber, less than 12%
Crude fat, more than 5%

Source: "Catfish Food Formulation for Hard Pellet (Sinking) Pond, Raceway and Cage Ration." Stuttgart, Arkansas: Fish Farming Experimental Station, 1977, p. 1.

Expanded pellets which float on the water are preferred by some farmers. The procedure by which expanded pellets are manufactured may destroy some of the vitamins and amino acids in the ingredients. However, after pelletizing and before packaging, it is possible to spray certain vitamins, amino acids, and fats onto the feed. Floating feed is generally more expensive than hard pellets but is considered to be a management tool in that the feeding activity of the fish can be observed when the feed is thrown on the water.

Other forms in which feed for catfish is manufactured are dry meals, crumbles, blocks, semi-moist pellets, and agglomerates. Fry are often fed finely ground forms of meal and are occasionally fed crumbles. Crumbles do not float and are prepared by cracking hard pellets into crumb-sized particles. Semi-moist pellets contain 25 to 30 percent water and, therefore, are not hard. The cost of semi-moist pellets is greater than that of some other forms. Agglomerates are prepared by rolling finely ground dry-formula

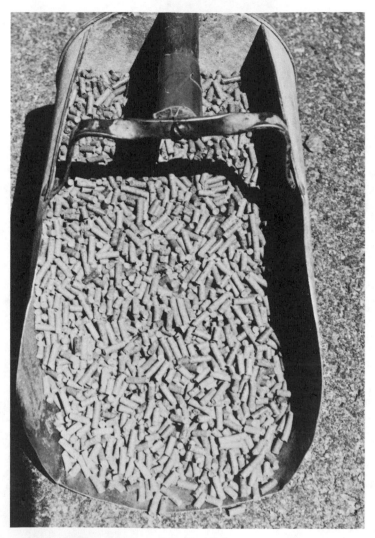

Figure 7-2. Hard Pellets.

feed into balls and are sometimes known as "balled-up feed."
Some consideration has been given to the use of dough-type feeds,
but since the moisture content is relatively high, such feed might
tend to spoil rapidly.

Size of feed particles, or pellets, is important. Fry cannot eat
pellets and must be fed a meal form of feed. Fry feed (starter meal)

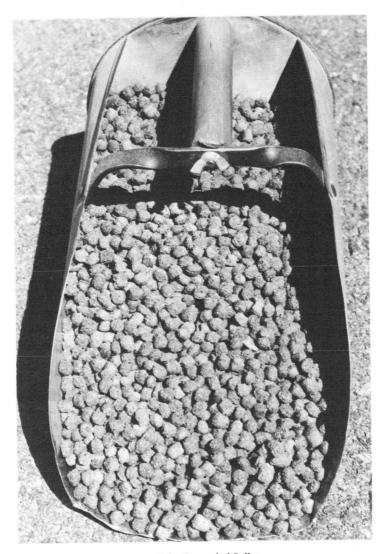

Figure 7-3. Expanded Pellets.

must have particles small enough to pass through a No. 30 sieve. Pellet sizes are numbered as follows:

No. 2 pellet	$1/8''$ diameter and $1/8''$ long
No. 3 pellet	$1/8''$ diameter and $1/2''$ to $3/4''$ long
No. 4 pellet	$3/16''$ diameter and $1/4''$ to $1/2''$ long
No. 5 pellet	$1/4''$ diameter and $1/4''$ to $1/2''$ long

The most commonly used size is the No. 4 pellet. The optimum size to use is the largest that the catfish will eat readily because less feed is wasted. The use of small pellets wastes more feed because more surface is exposed to water, thereby increasing the amount of leaching and erosion of nutrients from the pellets.

Feeding Fry, Fingerlings, and Stockers

Young catfish, like other young animals, should receive rations that are somewhat different from those of older animals near maturity. The primary difference relates to meeting the needs for growth. Proteins and vitamins are especially important.

An egg yolk sac is attached to fry when they are hatched. This sac contains nourishment that will last 5 to 10 days depending on water temperature. Fry will begin to eat feed when this nourishment is gone. The feed should be in meal form, primarily of animal origin, and about 36 percent protein. The feed needs to be high in fat and should be palatable to the fry. This feed may be made from a formula that is high in fish oil, chopped liver, and egg yolk. It is essential that fry feed be nutritionally complete. (Additional information on feeding fry is presented in Chapter 11.)

Most commercially prepared feeds for fingerlings contain 26 to 32 percent protein and are satisfactory for growing fingerlings. Some growers prefer rations containing around 40 percent protein, but these are more expensive and may result in feeding more protein than is efficiently used by the fish. However, a level near 40 percent may be needed in intensive culture systems. The source of the protein and other nutrients may vary, and a variety of feed ingredients is acceptable, including soybean meal, alfalfa meal, bran, and poultry by-product meal. Feed for fingerlings should contain fish meal, salt (which may be iodized), and a vitamin premix. Most commercial feeds contain a preservative to retard spoilage. Small fingerlings (less than 2 inches long) should be fed crumbles which are a particle size slightly larger than a meal. Particle size for fingerlings ranges from 1/8-inch pellets for small fingerlings to 1/4-inch pellets for medium and large-sized fingerlings and stockers.

Determination of Amount to Feed. The rate of feeding fingerlings is 3 to 5 percent; that is, fingerlings are fed at the rate of 3 to 5 percent of body weight at each feeding. To determine the

Figure 7-4. Feed for Fry.

amount to feed, the weight of the fingerlings in a pond should be estimated, then, 3 to 5 percent of the total fingerling weight should be fed. Samples of fish should be taken regularly to estimate the weight of the fish in a pond. The weight can be estimated by weighing a sample of fish, dividing the weight by the number of fish in the sample to get the weight per fish, and then multiplying the weight per fish by the number of fish stocked in the pond. For example, if a sample of 100 fish (the recommended size of the sample) weighs 50 pounds and the number stocked in the pond is 3,000, the total weight of the fish would be found by dividing 50 by 100 and multiplying by 3,000. In this case the weight of the fish in the pond is 1,500 pounds. The amount of feed would be 3 percent of 1,500 or 45 pounds. *(Note: It has been recommended that no more than 30 to 35 pounds of feed be fed per acre of pond each day.)* Some farmers have fed as high as 100 pounds per acre each day. Water problems are more likely to develop above the rate of 30 pounds per acre. If fresh water flows into the pond, and with additional aeration, it is permissible to exceed 30 to 35 pounds.

Another method of estimating the weight of the fish in a pond is to determine the average length of a sample of fish and refer to the length-weight table appearing in Appendix A to determine the weight of fish by length. The average weight of each fish is multiplied by the number stocked in the pond to estimate the total weight of the fish in the pond.

The following is an example of how to estimate the amount of feed per feeding using a length-weight table.

Conditions:

- Pond contains 20 acres of surface water.
- Stocking rate is 3,000 fingerlings per acre.
- Fish average 8 inches in length.
- Water temperature is 80°F.
- Rate of feeding is 4 percent.

Amount to Feed:

- Weight of 8-inch fish is .112 pound (refer to table in Appendix A).
- Weight of fish per acre is .112 multiplied by 3,000 which equals 336 pounds.
- Total weight of fish in pond is 336 pounds multiplied by 20 acres which equals 6,720 pounds.
- Amount of feed is 6,720 multiplied by .04 which equals 268.8 pounds.

CAUTION: *Do not exceed 30 to 35 pounds of feed per acre each day unless the water is carefully managed.*

Frequency of Feeding. Some growers feed six days per week rather than every day. By not being fed one day each week the fish are encouraged to consume any surplus feed that may remain, and there is less tendency of overfeeding, thus causing the fish to go off feed.

Form of Feed. Fingerlings and stockers may be fed either floating feed or sinking feed. Many growers prefer floating feed because the fish come to the surface to eat, thus making it possible to observe the activity of the fish; therefore, the general health conditions and growth can be observed more readily. Two common methods of feeding fingerlings are to mechanically blow the feed out into the water and to hand throw the feed out into the water.

Effects of Temperature. Water temperature is a factor to be considered in feeding. Catfish consume the most feed and make the best gains when the water temperature is between 70 and 90°F. The most efficient growth is obtained when water temperature is 84 to 88°F. Water temperatures in the summer are usually near the optimum range. The amount of feed should be reduced when the temperature is below 60°F or above 90°F, because catfish do not feed regularly during these times. When the temperature is below 55°F, the rate of feeding is reduced to .5 percent of the body weight. In the winter, it is necessary to feed only on the warm days once or twice a week. The winter rate of feeding is about one-fourth that of the summer rate. The rate of feeding may be reduced to less than 3 percent of body weight when the water temperature is unusually warm (above 90°F) and on rainy days in the summer. Incidentally, the rate of feeding may also be reduced when plankton bloom is heavy.

The feeding of catfish most often occurs in spring, summer, and early fall, even though research has shown some benefit in winter feeding. The problem of the water being too cool at this time of year is unlikely in areas where catfish are grown, except at the beginning or at the end of the growing season. Watching the feeding activity of the fish will determine whether or not to feed them. A small amount of feed, preferably a floating pellet, can be thrown into the water. If fish rapidly and vigorously consume the sample provided, they should be fed.

Feeding for Food Fish Production

The feeding of fish in growing ponds is essentially a continuation of the feeding program followed with fingerlings and stockers. The goal in feeding is to secure the maximum rate of growth as efficiently as possible. Successful food fish production often hinges on the feeding practices that are followed.

Catfish should be fed at the time of day that will be most beneficial for efficient growth and that will reduce water problems. Dissolved oxygen in pond water is lowest between 4:00 and 6:00 A.M. and highest between noon and 2:00 P.M. Research has found that low levels of oxygen depress feeding activity. A further consideration is that oxygen requirements of catfish are increased one to eight hours after feeding. This increase is due to the absorption and metabolism of the nutrients by fish. This means that feeding should occur so that at least eight hours pass before the level of oxygen becomes low. On this basis, catfish should be fed in midday between 10:00 A.M. and 2:00 P.M. (Figure 7-5 shows the relationship of time of day to level of dissolved oxygen.)

The amount of feed each day is calculated on the basis of the weight of the catfish. Fish should be fed all they will consume but no more. It is not always easy to know how much is eaten and how much is wasted. (Feeding activity is easier to observe with floating feed.) Factors influencing the amount catfish will eat are temperature, water quality, density of the feed, "flavor" of the feed, amount eaten the previous day, and the number of times they are fed each day.

During the summer, food fish are fed a 28 to 32 percent protein feed at the rate of 3 to 5 percent of body weight each day. Catfish weighing over 1 pound are fed at a lower rate, or approximately 2 percent. In the early spring and in the fall when the water is cooler, the rate of feeding should be reduced.

The ideal water temperature for catfish growth and feed conversion is 85°F. Growth and feed conversion decrease when the temperature is above or below the ideal. The rate of feeding should be adjusted according to temperature. Feeding rates should be reduced when the water temperature is above or below 85°F. Winter feeding encourages some growth and keeps the catfish healthy.

Research has shown that catfish need some feed the year round. Catfish weighing 1 pound in November will lose 9 percent

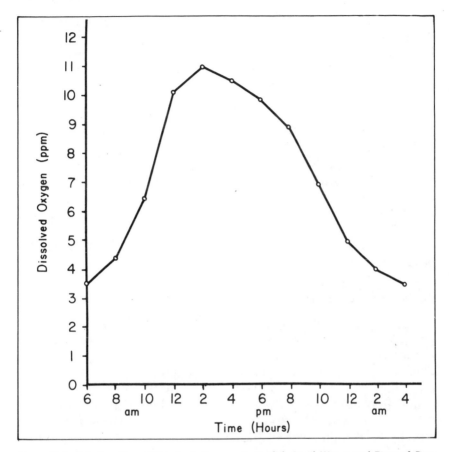

Figure 7-5. Relationship of Dissolved Oxygen in Catfish Pond Water and Time of Day.
(Source: "Nutrition and Feeding of Channel Catfish," Bulletin 218. Auburn,
Alabama: Agricultural Experiment Station.)

of their weight by March if they are not fed. If they are fed at the
rate of 1 percent of body weight on alternate days, or when the
water temperature is 54°F or warmer at a depth of 3 feet, they may
gain as much as 20 percent or more in weight in the winter.

The usual procedure is to feed fish one time a day, 6 days a
week. Catfish will eat more feed if they are fed twice each day. It
has been felt that by skipping a day, the fish will clean up any
surplus feed and reduce the possibility of oxygen depletion
caused by overfeeding.

Catfish should be fed at about the same time each day. They

should probably not be fed the full amount when it is raining or if the weather has been overcast for four consecutive days. In the latter case, feeding should not be resumed until after one day of sunshine. Also, catfish should not be fed within 24 hours of harvesting.

Catfish should be fed only when they will eat. If a small amount of feed is thrown into the water and the fish do not consume it, feeding should be delayed. Fish should be fed only the amount that is consumed in about 20 minutes. Overfeeding wastes feed and increases the chances of oxygen depletion.

Catfish in growing ponds may double their weight every 30 days if properly managed. Therefore, slight increases in rate of feeding are frequently needed. These increases should be based on fish size and rate of feed consumption.

The rate at which catfish are fed is variable and influences the profitability of catfish farming.

Ratio of Feed to Gain

Since one of the major costs in catfish farming is feed, the efficiency of catfish growth is related to the amount of feed required to produce a pound of gain. This is frequently referred to as a "feed conversion ratio." Feed conversion efficiency declines as fingerlings increase in size. Hot weather will also cause feed efficiency to decline. Fingerlings may have a feed conversion ratio of 0.9 pound of feed to 1.0 pound of gain the first year of life. The ratio in the second year, when the fingerlings are being grown into food fish, ranges between 1.5 and 2.5 pounds of feed to 1.0 pound of gain. With food fish, most commercial catfish farmers expect to get a pound of weight gain for 1.75 pounds of feed. Some of the better farmers, through proper feeding and efficient management, are getting a pound of gain on less feed. Large catfish held for more than two growing seasons are less efficient in weight gain and require more feed to produce a pound of gain.

Methods of Feeding

Catfish are fed in different ways with five methods of feeding being commonly used: (1) hand feeding, (2) blow feeding, (3) boat feeding, (4) self-feeding, and (5) air feeding. Each method has characteristics which make it suitable for certain farmers.

Hand Feeding. Hand feeding is a method by which feed is thrown out into the water by hand. A person walks along the edge of the pond and throws feed out with a bucket, a small scoop, or by the handful where the catfish will feed, 15 to 30 feet from the edge. Fish are usually fed in the same locations each time. Feeding locations which are accessible to the fish and free of aquatic weeds and deep mud are preferable. Hand feeding is best suited to small fish farms and small ponds. Ponds of 1 acre or less in size can be fed from one feeding location. However, it is a good practice to cover 10 to 25 percent of pond area when feeding. Feed should be placed in ponds so that all fish have access to it. Feed that sinks should be fed in shallow areas so that the feeding activ-

Figure 7-6. Hand Feeding. (Courtesy, Louisiana Wildlife and Fisheries Commission)

ity of the fish can be observed through the water. Fish that do not vigorously consume the feed should not be fed.

Blow Feeding. Blow feeding is a process by which feed is blown out into a pond with a mechanical blower. Blowers may be powered by an auxiliary engine or operated from the PTO of a farm tractor. Blower feeders are suited to medium- and large-sized fish farms.

Figure 7-7. Tractor Mounted PTO-Operated Blow Feeder. (Courtesy, Ralston Purina Company)

Boat Feeding. Boat feeding means simply that one feeds the fish from a boat. The feed may be distributed by hand or from a mechanical feeder. Boat feeding allows fish to be fed in any part of a pond. This type of feeding is suited to small- and medium-sized fish farms.

Self-Feeding. Self-feeding permits fish to secure feed when they want it. Special kinds of feeding equipment are required. Activity of the fish in bumping a trigger or tray suspended in the water causes feed to be released from the feeder. This method of

feeding is suited to fish farms of all sizes. Large ponds may require several feeders. One feeder is usually sufficient for 4 surface
acres of water. Some of the feeder bins are manufactured of see-
through materials that permit observation of feed level from a distance. Self-feeders are also known as "demand feeders."

Figure 7-8. Self-Feeder with Suspended Trigger.

Figure 7-9. Mounted Self-Feeder in a Drained Pond. (Courtesy, USDA, Soil Conservation Service)

Air Feeding. Feeding by air involves the use of an airplane to release feed while it flies over the pond a few feet above the water. This method of feeding is suited to large ponds and large farms.

Storing Feed

Improper storage of feed can result in damage to the feed due to loss of nutrients. Large catfish farmers may purchase feed in bulk and store it in a bin. Other farmers may purchase bagged feed. Regardless of how it is purchased, several practices should be followed in storing and handling feed.

- Feed should be handled carefully so as not to break pellets into small pieces.
- Feed should be stored in a dry place. (High humidity encourages the growth of mold and attracts insects.)

- Feed should be stored in a cool place. (High temperatures cause oils in the feed to become rancid and cause vitamins in the feed to deteriorate.)
- Rodents should be controlled in the storage area.
- Bags which retard moisture entry and protect the feed should be used. (Bags with plastic liners or multiple walls are preferable.)

Figure 7-10. Bulk Storage Facility for Feed.

Questions and Problems for Discussion

1. What are the foods of wild catfish?
2. Why do cultured catfish need to be fed?
3. What are the types of rations? Distinguish between each.
4. What are the basic nutrient requirements of catfish?
5. What is a vitamin premix?
6. What ingredients are used in making catfish feed?
7. What forms of feed are commonly used?
8. What are the advantages and disadvantages of extruded and expanded pellets?
9. How is water temperature related to the feeding of fingerlings?
10. What is meant by "feeding at the rate of 3 to 5 percent"?
11. Describe when to feed food catfish.
12. What is meant by "ratio of feed to gain"?
13. What are the common methods of feeding used with catfish?
14. What practices should be followed in handling and storing feed?

8

Controlling Diseases of Catfish

Catfish live in an environment which tends to be ideal for diseases. Warm water with high populations of fish harbors many potential problems for the catfish farmer. Disease outbreaks occur more frequently following a time when the catfish have been under stress. Preventing stress goes a long way toward preventing disease problems.

The conditions under which catfish are grown are somewhat different from their native habitats at the bottom of streams and lakes. Fortunately, various managerial and cultural practices are available to reduce the occurrence of and losses from diseases. This chapter presents information on the following:

The nature of disease in catfish
Characteristics of diseased catfish
Stress
Seasonality of disease outbreaks
Managerial considerations in fish disease control
Treatment methods
Common diseases of catfish: identification and treatment
Common parasites of catfish: identification and treatment
Chemicals used in disease and parasite control
Calculation of treatments

The Nature of Disease in Catfish

A disease is a condition that impairs normal body functions. Some diseases are transferred readily from fish to fish and are known as "contagious diseases." Others are not transferred readily and are known as "noncontagious diseases." Many of the problems in commercial fish culture are caused by contagious diseases.

There are several types of diseases in catfish: infectious, nutritional, environmental, and parasitic. Infectious diseases involve microorganisms such as bacteria, viruses, and protozoa. These are commonly known as "germs." Infectious diseases attack the living tissues of catfish. Some of the germs live in the tissue and multiply rapidly, thereby killing it. Other germs produce poisons which kill the catfish.

Nutritional diseases are due to improper diet. Feeding foods which provide the needed nutrients will prevent nutritional diseases. (Chapter 7 contains information on proper nutrition, including symptoms of catfish with certain deficiencies.)

The significance of environmental diseases in catfish is unknown. The environment may be one conducive to other diseases as well as one having certain elements in it which cause disease. For example, the effect of radiation from the sun on catfish is unknown. In many other animals, excessive exposure to the sun can destroy body tissues. With catfish, the presence of pesticide residues and other pollutants in the water may be harmful, and may even cause their deaths.

Parasites are organisms that live in or on other animals, known as hosts. Parasites may be internal or external. Internal parasites live in the digestive tract and various organs of the body. External parasites are attached to the gills, skin, or fins of catfish and secure food by sucking or eating. The term *parasitic disease* may be used to describe diseased conditions caused by parasites.

The more intensively catfish are cultured, the greater the potential for disease outbreaks. High-density fish populations tend to magnify some problems. Up to 10 percent of all cultured catfish are lost to disease each year. Some farmers may lose their entire crop. Much of this loss can be prevented.

Characteristics of Diseased Catfish

Catfish with diseases or parasites usually exhibit certain characteristics, known as symptoms. The symptoms depend on the kind of disease and on the stage of the disease. It is possible for mild cases of some diseases to go unnoticed. Also, fish that receive adequate feed and are managed properly are more resistant to diseases.

Some of the characteristics of diseased fish are observable without detailed examinations. At other times, microscopic and

Figure 8-1. Disease Outbreaks May Cause the Loss of Fish As Is Shown by the Pile That Has Been Raked Out of a Pond. (Courtesy, Thomas Wellborn, Mississippi State University)

laboratory examinations are necessary before a diagnosis can be made. Fish should be observed closely each day for characteristics indicative of diseased conditions. The characteristics that do appear in diseased fish may not permit accurate on-the-spot diagnosis. Several diseases may produce similar appearances in fish necessitating laboratory examination for identification. If fish begin to take on characteristics denoting disease, steps should be taken promptly to secure a diagnosis. Common symptoms of diseased fish are changes in normal behavior, reduced vigor, failure to consume feed, skin lesions or discoloration, death, and abnormalities in body shape.

Change in Behavior. Disease outbreaks usually cause fish to exhibit behavior which is atypical of healthy catfish. Fish that are in good health cannot be seen except during feeding. The gathering of fish near the surface of the water, in vegetation, or near an incoming water supply should be sufficient evidence to suspect disease. However, a deficiency of oxygen or other water problems may cause fish to come to the surface. Testing the water will be helpful in determining the cause of abnormal behavior. Fish scratching on vegetation may be attempting to remove parasites which are irritating them.

Reduced Vigor. Catfish that appear to be lifeless may be diseased. Fish normally swim away very rapidly when apparent danger approaches or a disturbance occurs nearby. If fish do not swim away quickly when a person approaches, some type of disorder should be suspected. Reduced vigor is also indicated by drooping or folded fins, loss of balance, and sluggishness.

Failure to Feed. Healthy fish normally come for feed within a few minutes after it is put in the water, if the water conditions are proper. Failure to feed may indicate that the oxygen level is low or that the fish are diseased. The cause of nonfeeding should be determined as quickly as possible. Emaciation of fish may be due to failure to feed or to the presence of parasitic diseases. Diseases associated with emaciation may cause diarrhea, which is often accompanied by a string of mucus trailing from the vent of fish.

Skin Lesions or Discoloration. The presence of bloody areas on the skin and the presence of sores, cysts in the skin or muscles, blisters, or open ulcers are symptoms of certain diseases. Inflamed areas on the skin may indicate external parasites. The presence of any lesions is sufficient evidence for a careful examination of the fish.

Death. The death of fish is an expensive way to learn that there has been a disease outbreak. Dead fish floating on the water

Table 8-1

Summary of the Signs (Symptoms) of Diseased Catfish

Behavioral Signs	Physical Signs
Slowing down or complete cessation of feeding	Excess mucous production giving the fish a grayish or bluish color
Loss of equilibrium and swimming erratically or in spirals	Abnormal color
	Erosion of skin or fins
Schooling just below the surface	Swollen or eroded gills
Swimming lethargically	Pale gills
Scraping against the bottom or some object in the pond	Swollen abdomen filled with cloudy, bloody, or clear fluid
Death	Bulging eyes (exophthalmia)

Source: John A. Plumb. "Principal Diseases of Farm-Raised Catfish," Bulletin 225. Auburn, Alabama: Agricultural Experiment Station, 1979, p. 6.

around the edges of the pond may be caused by one of several conditions. Death may be due to disease among the fish, oxygen depletion, or to the presence of toxic substances in the water. The cause of the death of fish should be determined as quickly as possible.

Abnormalities in Body Shape. Protruded eyes and swollen bellies are abnormal body shapes that certain diseased fish may acquire. Sometimes diseased fish may have tumor-like growths which protrude from the body, especially around the mouth and fins.

Table 8-1 presents a summary of the signs (symptoms) of diseased catfish.

Stress

Stress means that catfish have been exposed to conditions that strain the body. Stress occurs when the environment of catfish is suddenly changed or when conditions become less than ideal. Examples of situations causing stress include low oxygen levels, the hauling of fish, high water temperatures, inadequate diet, crowding, insecticides getting into the water, and excessive accumulations of wastes. When stress occurs, the fish are weakened and become more susceptible to disease.

Stress reduces the resistance of catfish to infectious and parasitic diseases. There is a range of conditions in which catfish thrive. Stress begins any time the outer limits are reached. One of these limits is temperature. The ideal temperature for catfish is 83 to 85°F. When the temperature is above 90°F, catfish have difficulty adjusting. When it is above 85°F, catfish eggs will either hatch premature fry that have a poor survival rate or produce a high percentage of deformed fry.

Handling and transporting catfish usually create stressful conditions. Rough handling is usually followed by disease. Fish should be handled gently and transported under conditions which reduce stress possibilities. (Chapter 13 presents additional information on handling catfish.)

Good managers can control these situations and, thereby, avoid stressing catfish. When stress is avoided, disease problems are minimized.

Seasonality of Disease Outbreaks

Certain times of the year tend to be more troublesome in terms of disease problems with catfish. This may be due to a complex combination of factors associated with stress in the fish. The organisms causing disease are usually present in a pond throughout the year, but epizootics (outbreaks affecting many fish at the same time) occur at scattered intervals, most often in the spring. Because of this seasonality, a farmer should be on guard for abnormal behavior during this season.

The spring seasonality of disease outbreaks may be due to increased handling as related to spawning, stocking, and other activities. These are often conducted at times when water temperatures may be fluctuating. In the lower Mississippi River Valley, April is the most troublesome month. The period of March through July is the time of greatest continuous danger. Some farmers use routine prophylactic treatments each time fish are handled. Such treatments reduce the likelihood of disease problems. The fish may be dipped or held in a solution containing an appropriate chemical.

Disease outbreaks often occur at times other than in the spring. Outbreaks in the fall may be attributed to changes in the water temperature or increased stress due to harvesting. Outbreaks in the winter are less common and can be reduced if the fish are properly fed and are not overcrowded. Most all outbreaks can be prevented by avoiding placing fish under stress (such as in hauling or with an oxygen deficiency), introducing only disease-free fish into a farm, and using prophylactic treatments when fish are handled.

Managerial Considerations in Fish Disease Control

There is no substitute for good management in preventing disease outbreaks. Prevention of disease problems is much preferred over attempting to treat them after they arise. Prevention involves a combination of quarantine, isolation, and sanitation procedures. Proper nutrition and the prevention of stress are also important in keeping catfish healthy.

Poor management may result in disease problems that otherwise could have been avoided. Several practices that are helpful in preventing disease outbreaks are listed here:

1. An abundance of disease-free water should be used.
2. Aquatic weed growth in ponds should be controlled.
3. Only healthy fish should be stocked.
4. New fish should be treated and quarantined for two weeks before being placed with other fish.
5. Fish of the same size should be kept together. This means that fingerlings and broodfish should be kept separately. Mixing the sizes may result in diseases and parasites being passed from adult fish to young fish. Also, the adult fish will compete with the younger fish for feed, and this competition may result in lack of growth of the younger fish.
6. Sufficient room should be provided for fish. They should not be overcrowded.
7. They should be fed properly. Overfeeding or underfeeding should be avoided.
8. Equipment should be disinfected to prevent the spread of diseases from one pond to another.
9. Pond bottoms should be allowed to dry between uses. This destroys parasites and their eggs, and may increase fish yields.

In dealing with fish disease problems, it is essential that the problem be accurately diagnosed. Once the disease has been diagnosed, treatments are administered based on the chemistry of the water, characteristics of the fish, and the chemical to be used. The toxicity of many chemicals is related to water chemistry; therefore, before treating a large number of fish, it is a good idea to try out the treatment on a sample of fish to be treated. If no harmful side effects develop with the sample, it is likely that the chemical is safe to use.

The method of treatment used depends upon the nature of the disease. Systemic, or internal, infections are treated by feeding medicated feed or by finding other means of getting medications inside the fish. External diseases may be treated by adding medications or chemicals to the water in which fish exist. Treatments must get to the site of the infection to be effective.

Very few chemicals have been approved by the Food and Drug Administration (FDA) for use on food fish. Treatments that are not approved are sometimes used, but it is risky. Food fish treated with chemicals that have not been approved are subject to condemnation by the FDA. The approval regulations do not apply to fish not used for human consumption, such as broodfish. Fish farmers should exercise caution in using chemicals. Food fish on the way to market should not be treated.

It is a generally accepted practice to treat broodstock and fingerlings during hauling regardless of whether or not a disease is suspected. Such prophylactic treatments prevent the spread of disease and reduce die-off of fingerlings after stocking. The small tanks in which fish are hauled make it convenient and economical to treat with chemical solutions at this time. Broodfish may be treated at any time, especially prior to being placed in spawning ponds. Fish may also be treated in vats and other small facilities more economically and with better results than in ponds. The tanks and vats in which fish are treated should be equipped with aerators and conveniently located near a source of water. Treatment facilities should be easily drained.

Treatment Methods

The best treatment is prevention! It is much easier to prevent a disease than it is to cure it after an outbreak. There are treatments for most catfish diseases. Some are fairly effective, while others are not very effective at all. Several methods of treatment are used.

Dipping into a Concentrated Solution. This method involves dipping the catfish into a strong solution of a chemical for a relatively short period of time. Dipping is good for treating a small number of fish, specifically fingerlings and broodfish. The fish are usually placed in a net and dipped into the solution for 15 to 45 seconds. The length of time catfish can be held in a dip depends on the kind of chemical used and on the concentration of the solution.

Flushing. This method is best suited to vats, tanks, raceways, and egg incubators. It involves adding a chemical solution at the upper end of the container and allowing it to move through the unit. Sufficient water must be available in order for all of the solution to be flushed out.

Bathing. This method involves adding the chemical to the holding unit and leaving it for a period of time. It is then flushed out with fresh water. Catfish should be carefully observed during bath treatments because the oxygen may become low or the chemical may have a stronger reaction than expected. Bath treatments may last up to one hour or more, depending on the chemical. Care should be used to distribute the chemical evenly throughout the water.

Indefinite. The indefinite method of treatment involves using low concentrations of chemicals. It is used with ponds and hauling tanks. Since the concentration is low, no effort is usually needed to flush away the chemical. The treatment naturally breaks up and disappears with the passage of time. With the indefinite treatment method, it is important to mix the chemical evenly in the water. Special boats may be used to apply chemicals to large ponds. Smaller ponds can be treated by using hand or power sprayers or by putting the chemical in a burlap bag and towing it behind a boat.

Feeding. Some diseases can be treated by adding the medication to the feed. It is important to have the medication dispersed evenly in the feed so that all of the catfish receive it. With a small number of larger fish, the medication can be put in a capsule and inserted in the stomachs of the fish with a balling gun.

Injecting. When a small number of large catfish are involved, medications can be injected with a hypodermic needle and syringe. Most drugs will act more rapidly when injected than when added to feed, bath, or dipping solution. Of course, not all diseases are best treated with injections.

Two types of injections are commonly used with catfish. Intraperitoneum (IP) injections are used to get medication into the body cavity. Intramuscular (IM) injections are used to get medication into muscle tissue. In making injections, care should be used not to damage internal organs.

IP injections are given by inserting the needle at the base of the pelvic fin. The needle is inserted at a 45-degree angle parallel to the long axis of the body.

IM injections are made by inserting the needle at the base of the dorsal fin. The needle should be inserted 3/4 to 1/2 inch deep at a 45-degree angle with the long axis of the body.

Common Diseases of Catfish: Identification and Treatment

The precise identification and treatment of most of the diseases of catfish cannot be accomplished without microscopic examinations and laboratory tests. Persons such as veterinarians, who have traditionally been qualified to assist in the identification and treatment of animal diseases, may not be qualified to assist with fish problems. Live fish with typical symptoms of the diseased condition should be sent to a laboratory with the facilities to identify fish diseases.

Some states have veterinary diagnostic laboratories which are equipped to diagnose fish diseases. In other states, departments of fisheries and wildlife associated with the land-grant universities will diagnose fish disease problems. A few county agents have set up small laboratories and can diagnose catfish diseases fairly accurately. A list of laboratories in the United States which can assist with catfish disease problems is presented in Appendix D.

The most common diseases are caused by bacteria, viruses, fungi, algae, nutritional deficiencies, and environmental problems.

Bacterial Diseases. Three main bacterial diseases affect catfish: columnaris disease, motile aeromonas septicemia, and edwardsiellosis. Each causes lesions on the skin and requires laboratory analysis for precise identification.

Columnaris is a severe disease of catfish, occurring primarily between the months of March and October. It is caused by the myxobacterium, *Flexibacter columnaris.* Most columnaris infections are associated with stress, especially high water temperatures, crowding, injury in handling, and other environmental disorders. Young fish are most severely infected. High mortality rates may occur.

Columnaris disease is visible as lesions on the external areas of the body or in the mucous membranes, such as those in the mouth. At first, grayish-white or yellowish-white patches appear on the skin. These change to shallow ulcerations, and the fins may become frayed. The bacteria form mounds or columnar masses of cells on fish tissue. This disease is common in both adult and fingerling catfish, especially under crowded conditions. Identification is made by scraping infected cells from the edge of a lesion and viewing in a living state with a microscope. Control of columnaris is difficult. Columnaris is sometimes known as "saddleback disease" or "cotton mouth disease."

Aeromonas infections, commonly known as hemorrhagic septicemia, are serious diseases in fingerlings and subadult catfish.

Figure 8-2. Catfish with Bacterial Disease *(Aeromonas liquefaciens)* and Trichodina. (Courtesy, Thomas Wellborn, Mississippi State University)

Broodfish may die just before or during the spawning season or, in milder cases, may fail to spawn. Symptoms may include grayish patches on the skin or bloody areas that erode away. Other symptoms are the presence of fluid in the body cavity and protruded eyes. It is caused by the bacterium, *Aeromonas liquefaciens*. Wild fish that are captured and confined are particularly susceptible to this disease when making the adjustment from a natural to an artificial environment. Identification of these bacteria cannot be done with a microscope but requires biochemical tests.

The *Pseudomonas* infections are caused by the bacteria in the *Pseudomonas* genus. The symptoms are similar to those of fish with the *Aeromonas* infection and require the same laboratory analysis for identification, which is often difficult. Epizootics of this disease may occur among cultured catfish.

Edwardsiellosis is a relatively new disease of catfish, first being identified in 1969. It is caused by the bacterium, *Edwardsiella tarda*. The signs include the presence of gas-filled lesions in the muscle tissues of mature catfish. In mild stages, small lesions resembling puncture wounds appear on the skin. These lesions originate deep within muscles. Death occurs when the kidneys and liver cease to function. Fish that survive have scars left by the lesions. Mortality rates are usually no more than 5 percent when the fish are in ponds. Mortality may be 50 percent when the fish are held in tanks. Edwardsiellosis is most frequently observed during the months of July through October.

Inadvertently processing an infected fish creates serious problems. When lesions are ruptured, the processing equipment and nearby fish may become contaminated. The contaminated fish are unfit for food.

Table 8-2 presents possible treatments for bacterial diseases.

Viral Diseases. Catfish virus disease, also known as "channel catfish virus" (CCV), is a highly infective and contagious disease which may cause large losses of fry and fingerlings. The virus will pass through a filter that retains bacteria. It is transmitted from infected catfish through the water to healthy fish. Fry and fingerlings will develop the disease in 72 to 78 hours after exposure, depending on water temperature. A 100 percent mortality rate can be expected over a period of three to seven days with fry. As fish

Figure 8-3. Catfish with Virus Disease. (Courtesy, Thomas Wellborn, Mississippi State University)

become larger, the mortality rate is reduced. With fish three to four months old, mortality may be between 40 and 60 percent. Signs include hemorrhage at the base of fins and in the skin, enlarged abdomen filled with fluid, bulged eyes, and pale gills. Be-

Table 8-2

Possible Treatments for Common Diseases of Catfish

Disease	Possible Treatment[1]
Bacterial Diseases	
(Columnaris, Aeromonas septicemia, and Edwardsiellosis)	Maintain a favorable environment for catfish, especially sufficient oxygen in the water. Avoid overcrowding when water is warm. Dip fish in a 1 to 3 percent salt solution until signs of stress appear or in a 10-ppm solution of acriflavine for one hour. A medicated feed containing Terramycin at 83 grams per 100 pounds of feed may be fed for 10 to 12 days following stocking. Valuable broodfish may be injected with Terramycin at the rate of 25 mg per pound of fish. Treat with 2 ppm potassium permanganate as a pond treatment.
Fungal Diseases	Sanitation and hygienic cultural practices are essential. Dip fish for 10 to 30 seconds in a 67-ppm solution of malachite green or up to one hour in a 3-ppm solution of malachite green. Potassium permanganate may be used at the rate of 2 ppm in ponds.
Catfish Virus (CCV)	Only control is prevention. No known effective treatment. Adding cool water to a pond may reduce mortality.
Algal Diseases	In case of algal toxicoses, treat pond water to reduce algae population.
Environmental Diseases	
(Brown blood disease)	Prevent by not overfeeding and by flushing ponds when nitrite content exceeds 0.5 ppm in pond water.

[1]The possible treatments given here are not recommendations but are those which have been used to aid in controlling fish diseases. Some of the chemicals listed have not been approved by the Food and Drug Administration for use with food fish.

Sources: "Report to the Fish Farmers." Washington: U.S. Department of the Interior, Bureau of Sport Fisheries and Wildlife, 1970, p. 55. Fred P. Meyer, "Parasites of Freshwater Fishes." Washington: U.S. Department of the Interior, FDL–2, 1966. "The Biology of Channel Catfish Production," Circular 535. Fayetteville: University of Arkansas, Cooperative Extension Service, 1969. "Principal Diseases of Farm-Raised Catfish," Bulletin 225. Auburn, Alabama: Agricultural Experiment Station, 1979.

havioral signs include erratic swimming and floating head-up just prior to death.

There is no known treatment for catfish virus. Once the disease is confirmed, lowering the water temperature may lessen mortality. Practical control involves isolating new fish, introducing fish from disease-free sources, and employing good sanitation practices. The spread of catfish virus to other places can be prevented by disinfecting the ponds with 20 ppm chlorine and by destroying the affected fish. Destroyed fish should be buried immediately and ponds and equipment should be sterilized.

Fungal Diseases. Fungi ordinarily grow in decaying organic matter. Fungal infections result from an injury or from a lack of proper nutrition. Occasionally, patches of fungi will be seen growing on fish creating a fuzzy appearance. Fungi are usually associated with discolored areas or lesions. Injuries to fish, such as those caused by handling and hauling, may cause the necrosis, or death, of tiny patches of flesh. Fungi attach themselves to the necrotic tissue. Treatment of fish in tanks with formalin, potassium permanganate, or malachite green will reduce the incidence of fungal infections. The control of fungal diseases is usually not a problem since fungi seldom grow on healthy fish unless the fish are subject to stress or injury. (Note: Formalin and malachite green are not registered for fishery use even though they have been used in the past.)

Fungi may attack dead eggs in an egg mass and spread to the living eggs, eventually killing the entire egg mass. It is thought that fungi start in organic matter that settles on the egg mass. In this case, keeping the egg mass clean will prevent a buildup of fungi and prevent the loss of eggs.

Algal Diseases. Catfish are usually not directly affected by algae. The most serious problems are indirectly associated with heavy blooms of blue-green algae which may cause algal toxicosis, or poisoning. Symptoms of algal toxicosis are similar to the symptoms of oxygen depletion but can be distinguished by the fact that the smaller fish die first and the losses occur in the afternoon. These conditions are more likely to develop when only one species of alga is dominant. Control of blue-green algae will prevent the problems associated with it.

Nutritional Diseases. Catfish are susceptible to nutritional diseases, but the extent of this problem has not yet been determined. Feeding complete rations should help to eliminate these problems. At the present time, the exact requirements for a complete ration are unknown. More research is needed in this area.

Environmental Diseases. Some disease problems are attributed to the environment of the fish. These include diseases caused by industrial and agricultural chemicals that are found in water. Gas bubble disease is also included here. It may result when the water saturation with oxygen is 150 percent or more.

A new environmental disease first observed in 1978 is brown blood disease. It is caused by excess amounts of nitrites in the water. The nitrite combines with the hemoglobin in the red blood cells and forms a brown-colored compound known as methemoglobin. The ability of the red blood cells to carry oxygen is destroyed. Catfish tend to have the same symptoms with brown blood disease as they would with oxygen deficiency.

The best way to prevent brown blood disease is to avoid overfeeding and to periodically flush the pond. A good procedure is to test pond water for nitrite content every two weeks. When the concentration of nitrite exceeds 0.5 ppm, the pond should be

Figure 8-4. Catfish with Gas Bubble Disease. (Courtesy, Thomas Wellborn, Mississippi State University)

flushed to bring the nitrite level down. The test kit to use is the Hach Nitrate-Nitrite Test Kit Model NI–12. Some research has been done concerning the addition of salt to the water at the rate of 67.5 pounds per acre-foot. This is unproven and should be used cautiously.

Common Parasites of Catfish: Identification and Treatment

Losses from parasites can be considerable. However, such losses are usually not so great as with bacterial diseases, except with "Ich" disease. It is possible that low and moderate infestation of some parasites may go unnoticed. Any level of infestation will reduce the efficiency of production.

Parasites often cause more serious problems in the production of fry and fingerlings and in the production of fish that do not receive proper nourishment. Fry are particularly susceptible to some parasites. The most common groups of parasites are protozoa, flukes, tapeworms, roundworms, leeches, and copepods.

Protozoa. Protozoa are one-celled animals of microscopic size. The infections caused by the protozoa may be external, internal, or both. Of the external diseases caused by various protozoa, "Ich" or "white spot" disease is by far the most difficult to control. "Ich" disease is caused by the *Ichthyophthirius multifilis* organism. It is a highly contagious disease and affects the entire external portion of the body, including the gills. Fish with this disease attempt to scratch themselves on anything available. Diseased fingerlings may congregate in a large mass near the incoming water supply. "Ich" occurs most often in the spring when water temperatures begin to rise.

Control of "Ich" is dependent upon early detection and proper treatment. Detection involves microscopic examinations of affected fish. Identification of the organisms is relatively simple in that they contain a horseshoe-shaped nucleus. No chemical treatment which always produces satisfactory results is available. The effectiveness of chemical treatments is related to differences in the mineral content of the water. The best control is prevention. New fish should be quarantined for two weeks in water with a temperature near 70°F. Ponds in which outbreaks of "Ich" have occurred should be thoroughly dried and the bottoms should be

Figure 8-5. Catfish with "Ich." (Courtesy, Thomas Wellborn, Mississippi State University)

disked or sterilized with calcium hypochlorite. One of the stages in the development of "Ich" involves the formation of cysts in the bottoms of ponds in which many new young may be formed.

Several external protozoa, in addition to "Ich," may cause problems with catfish. These include *Trichodina*, *Chilodonella*, *Costia*, *Trichophyra*, *Scyphidia*, and *Epistylis*. The first two are particularly dangerous to fry and fingerlings. The symptoms of these protozoan infections tend to be the same and may include small bloody spots on the fins and body, ragged fins, loss of appetite, and the formation of bluish-gray patches on the body. In-

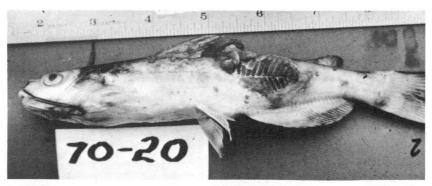

Figure 8-6. Fish Infected with Three Disease Problems: "Ich," Fungus, and *Aeromonas liquefaciens*. (Courtesy, Thomas Wellborn, Mississippi State University)

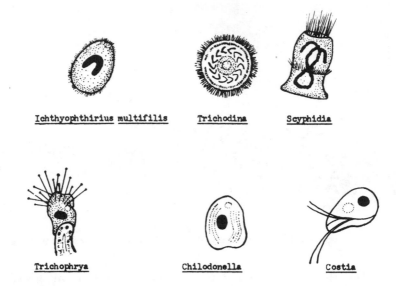

Ichthyophthirius multifilis   Trichodina   Scyphidia

Trichophrya   Chilodonella   Costia

Figure 8-7. Enlarged Drawings of Microscopic-Sized Protozoa. (Courtesy, Bureau of Sport Fisheries and Wildlife, U.S. Department of the Interior)

fected fish may also tend to lose their balance and come to the surface, roll over (known as "flashing"), and swim away. These protozoa often infect the gills, blocking the exchange of gases. Fish with chronic infections may become emaciated. One of the protozoa, *Epistylis*, may cause eroded areas on the head which resemble fungal infections. Protozoan diseases can be prevented largely by treating the broodfish prior to spawning, by using good water, and by following good management practices.

Internal protozoan diseases have not been considered to be so costly so far as losses of catfish are concerned. The extent of the damage caused by internal protozoan diseases is not known.

Flukes. Two main groups of flukes, or trematodes, affect catfish: monogenetic and digenetic. The monogenetic group can reproduce on a fish without additional hosts, while the digenetic group requires one or more hosts in addition to fish. Catfish may carry a number of tiny flukes on the gills. *Gyrodactylus* and *Cleidodiscus* are the two monogenetics which cause the most problems in fish culture. *Gyrodactylus* is generally found on the body and fins and possibly on the gills; however, it is very seldom found on catfish. There has never been a recorded case of

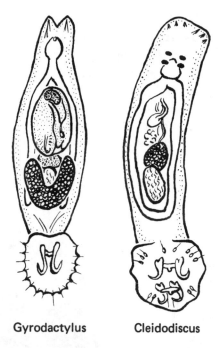

Gyrodactylus   Cleidodiscus

Figure 8-8. Enlarged Drawings of Monogenetic Trematodes. (Courtesy, Bureau of Sport Fisheries and Wildlife, U.S. Department of the Interior)

Gyrodactylus causing the death of catfish. It is identified by the presence of a pair of large hooks and the absence of eyespots. This fluke gives birth to its young which, prior to birth, can be seen within the living parent. *Cleidodiscus* is found only on the gills, except in extremely heavy infestations when some may be found on the body and fins. It has two pairs of hooks and eyespots, and it lays eggs. It is possible to see the unlaid eggs inside the adult.

Digenetic trematodes are of two forms. One form lives in or on the catfish as an adult parasite. Another form lives in or on the catfish in a preadult stage of parasitic growth. The adult digenetic flukes may live in the intestines, air bladder, or urinary bladder of catfish and appear to be flat and wormlike. A microscopic examination will reveal an oral sucker at the anterior end and a ventral sucker near the midsection of the body.

Certain flukes may spend the intermediate stage of their development in catfish and spend their adulthood as parasites of birds. In the larval or intermediate stage these flukes form cysts in the flesh of catfish. Fish with cysts may have a "grubby" appearance. Control may be partially accomplished by removing nearby roosts which may be used by birds.

Tapeworms. Tapeworms, or cestodes, may be found in the intestines of catfish. Tapeworms are typically long, flat, and segmented and are tapered toward one end. Four small suckers are present on the small end, or head, of each tapeworm. Each segment of a tapeworm contains a set of reproductive organs and eggs. Tapeworms are seldom a problem unless a high population develops in catfish.

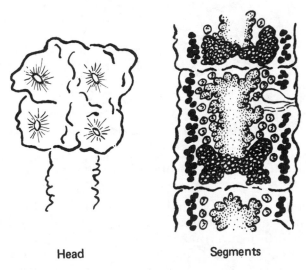

Head   Segments

Figure 8-9. Enlarged Drawings of Tapeworm Head and Segments. (Courtesy, Bureau of Sport Fisheries and Wildlife, U.S. Department of the Interior)

Roundworms. Roundworms, also known as nematodes, are less common in the intestines of catfish than are flukes or tapeworms. Roundworms do not have segments and are recognized by the long, round, smooth body. The larval form may develop in fish-eating birds; therefore, partial control involves keeping birds away from fish ponds.

Leeches. The leeches affecting catfish are described as small worms which attach themselves to fins or at the base of fins. Older fish kept through the fall and winter are most susceptible to

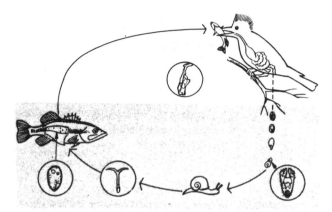

Figure 8-10. Life Cycle of Certain Worm Parasites. (Courtesy, Illinois Division of Fisheries, Department of Conservation)

leeches. Adult leeches leave the fish host in the summer to lay eggs. Treating fish by dipping them in a 3 percent solution of salt (NaCl) may release leeches from the fish and cause them to fall to the bottom of the container. Fish should be removed from the salt solution when signs of distress appear. Other treatments that are used to control external parasites may be effective.

Copepods. Copepods, seldom a problem in natural waters, may reach epizootic proportions in cultured fish operations. The appearance of copepods varies considerably. Some attach themselves to the gills of catfish. "Fish lice," another form of copepods, resemble scales and feed on blood and juices of the fish. Irritations caused by copepods are primary factors in the entrance of bacterial infections.

Table 8-3 presents possible treatments for common parasites of catfish.

Table 8-3

Possible Treatments for Common Parasites of Catfish

Parasite	Possible Treatment[1]
"Ich" disease	Prolonged treatment with one or more of the following may be required: Formalin—200 ppm daily for one hour in vats or 25 ppm in ponds on alternate days for two weeks.

(Continued)

Table 8-3 (continued)

Parasite	Possible Treatment[1]
	Malachite green—1.25 ppm daily for 30 minutes in vats or 0.5 ppm in ponds weekly.
	Combination of 0.1 ppm malachite green and 15 ppm formalin—one to three treatments at two-day intervals.
	The bottoms of dry ponds may be disked to destroy the encysted stage of "Ich" disease.
Trichodina, Chilodonella, Costia, Trichophrya, and Scyphidia	Formalin—one application in ponds at 15 to 25 ppm, or 250 ppm in tanks for so long as fish will tolerate.
	Malachite green—one application at 0.1 ppm in ponds.
	Potassium permanganate in ponds at 2.0 ppm or as dictated by water chemistry. Broodstock should be treated before being transferred to spawning ponds to prevent spreading to fry.
	Copper sulfate—0.25 to 0.5 ppm depending on water hardness. (Copper sulfate is much more toxic in water with low alkalinity.)
Blood suckers (Leeches)	Use 0.1 percent salt solution in holding tanks.
Epistylis	Use 0.1 to 1.0 percent salt solution in holding tanks.
Monogenetic trematodes	Formalin—15 to 25 ppm in ponds or 250 ppm in tanks for one hour.
	Potassium permanganate—2.0 ppm in ponds.
	Dylox—0.25 ppm active ingredient in ponds.
	Potassium dichromate—20 ppm.
Digenetic trematodes	Place in feed 0.3% di-N-butyl tin oxide active ingredient for three days.
Cestodes (tapeworms and other intestinal worms)	Feed 125 milligrams of di-N-butyl tin oxide per pound of fish, or add 1% to the ration of feed for three days.
Copepods	Apply Dylox weekly at the rate of 0.25 ppm active ingredient.

[1]The possible treatments given here are not recommendations but are those which have been used to aid in controlling fish diseases. Some of the chemicals listed have not been approved by the Food and Drug Administration for use with food fish.

Sources: Fred P. Meyer, "Parasites of Freshwater Fishes." Stuttgart, Arkansas: Fish Farming Experiment Station, 1966. "Report to the Fish Farmers." Washington: U.S. Department of the Interior, Bureau of Sport Fisheries and Wildlife, 1970, p. 55. "The Biology of Channel Catfish Production." Fayetteville: University of Arkansas, Cooperative Extension Service, Circular 535, 1969. "Principal Diseases of Farm-Raised Catfish," Bulletin 225. Auburn, Alabama: Agricultural Experiment Station, 1979.

Chemicals Used in Disease and Parasite Control

A number of different chemicals have been used in attempts to control diseases and parasites. Some have been relatively effective. Of those which are effective, only a few have been approved by the Food and Drug Administration for use on catfish for human consumption. A brief summary of the chemicals used is shown in Table 8-4.

Table 8-4

Summary of Chemicals Used to Control
Diseases and Parasites

Chemical	Summary
Oxytetracycline	Commonly known as Terramycin, this chemical is used in controlling systemic bacterial diseases. A premix for addition to feed is available when needed. Since oxytetracycline is usually expensive, it should be fed only when needed. (Some diseases are developing resistance to oxytetracycline, one of which is *Aeromonas.*)
Copper sulfate	Copper sulfate is often used to control external parasites and, sometimes, aquatic vegetation. The rate of usage ranges from 0.25 to 1.5 ppm, depending on water chemistry. Copper sulfate is more toxic in soft water than in hard water; therefore, a lower rate is used in soft water. Since chemicals are more active in warm water, the rate used may be reduced with warm water. Plastic containers should be used with copper sulfate because of its corrosive effects. Galvanized containers should never be used. Also, copper sulfate will cause a die-off of plankton which may contribute to oxygen problems in ponds.
Malachite green	This chemical is often used with external parasites. A rate of 0.1 ppm is normally used for both tanks and ponds. The toxicity of malachite green is greatly increased in zinc containers and, therefore, plastic or nonmetallic containers should be used.
Acriflavine	Acriflavine is often used as a prophylactic treatment in haul tanks to control bacteria at the rate of 3.0 ppm. It is considered to be too expensive for use in ponds. It should be

(Continued)

Table 8-4 (continued)

Chemical	Summary
	mixed and used right away. If allowed to stand in water for several hours, it will become toxic to fish.
Formalin	Better known as formaldehyde, formalin is used in treating for external parasites. The rate of usage may range from 15 to 30 ppm in ponds to 150 to 250 ppm in vats for one to two hours.
Salt	Common salt (NaCl) is used to cause external parasites to release from fish and fall to the bottom of the tank in which it is used. It is used as a 3 percent solution. The fish should be removed when they begin to show signs of distress.
Potassium permanganate	Potassium permanganate is used for a number of purposes in fish culture. It is used to control external parasites at the rate of 2 to 6 ppm, depending on water chemistry. The effectiveness is related to water pH, hardness, and temperature. It should be used with care in water with a hardness less than 40 ppm.
Dylox (masoten)	Monogenetic trematodes, copepods, and anchor parasites have been controlled with Dylox. A rate of 0.25 ppm active ingredient is often used. Dylox breaks down rapidly in water with a high pH and at high temperatures.
Calcium hydroxide	Calcium hydroxide is commonly known as slaked or hydrated lime. It can be used as a disinfectant in drained ponds. It is used at the rate of 1,000 to 2,500 pounds per acre spread over the pond bottom.
Di-N-Butyl Tin Oxide	This chemical is used to control intestinal parasites. It should be fed at the rate of 0.3% for 5 days. (This equals 0.3 lb. per 100 pounds of feed.)
Furance	Furance is used on a limited basis to treat bacterial infections. It is used at 0.25 ppm for one hour on three consecutive days in vat treatment. It can be fed at 100 to 200 mg active per 100 pounds of catfish for three to five days. (This is equivalent to 3.3 to 7.6 g active per 100 pounds of feed.) Warning: Continued treatment may cause injury to skin.

Sources: Fred P. Meyer, "Parasites of Freshwater Fishes." Stuttgart, Arkansas: Fish Farming Experiment Station, 1966. "Report to the Fish Farmers." Washington: U.S. Department of the Interior, Bureau of Sport Fisheries and Wildlife, 1970, p. 55. "The Biology of Channel Catfish Production." Fayetteville: University of Arkansas, Cooperative Extension Service, Circular 535, 1969. "Principal Diseases of Farm-Raised Catfish," Bulletin 225. Auburn, Alabama: Agricultural Experiment Station, 1979.

Calculation of Treatments

The treatment of fish for diseases and parasites involves calculating the amount of chemical to use per given volume of water. Water treatments for catfish diseases and parasites are usually stated in terms of parts per million (ppm). One ppm means that 1 part of a chemical should be added to 999,999.0 parts of water by weight. Weight is always used as the basis for formulation. In order to determine the amount of chemical to use, it is necessary to know the amount of water in a vat, tank, or pond. Records of the size of water facilities should be readily available. One ppm requires the following amounts:

2.7 pounds per acre-foot of water
0.0038 gram per gallon of water
0.0238 gram per cubic foot
1.0 pound in a million pounds
1.0 gram in a million grams

A table containing other useful conversion information is located in Appendix B.

Vat and Tank Calculations. The volume of water in a vat or tank is determined by measuring the length, width, and depth of the water in feet. By multiplying length times width times depth, the volume in cubic feet is determined. For example, the amount of water in a vat with inside measurements of 12 feet long and 4 feet wide and a water depth of 3 feet is $12 \times 4 \times 3 = 144$ cubic feet. If a chemical is to be used at 0.5 ppm, the amount needed is $144 \times 0.0283 \times 0.5 = 2.0376$ grams of chemical for the vat (0.0283 grams = 1 ppm per cubic foot). The volume of water in a round tank is determined with the following formula:

$$\text{Volume} = 3.1416 \, (\frac{\text{diameter of tank}}{2})^2 \times \text{water depth in tank}$$

Of course, an allowance must be made if the bottom of a round tank slopes or is recessed.

Fish should be regularly observed during treatment in vats and tanks. If fish show signs of distress, fresh water should be added. Aerators should operate during the treatment period.

Pond and Raceway Calculations. Determining the amount of water in a pond or raceway section involves essentially the same procedure as that for a vat or tank. The average depth of the water must be determined. Water depth is estimated by measuring at regular intervals along straight lines in all directions across the surface. Measurements should be made in both deep and shallow water. The average depth is determined by adding all of the measurements and dividing the sum by the number of measurements taken. The volume of rectangular ponds is more easily determined than that of irregular ponds. The following is an example of how to determine the amount of water in a rectangular pond. (A similar procedure may be used with raceway sections.)

EXAMPLE: A pond measures 207.5 feet long by 77.5 feet wide; levees have a 3-to-1 slope; the depth at the foot of the levee at the shallow end is 2 feet, and 3 feet at the deep end. Since the levee has a slope of 3-to-1, it is a distance of 6.0 feet from the edge of the water to the foot of the levee at the shallow end and 9.0 feet from the edge of the water to the foot of the levee at the deep end. Average length is found by adding 6.0 and 9.0, dividing by 2.0, and subtracting from 207.5, which equals 200.0 feet. The average width of the volume of water is calculated in the same way and is 70.0 feet. (If the slope of a levee is unknown, the distance the foot of the levee extends into the water can be located by sounding from a boat with a weighted line and the distance measured from the edge of the water.) The measurements used in making the calculations are 200 feet by 70 feet by 2 feet deep at the shallow end and 3 feet at the deep end. Volume of the pond is $200 \times 70 \times 2.5 = 35,000$ cubic feet. The volume in cubic feet can be used to determine the amount of chemical needed, or cubic feet can be converted to acre-feet by dividing the cubic feet by 43,560. The acre-feet in the pond is 35,000 divided by 43,560, or 0.8 acre-foot. The amount of chemical to use at 1.0 ppm is 2.7×0.8, or 2.16 pounds. (The number of pounds needed to give 1.0 ppm per acre-foot is 2.7.)

A simple formula has been devised for estimating the volume of water in a pond constructed by damming a hollow: Volume = .4 (maximum depth) × surface area.

The percentage of active formulation in a compound must be known to calculate the amount of chemical needed. For example, a chemical containing 50 percent of active formulation requires two times the amount as a chemical of a 100 percent active formulation. If 2 pounds of a 100 percent active formulation are required, 4 pounds of a 50 percent active formulation would be re-

Dimensions of Surface Area:

Length	207.5 Feet
Width	77.5 Feet

Depth of Water:

Shallow End	2 Feet
Deep End	3 Feet

Levee:

3:1 Slope

Average Dimensions of Volume of Water:

Length: 200.0 Feet (207.5 Minus $\frac{6+9}{2}$)

Width : 70.0 Feet (77.5 Minus $\frac{6+9}{2}$)

Depth : $\frac{2+3}{2}$ = 2.5 Feet

Approximate Volume of Water:

Length X Width X Depth = Cubic Feet

200.0 X   70.0 X   2.5   = 35,000

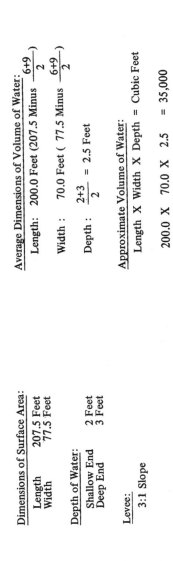
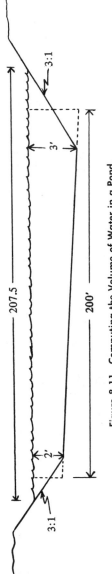

Figure 8-11. Computing the Volume of Water in a Pond.

quired. The percentage of active formulation is stated in the label attached to containers of chemicals.

Applying chemicals to ponds for the treatment of diseases may pose a problem. Chemicals need to be evenly distributed throughout all of the water in order to be effective and to reduce the risk associated with excess concentration in some areas. Formalin and other liquid treatments may be applied by placing a drum containing the desired amount of liquid in a boat. A faucet should be located on one end of the drum and a piece of garden hose long enough to reach the water should be attached to the faucet. The boat should move around the pond starting at the outer edge and gradually reducing the size of the circle until all of the formalin has been applied. The drum should be tilted so that the formalin will flow into the water. Rate of flow will be regulated by the faucet. It may be necessary to make extra passes with the boat over deeper water. Care should be used so that the proper amount of formalin will be evenly distributed.

Dry materials, such as malachite green and potassium permanganate, may be applied by placing the amount required for the pond in a cloth sack and then towing it behind a boat in the water. The boat should circle around the pond until all of the dry material has been dissolved. Movement of the boat should facilitate mixing the chemical with the water.

Questions and Problems for Discussion

1. What is the distinction between infectious, nutritional, environmental, and parasitic diseases?
2. What is the relationship of intensive culture to disease problems?
3. What are the symptoms of diseased fish?
4. What is stress? How is it related to disease?
5. How is the occurrence of disease outbreaks related to the season of the year?
6. What are some good management practices that may reduce disease problems?
7. What are prophylactic treatments?
8. What treatment methods may be used?
9. What are the common diseases of catfish?
10. What are the common parasites of catfish?
11. Explain what is meant by ppm.
12. What are some of the chemicals that are commonly used in controlling diseases?
13. Calculate the amount of water in a vat that is 20 feet long, 6 feet wide, and 3 feet deep. (Determine cubic feet and gallons.)

9

Controlling Predators, Trash Fish, and Other Pests

Catfish are occasionally subject to attack from a number of other animals, including other fish. Sometimes the damage may be confined to the facilities with no direct effect on the catfish. Considerable losses may result from some pests. The extent of such losses can be minimized through the use of various managerial and technical practices.

This chapter discusses the following areas:

> Predator control
> Trash fish control
> Pest control

Predator Control

A "predator" lives by preying on other animals. Catfish have predators and are predatory themselves. Most fish farmers are not concerned with the fact that catfish are predatory, since authorities agree that an animal source of protein is required for growth. However, the predators of catfish do cause concern, since catfish populations and profits may be reduced because of them.

The common predators of catfish are snakes, fish-eating birds, insects, and certain species of turtles. Occasionally, even alligators have been known to poach catfish. Each of these may cause considerable losses if present in large numbers. The greatest losses are to fingerling-size catfish.

Snakes. Several species of snakes may be present in and around fish ponds. In addition to causing fish losses, some of the species are poisonous to man. The best control involves keeping the banks around ponds closely mowed and free of debris, such as boards and brush. Snakes can be controlled reasonably well by removing their lurking places and by killing them when they are accessible.

Birds. Certain water birds are serious problems if present in sufficient numbers. Those which most commonly prey on catfish are kingfishers, little green herons, grebes, mergansers, and great blue herons. Federal and state laws protect most water birds, thereby eliminating certain control measures. Loud noises, such as exploding fireworks, have been used with limited success in attempts to drive water birds away. Ponds should be constructed with a minimum of shallow water so that there are no places in which birds can stand for the purpose of catching fish.

Turtles. Losses are caused by turtles preying on catfish and competing with catfish for space and feed. The snapping turtle is the only turtle that actively preys on catfish. The "slider" turtle is the most common turtle found in fish ponds, but it does not prey on catfish. Turtles compete with catfish and are objectionable at the time of harvest, because they must be separated from the catfish. Some turtles bite and should be handled carefully. Turtles are often controlled by trapping them or by shooting them with a rifle.

Figure 9-1. A Box Trap May Be Effective in Controlling Turtles. (Courtesy, Extension Service, Auburn University)

Trash Fish Control

A "trash fish" is a fish other than the species being grown. In a way, a trash fish is similar to a weed in a row crop. Catfish farmers frequently consider scale fish, such as sunfish, carp, and bullheads, to be trash fish. Trash fish compete with catfish for food, space, and oxygen. Feed costs are increased, and the rate of growth of catfish may be reduced by the presence of trash fish. Labor requirements at the time of harvest are increased, because the trash fish must be sorted from the catfish. Trash fish may introduce diseases and parasites into growing ponds. Trash fish are sometimes referred to as wild or undesirable fish.

Sources of Trash Fish. Trash fish may gain entry into a fish farm in several ways:

1. Water secured from streams or lakes may contain trash fish.
2. Overflow or backwater from nearby streams or lakes that enters a pond may carry undesirable fish.
3. A new pond that is built across a stream, spring, or drain may get trash fish from puddles of water present in the construction site.
4. Improper construction of spillways may allow trash fish to enter when the water level below a pond rises and water flows into the pond.
5. Fingerlings may contain trash fish.

Removal of Trash Fish. Water used for catfish culture may need to be filtered to remove wild fish, especially if it is obtained from streams or lakes. Two types of filtering devices are commonly used: a saran sock filter and a box filter. The filters are ordinarily made of saran screen, a product available commercially.

Sock-type filters are placed over the ends of pipes. The sock is constructed by sewing together two pieces of saran screen 12 feet long and 3 feet wide to form a cylinder. A draw-string closure arrangement is placed at each end. One end of the screen filter is placed over the end of the incoming water-supply pipe. The other end is drawn tightly together to close the sock and prevent the passage of fish. This type of filter should be used on inlet pipes that discharge water near the surface to prevent strain on the screen. The filter should be regularly cleaned to remove the fish which have been filtered from the water.

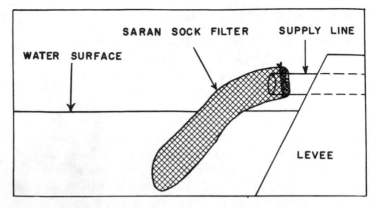

Figure 9-2. A Sock-Type Filter. (Courtesy, Bureau of Sport Fisheries and Wildlife, U.S. Department of the Interior)

Box filters are usually constructed of wooden frames and screen. Common dimensions of box filters are 8 feet long, 3 feet wide, and 2 feet deep. A filter of this size will handle 1,000 gpm. The bottom is covered with screen. Boards should be placed across the bottom at 1- to 2-foot intervals to reduce the strain on the screen. Box filters may be permanently stationed in a pond or constructed so that they float. Floating box filters change with the

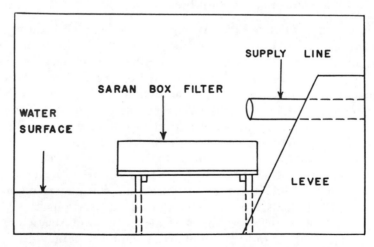

Figure 9-3. A Box-Type Filter. (Courtesy, Bureau of Sport Fisheries and Wildlife, U.S. Department of the Interior)

water level and may have a longer life, because the filter is at or below the water level.

Trash fish may be chemically removed if filtering is impractical. Rotenone is commonly used to rid ponds of unwanted fish. It is a non-selective pesticide that also will kill desirable species of catfish. Certain species of fish tend to be resistant to rotenone; but when it is used at a rate of 0.5 to 2.0 ppm, most fish will be killed. A major disadvantage of rotenone is that it may remain poisonous for two weeks in warm water and longer in cold water.

Antimycin A is a selective poison for eliminating scale fish in the presence of catfish. It may be used in ponds or troughs. Its major disadvantage is that it does not kill bullheads without also killing other catfish. The effectiveness of Antimycin A is related to the chemistry and temperature of the water. Instructions on the label may be sufficient for most pond conditions; otherwise, the advice of experts should be obtained. This poison may be used in troughs and vats to rid catfish of scale fish at the rate of 5.0 ppb (parts per billion). The rate to use varies with the pH of the water. Antimycin A is marketed under the registered trade name of Fintrol-5, which is a formulation containing 1 percent of the active ingredient.

Attempts have been made to control trash fish by stocking 50 to 75 large-mouth bass per acre. The bass will supposedly prey on the trash fish and leave the catfish unharmed. Bass do not compete with catfish for commercial feed, but they do compete for oxygen. Fingerling-size bass are usually stocked at about the time the catfish are stocked. The bass must be sorted from the catfish during harvest.

Pest Control

Several pests that are not predators or trash fish may compete with catfish or cause damage to the facilities in which catfish are produced. These include bullfrogs, "walking catfish," crayfish, muskrats, beavers, and ordinary livestock.

Bullfrogs. Adult bullfrogs may be controlled by using techniques similar to those used for snakes, that is, removing places in which they may hide. Other effective means of controlling frogs include removing and destroying eggs or poisoning the eggs by placing several crystals of copper sulfate on the egg masses. Tadpoles, which are immature frogs, compete with catfish for space and consume fish feed.

Walking Catfish. The "walking catfish" is a very undesirable type of fish that has the ability to move across land without water. This fish was imported into Florida from Asia for exhibition in aquariums. At the present time, it is pretty much confined to Florida and the immediately surrounding area. It is best adapted to climates that are warm year-round.

The "walking catfish" can travel 5 feet a minute by using its fins, arching its back, and throwing its tail forward. It can remain out of water for more than 24 hours by breathing through a rudimentary lung behind its gills. This pest has a tremendous appetite, and a few will completely consume all of the minnows, shellfish, frogs, and insects in a small pond in a few days. In addition to competing with catfish for food, it may attack and kill the entire desirable catfish population. "Walking catfish" are difficult to control, because they jump out of the water when a chemical is added to a pond. The transportation of "walking catfish" into some states is prohibited by law.

Crayfish. Certain species of crayfish may cause problems by burrowing into pond dams. These burrows may weaken dams and cause leaks. Crayfish may be eliminated by placing a poison in their burrows. A crayfish poison that has been used is made by dissolving 12 common moth balls in a gallon of kerosene to which 2 gallons of warm water and 1 tablespoon of detergent are added. Control is accomplished by pouring 1 cup of this mixture into each burrow and sealing the burrow by pressing mud from the chimney over the opening.

Muskrats. Damage by muskrats is done by their burrowing into levees and digging dens. Levees are weakened and may become rough for walking and vehicle movements as the burrows and dens collapse. Control of muskrats is primarily accomplished by removing their source of food, such as cattails and emersed vegetation. Pond levees should be closely mowed to remove hiding places. Levees may be riprapped with rock for 2 feet above and 3 feet below the waterline. Merely dumping broken concrete along a levee will not suffice, as this may make hiding places. Another possible method of control involves drilling small holes at 3- to 4-foot intervals on the upstream side of the levee. The holes should be 2 feet from the edge of the water and extend 2 feet below the waterline. Four to 5 ounces of creosote, calcium carbide, or naphthalene should be poured into each hole.

Beavers. Beavers rarely cause problems in catfish production ponds. However, their presence can result in considerable damage to levees and banks. Beavers dig large dens which may cause sizeable portions of pond levees to cave-in. It is possible for beavers to dam spillways, thus causing an excessive amount of water to build up in a pond. Excess water may cause a dam to collapse. Beavers may be controlled by being trapped.

Livestock. Damage to ponds may be caused by livestock. Hogs wallowing in a pond will cause the water to become muddy and make the bottom of the pond uneven. The movement of cattle into a pond to secure water may result in deep paths being cut in banks and levees which make the ground uneven and weaken levees.

Questions and Problems for Discussion

1. What is a predator?
2. What are some predators of catfish and how are they controlled?
3. What is a trash fish?
4. What are the sources of trash fish?
5. How are trash fish removed and prevented?
6. What pests may be present in catfish farming?

10

Selecting and Managing Broodfish

Efficient catfish production requires fingerlings that can be quickly and economically grown into marketable food fish. The performance of fingerlings can be no better than their biological inheritance permits. Nutrition, water management, and disease control are important and have received considerable emphasis in the past.

Crop farmers would not think of using unimproved crop varieties, and now the catfish farmer's interest is turning to the use of genetically improved broodfish. In the future, broodfish will be more carefully selected on the basis of their ability to produce fingerlings with superior performance.

The following topics are discussed in this chapter:

Determination of sex
Desirable characteristics of broodfish
Sources of broodfish
Care of broodfish
Number of broodfish needed
Improvement of fish stocks
Research needs in catfish genetics

Determination of Sex

As with other animals, there are two sexes of catfish—male and female. Both sexes are required if eggs are to be produced and fertilized. The ability of distinguish between the sexes is essential. Distinction is made by observing the primary and secondary characteristics of sexual difference. Primary sexual characteristics are directly concerned with reproduction. Secondary sexual characteristics may or may not have any relationship to reproduction.

In catfish, the primary sexual characteristics are not readily observable. Dissection of the fish is often necessary in order to determine some of these characteristics. In the male catfish, testes and the attached ducts are the primary sexual characteristics, whereas in the female, the ovaries and the attached duct system are primary. Testes produce milt, or sperm cells, and ovaries produce eggs, or spawn.

Sexual distinction can be made by observing the external portion of the primary sexual organs, or genitals, on the belly, or ventral side of a fish. Two openings are present: the anus and the genital opening. The opening nearest the head is the anus while that nearest the tail is the genital opening. In the male, the genital opening has the appearance of a tiny raised nipple, known as a "genital papilla." In the female, the genital is rounded and flat. Prior to spawning, the genital opening of the female catfish may be swollen and reddish in color with folds of skin appearing on each side of the urinary and genital openings. These folds may be

Figure 10-1. Ventral View of a Female Channel Catfish. (The arrow is pointing to the flat and rounded genital opening. The full abdomen indicates that the fish is soon to spawn.) (Courtesy, Bureau of Sport Fisheries and Wildlife, U.S. Department of the Interior)

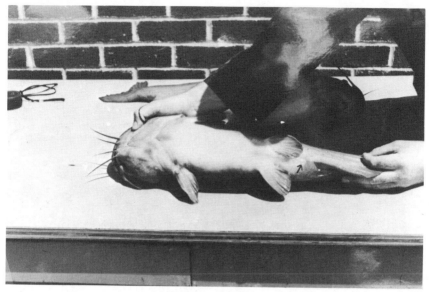

Figure 10-2. Ventral View of a Male Channel Catfish. (The arrow is pointing to the raised nipple-like genital papilla. Note the broad head and slender abdomen.) (Courtesy, Bureau of Sport Fisheries and Wildlife, U.S. Department of the Interior)

divided by a groove or slit. Sometimes a pulsating motion of the genitals is observed.

Catfish farmers often make use of the secondary sexual characteristics in sexing fish. The most distinguishing secondary characteristics have to do with the shape and proportions of the body. Male catfish have wider heads than females. Females tend to have a full abdomen, or "potbellied" appearance, especially if observed just prior to spawning. Males have darker pigment on the under side of the body. Sometimes it is difficult to determine the sex of catfish not having distinctive secondary sexual characteristics. In this case, other means of sexual distinction must be used.

Several techniques may be used if a fish's sex is not clearly evident. One of these involves rubbing a broom straw longitudinally over the vent, or genital opening. A straw will hang on the vent of a male. Another technique in sexing involves inserting the point of a lead pencil into the genital opening. If the tip of the pencil catches in the opening and is perpendicular to the body, the fish is a female; but if it does not catch or if it catches and angles toward the tail, the fish is a male.

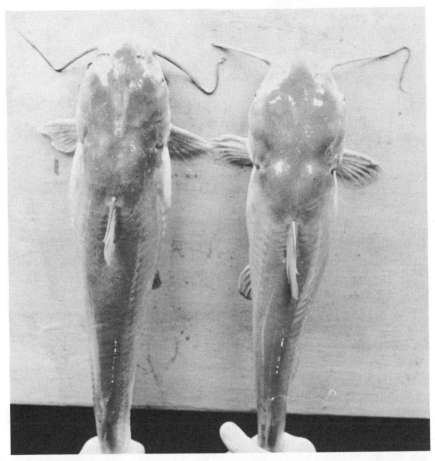

Figure 10-3. Secondary Sexual Characteristics of Catfish. (The fish on the right is a male and is characterized as having a large, wide head and a relatively thin abdomen. The fish on the left is a female and is characterized as having a small head and a full abdomen.) (Courtesy, Louisiana Wildlife and Fisheries Commission)

Desirable Characteristics of Broodfish

Broodfish should be selected on the basis of spawning potential. Many times in the past this has meant that greater attention has been given to the selection of females than to the selection of males. Of course, in any long-range program designed to improve the quality of catfish, the same attention should be given to selecting the male as to the female. This is obvious if one will remember that the offspring inherit the characteristics of both parents.

Female broodfish capable of producing large spawns should be selected. Spawning capability can be determined by observation of the fish. A full, well rounded abdomen, or "potbelly," is the best characteristic of spawning potential. The fullness should extend to the genital orifice. Physical manipulation of the abdomen of the fish should reveal that the ovaries are soft and palpable. The genitals are usually flat or slightly depressed and of a reddish color. Female fish should be examined before feeding so that abdominal fullness is readily attributable to egg development and not to the feed that has been consumed.

Male broodfish with prominent secondary sexual characteris-

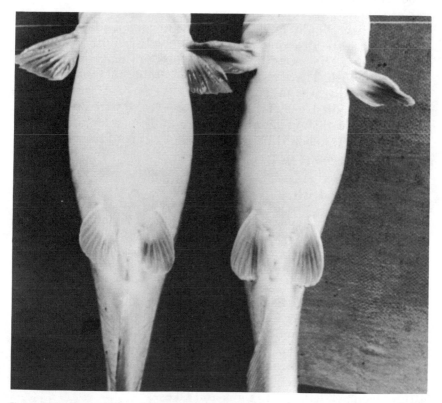

Figure 10-4. Ventral View of Male and Female Fish. (These are the same fish as in Figure 10-3. The female is on the left.) (Courtesy, Louisiana Wildlife and Fisheries Commission)

tics are preferred. These characteristics include (1) a head wider than the body, (2) the presence of darker pigment under the body, and (3) a large and protruded genital papilla.

Size should be considered in selecting broodfish, especially in selecting the females. Large catfish usually spawn earlier and produce more eggs; however, most fingerling producers tend to prefer fish weighing less than 10 pounds. Fish weighing more than 10 pounds are not so easily handled as smaller fish. Also, the spawning behavior of large catfish cannot be so reliably predicted. Most fingerling producers prefer broodfish weighing from 2 to 10 pounds. This size fish can be produced in three years. Catfish may become capable of spawning at ¾ pound, but fish of this size are not usually kept as broodstock. Size of the male is not quite so important, but fish should be paired so that the male is of similar size or slightly larger than the female.

Broodfish should be healthy and in good body condition. Females that are diseased and in poor body condition produce small spawns. The proportion of eggs hatched may be less than with healthy fish. There is always the possibility that diseased fish may transmit diseases to fry.

Good broodfish are of the desired species. It is relatively easy for species of catfish to get mixed in handling or selection. Fish of the same species should be held together to avoid the possibility of mixing egg masses or fry.

Sources of Broodfish

Broodfish may be obtained from streams and lakes as wild fish or from fish producers who have cultured stock. A few years ago wild fish were used almost exclusively because no other sources were available. Preference is currently given to cultured broodfish.

The suitability of fish for broodfish depends upon the environment in which they were grown and upon the food which they had received. Good broodfish must have had a proper diet, including animal protein. Pond-reared broodfish must receive supplemental animal protein in addition to the regular commercial feed. Wild fish tend to secure the needed animal protein from the natural food available in streams and lakes.

Cultured broodfish may be selected from improved stocks, whereas the heredity of wild fish is unknown. Selective breeding may be used to improve the fish available. Certain strains of fish may be selected because of desired characteristics. Considerable attention is currently being given to improving fish stocks through hybridization, crossbreeding, and selective breeding.

The health conditions of wild fish are relatively unknown. Cultured broodfish are carefully tended during growth. Any evidence of diseases or parasitic conditions is immediately considered, and the appropriate treatment is provided. Reliable broodfish producers will relate all information pertaining to the health of fish produced. On the other hand, wild fish obtained as broodfish may introduce diseases and parasites into a fish farming operation.

The changing physical and chemical conditions in ponds may affect the spawning behavior of broodfish. Cultured broodfish are able to tolerate these changes better than wild fish are. Wild fish may not spawn for several years after being captured, whereas cultured broodfish will spawn more normally.

Occasionally broodfish from outside sources should be introduced into a fish farm to reduce inbreeding. Outside sources should be free of diseases and should vary from year to year. Continually obtaining broodstock from the same sources will result in inbreeding. A few broodfish unrelated to those presently on hand should be introduced each year. It may be necessary to travel a good distance from home to secure unrelated broodstock. Inbreeding may result in a number of variations in offspring, including crooked spines, the absence of tails and eyes, and malformed mouths.

Care of Broodfish

Proper care of broodfish throughout the year is necessary to insure healthy brooders when spawning season arrives. Small eggs and spawns, and even failure to spawn, may be the outcome of neglected broodfish. The same broodfish are used for three years.

At the end of the spawning season broodfish should be placed in holding ponds until the next spawning season. The number of fish to put in a holding pond depends upon size of the fish and whether additional growth is desired. Smaller fish weighing 2 to 3 pounds each are stocked in holding ponds at the rate of 300 to 400 pounds per acre. Therefore, 100 to 130 fish weighing 3 pounds each can be stocked per acre of holding pond. Larger fish which are not expected to grow can be stocked at the rate of 800 pounds per acre, or about one hundred 8-pound fish. Many farmers prefer small holding ponds of about ¼ acre. The smaller ponds facilitate feeding and reduce the possibility of losing all fish from an outbreak of disease when two or more small ponds are used. The smaller ponds also improve the percentage of fish that come for food, since broodfish are easily frightened. In a ¼-acre pond, 90 to 95 percent of the fish will come for food. In a 1-acre pond, 70 to 75 percent will come for food. Fish that do not receive food will be in poor condition for spawning; therefore, smaller ponds aid in maintaining the broodfish in good condition. Precaution should be exercised to avoid overstocking small holding ponds.

The most critical factor in maintaining broodfish is the availability of food containing sufficient nutrients. Research has not yet revealed the exact dietary requirements of broodfish, but it is known that certain foods are needed to produce big spawns. Adult catfish consume a variety of food materials. The natural food of a well fertilized pond will maintain 200 to 300 pounds of broodfish per acre. Greater stocking rates are often used and will require supplemental feeding.

Broodfish are usually fed five or six days a week in warm weather. The rate of feeding each day is somewhat less than 3 to 4 percent of the body weight, depending on the availability of natural foods in the pond. For example, 3 to 4 pounds of feed is fed for each 100 pounds of catfish when no natural food is available from the pond. In cooler weather when the water temperature is 45 to 65°F, broodfish may be fed at the rate of 1 percent of estimated weight five or six days each week. Regular, commercially prepared pelleted catfish rations are usually fed; but these alone are not considered sufficient to meet the dietary requirements of broodfish.

An important dietary supplement for broodfish is either fresh or frozen meat, including fish. Broodfish frequently feed on minnows, tadpoles, small bluegills, crayfish, and other readily available aquatic animals. Sources of supplementary meat include chopped up fish, fish liver, beef heart, beef liver, and similar economically priced meats. Condemned beef liver obtained from packing plants is sometimes used. It is usually considered a good procedure to feed meat at least once a week at the rate of 10 to 15 percent of the body weight of the fish. Meat should be fed at the higher rate in cooler weather when the water temperature is

Figure 10-5. Feeding Broodfish in Pens. (Courtesy, Master Mix Feeds)

below 55°F. Likewise, the amount of commercial type feeds high in cereal proteins is reduced. Fish consume less feed in cooler weather; however, research has shown that a greater percentage of proteins is needed when the weather is cool. Catfish will consume more feed and should be fed more in March and April, when the weather begins to warm. Goldfish are often stocked in holding ponds to serve as food and to supplement protein for the dietary needs of broodfish.

Catfish, especially channel catfish, do not eat when the water temperature is below 45°F; therefore, feeding is not usually necessary. However, some authorities recommend feeding .5 percent of the weight of the fish every four or five days when the water temperature is below 45°F. Other authorities on catfish recommend feeding only if the fish indicate a desire for feed. The feeding activity of fish can be determined by throwing a small amount of floating feed into the water. If it is consumed, the fish will feed and should be fed; otherwise, the fish should not be fed. Warm periods in the winter may result in increased feeding. Fish should be fed only the amount that they will consume.

It is often recommended that broodfish be treated for diseases and parasites each time they are handled. This is especially true prior to stocking in spawning ponds. Newly hatched fry are particularly susceptible to diseases and parasites. Precautions should be followed to insure that only healthy broodfish are used. (Diseases and parasites were previously discussed.)

Number of Broodfish Needed

The number of broodfish required depends upon the number of fingerlings to be produced, size of spawns, and cultural conditions under which the eggs hatch. Another factor is the economics of keeping broodfish and raising fingerlings versus the purchasing of fingerlings from other producers. Sometimes it is more economical to purchase fingerlings. In this case, the problem of not knowing the ancestry and health condition of fingerlings may arise.

Number of Female Broodfish. The size of spawns determines the number of female broodfish needed. "Size of spawns" refers to the number of eggs in a spawn. Size varies with the weight and health conditions of female catfish. Females weighing 3 to 4 pounds will produce around 4,000 eggs per pound of body weight. Females larger than 4 pounds will produce a smaller number of eggs per pound of body weight, usually about 3,000. Fish that are not properly fed and managed will produce smaller spawns. All of the eggs do not hatch. Some may fail to be fertilized by the male or may be destroyed in handling. After hatching, some of the fry may be lost. A general rule is that 2,000 eggs per pound of broodfish body weight will survive. It is important to know the average weight of female broodfish. A female fish in good body condition weighing 4 pounds should produce sufficient eggs to hatch 8,000 fry.

The number of female broodfish needed is estimated by multiplying the average weight in pounds of the female broodfish by 2,000 to determine the number of fry per female broodfish and by dividing the average number of fry per broodfish into the total number of fingerlings required. A minimum of 17 female broodfish weighing 3 pounds each is needed to produce 100,000 fingerlings. Most farmers maintain several extra broodfish to insure sufficient fingerlings in case several of the broodfish fail to spawn. A general rule is to keep 20 female broodfish for each 100,000

Figure 10-6. A Female Catfish in Good Condition. (Courtesy, Louisiana Wildlife and Fisheries Commission)

fingerlings needed. A convenient formula for determining the minimum number of female broodfish needed is:

$$\text{Minimum Number of Female Broodfish Required} = \frac{\text{Number of Fingerlings Needed}}{\text{Average Body Weight of Female Broodfish in Pounds} \times 2{,}000}$$

Number of Male Broodfish. The number of male broodfish needed varies with the number of females, sexuality of the males, and the method of spawning used. (Methods of spawning are discussed in another chapter.) Authorities do not agree on the number of males required with the open-pond method of spawning. However, it is generally agreed that a male fish with strong secondary sexual characteristics can fertilize more than one spawn. A male fish should not be expected to fertilize more than two spawns per season. Therefore, one to two males should be stocked for every two females. With the open-pond method, 20 female broodfish would require 10 to 20 male broodfish of equal or slightly larger size. When the pen method of spawning is used, one male and one female are placed in each pen. Thus, it appears

the same number of males as females will be required, but not
. :essarily. All females do not spawn at the same time; therefore,
males can be used more than once.

Improvement of Fish Stocks

Fish that grow efficiently and quickly are most desirable.
Through breeding programs it is possible to develop improved
fish stocks that have desirable characteristics. The culture of catfish is relatively new, and as a result, widespread experimental
work in improving stock has only recently been initiated. Improved strains of catfish may be obtained in four ways; introduction, selection, hybridization, and crossbreeding.

Introduction. This is a simple method of improving catfish
stocks. Introduction is simply bringing a new strain into an area.
Producers of fingerlings should secure a number of broodfish each
year from outside sources to reduce inbreeding and the malforma-
tions that may be associated with inbreeding. Fish that are introduced from other areas should be disease- and parasite-free.

Selection. This is a relatively easy method of improving catfish. The object of selection is to select fish which have, or tend to
have, the traits that are desired. These fish are further perfected
by breeding and continued selection. Catfish are frequently
selected on the basis of size, age, and growing conditions. A fish
may be larger because of feed and care during growth and not
because of genetic factors. In using selection, the conditions of
growth must be identical for all fish so that genetic superiority, if
present, is readily evident.

A selection program commonly involves the following steps:

1. Selecting the largest males and females in a group of fish.
   (The fish should be of the same age, preferably four years
   old, and of the same general stock.)
2. From the largest fish, selecting those which have the preferred body form, strong secondary sexual characteristics,
   and good color. (After this step, the fish are often branded
   or tagged for identification.)
3. Mating the best male with the best female and keeping the
   spawn completely isolated from other spawns. (An
   aquarium might be used to hatch the spawn.)

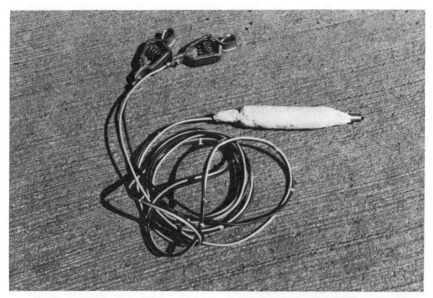

Figure 10-7. Fish-Branding Instrument Developed by the Fish Farming Experimental Station.

4. Growing the fry and fingerlings in isolation from other fry and fingerlings. (It is important that fish from other spawns not be mixed with this spawn.)
5. Selecting the largest 10 percent at one to two months of age.
6. Growing the selected 10 percent until the age of four to five months.
7. Selecting the best 5 percent at the age of four to five months.
8. Growing the best 5 percent to the age of 18 months and at that time selecting the best 5 percent of these for potential broodfish.
9. Growing the last fish selected to the age of 36 months.
10. Selecting at 36 months the best males and females and identifying them by additional branding or tagging. (At this time, only the fish with the most distinct secondary sexual characteristics, desirable body conformation, and color should be selected.)
11. Mating the fish selected at the age of 36 months. (A repeat of these 11 steps may be used to further select the fish.)

Hybridization. This is a process designed to produce catfish with desired characteristics by crossing two different species. Catfish produced by hybridization are known as "hybrids." Hybrids differ in constitution from their parents and are usually more vigorous, a trait which is known as "hybrid vigor," or "heterosis." Current attention is focused on the hybridization of channel catfish and white catfish (channel X white catfish) and channel catfish and blue catfish crosses (channel X blue catfish). The channel catfish and white catfish hybrid crosses show slightly better feed conversion and grow faster than the channel catfish and blue catfish hybrid crosses.

Figure 10-8. Improvement of Fish Stocks Is One Area of Research Conducted by the Fish Farming Experimental Station.

The hybridization of catfish involves "commercial crossing" and "synthetic crossing." Commercial crossing is used to produce first-generation hybrids for food fish purposes only. Catfish produced by commercial crossing are not usually retained as broodfish, because the second generation seldom has hybrid vigor. Synthetic crossing is used to develop new breeds of fish. It is more complex than commercial crossing and involves the mating of two or more kinds of fish in a long-term program of breeding and selection.

Crossbreeding. This involves the crossing of unrelated strains of the same catfish species to avoid inbreeding. Crossbreeding is considered to be a fast way of improving fish stock. Fish of unrelated strains showing the desired characteristics are selected and mated. Fish strains for crossbreeding may be selected because of a rapid rate of growth, disease resistance, high dressing percentage, resistance to adverse environmental conditions, or spawning at a low temperature. Fish used in crossbreeding should be banded or tagged for identification. Females should be crossed with unrelated males.

Research Needs in Catfish Genetics

Very little is known about catfish genetics—the passing on of the characteristics of parent broodfish to their offspring. Techniques used in developing healthier and more productive cattle, hogs, sheep, and poultry may be applicable to catfish. Since knowledge of catfish genetics is lacking, the practices followed in catfish breeding tend to be primitive.

The characteristics of catfish most in need of genetic research are:

- General growth information, including body weight, gain, and body conformation
- Feed efficiency, including nutrient requirements
- Viability (survival) and resistance to disease
- Reproduction, including spawning rate, egg size, fertility, and hatchability
- Processing and meat quality, including dressing percentage

It is likely that the farmers of the future will use hybrid catfish specifically bred to economically produce a high-quality product. Most of the past research has been on nutrition, water management, and disease control. For the catfish industry to continue to expand, research into the fish itself is needed. Much of the financial support for this research will need to be provided by Federal and state governments. The industry itself is not large enough to support the needed genetic research. Further, considerable time will be required to do the kind of long-term research that is needed.

Questions and Problems for Discussion

1. Why will more attention in the future be focused on the selection of broodfish?
2. What is the difference between primary and secondary characteristics of sexual difference?
3. What are the secondary sexual characteristics of male and female catfish?
4. What are the desirable characteristics of female broodfish? Male broodfish?
5. How is size of female fish related to spawning potential?
6. What are the sources of broodfish?
7. What are the advantages of using cultured fish as broodfish?
8. Describe the feeding program that should be followed with broodfish.
9. How are estimates made of the number of broodfish needed?
10. Describe four ways of improving catfish stocks.
11. What are the steps in improving fish stocks by selection?
12. What characteristics of catfish are most in need of genetic research?

11

Producing Fry, Fingerlings, and Stockers

Success in catfish farming is closely related to the quality of the fingerlings and stockers used in growing ponds. Small, diseased catfish are unprofitable and are not likely to survive. Healthy and high-quality fingerlings and stockers are desirable. They should be of an adequate size and of a uniform species.

This chapter presents information on the following:

    Methods of spawning
    Control of spawning
    Handling eggs
    Hatching eggs
    Rearing fry
    Classification of fingerlings
    Identification of stockers
    Rearing fingerlings and stockers
    Time required to produce fingerlings and stockers
    Number of fingerlings and stockers produced per acre
    Estimating number of fry, fingerlings, and stockers

Methods of Spawning

Spawning refers to the production of eggs by the female catfish and the subsequent fertilization by the male. Fish farmers have attempted to manipulate spawning behavior. This is because wild fish do not reproduce in sufficient numbers, and if they did, it would be difficult to obtain acceptable wild fingerlings for culture. In addition to the natural spawning of wild fish, three methods used by fish farmers are: pond, pen, and aquarium.

Natural Spawning. Wild channel catfish naturally spawn in streams and lakes when the water temperature is 70 to 85°F. Most often spawning occurs in May, June, and July. The water depth preferred for spawning may vary, but is usually not over 5 feet. Wild catfish make nests in holes in banks, beneath submerged stumps, and in similar secluded places. The male usually prepares the nest for spawning by smoothing and packing the mud. The eggs are about two-thirds the size of an average garden pea and are laid in a single mass that adheres together. Four to six hours may be required for spawning to be completed. Not all eggs are laid at the same time. A few eggs are laid, and the female moves aside. The male swims over the eggs releasing sperm cells, known as milt. Ferilization occurs as the sperm cells flow into contact with the eggs. One sperm cell enters each egg that is fertilized. The male moves aside, and the female returns and deposits another layer of eggs which is subsequently fertilized by the male. This procedure is repeated several times until all eggs have been laid and fertilized.

When spawning has been completed, the male drives the female away and assumes a position over the eggs. Through

Figure 11-1. Catfish Egg Mass. (Courtesy, *The Catfish Farmer* Magazine)

movement of the fins, the eggs are continuously fanned by the male until hatching occurs in 6 to 10 days. Occasionally, the male may touch the egg mass with his fins so that the eggs are shaken and lightly packed. After hatching, the male may continue to guard the nest and fry for about a week.

Pond Spawning. The pond method of spawning is the method most widely used by fish farmers. It makes greater use of the natural spawning process of wild fish than do other methods. Spawning ponds are usually 1 acre or less in size; however, the sizes being used range from $^{1}/_{10}$ acre to 5 acres. The number of ponds varies with the size of pond used and number of fingerlings needed. Spawning ponds are usually relatively shallow with a maximum depth of 7 feet.

The number of broodfish to stock in a pond ranges from 20 to 50 females per acre of water, depending on the method used to hatch the eggs. Twenty females should be stocked per acre when the eggs are hatched by the male and the fry are to remain in the pond. Fifty females may be stocked if the eggs are to be removed to troughs with mechanical hatching and the fry are to be placed in special rearing ponds. The number of males varies but frequently is identical to the number of females. Normally, broodfish should be placed in spawning ponds when the water temperature reaches 60°F.

Artificial nests, or spawning receptacles, are needed in most ponds. Depth of placement may range from 6 inches to 5 feet, but is usually about 30 inches. Nests placed more than 3 feet deep are difficult to observe for spawning activity. Spawning nests may be made of nail kegs, wooden boxes, hollow logs, 10-gallon milk cans, concrete tile, or similar materials. The opening of the spawning receptacles should be toward the center of the pond. Receptacles are usually placed around the edge of ponds at intervals of 20 to 30 feet. Authorities do not completely agree as to the number of spawning receptacles needed, but one receptacle for each 2 pairs of fish is a good rule of thumb to follow. It is possible to use fewer receptacles than pairs of fish, because all fish do not spawn at the same time.

Spawning receptacles should be checked at least every other day, or more often, to determine if spawning is occurring. A bare hand should not be thrust into a receptacle. The male catfish attempts to protect the nest from potential enemies and will attack when apparent danger comes near the nest. Male catfish can cause severe bites. Various techniques for checking receptacles include wearing gloves, gently raising the receptacle so that a visual observation can be made for eggs or fry without disturbing the male, and using various devices to restrain and remove the male fish. A few fingerling producers have made checking easy by constructing small doors in the tops of spawning containers. The doors are hinged and latched.

The eggs may be removed from the spawning receptacles and hatched mechanically or left in the receptacle for the male fish to hatch. The eggs will hatch in 7 to 8 days. After hatching, the fry may be removed and transferred to a rearing pond or allowed to remain in the brood pond. When fry are allowed to remain in the brood pond, it is preferable to remove the broodstock. It is generally considered best to remove the eggs for mechanical hatching so that the danger of the spread of disease and parasites is reduced.

New spawning ponds used for the first time should receive special treatment. Before being filled with water, a soil sample should be taken from the bottom of the pond. The pH of the soil should be neutral. If it is acidic, agricultural lime should be applied so that it has a pH of around 7.0. New ponds should be filled with water 30 days before the spawning season. Some authorities suggest that it is a good procedure, especially with soil of low fertility, to fertilize with 40 pounds of 20-20-5 per acre of water. One to three applications at 10-day intervals should be made. It is not necessary to fertilize ponds after spawning and feeding are underway.

Pond spawning is the most popular method. It is relatively inexpensive, since only a pond and spawning receptacles are required. Management by the farmer is not so critical as with the other methods. After the spawning season, the pond should be drained, allowed to dry, and the bottom disked lightly and smoothed. Such a procedure will reduce the buildup of disease and parasite infestations and aid in the oxidation of waste materials.

Pen Spawning. The pen method involves placing broodfish in pens for spawning. Pens are most often placed in ponds, but flowing streams can be used. The size of pens ranges from 4 to 6 feet wide and from 8 to 12 feet long. The height of the sides is based on the depth of the water in which the pens are to be used. Normally, the water should be about 3 feet deep. Pens are commonly constructed of wood and welded steel wire with a 1- by 2-inch mesh. Snow fences and concrete blocks are sometimes used. Concrete blocks are least preferred, because the movement of water is reduced. The sides of the pens are constructed so that they are embedded into the bottom of the pond and extend 1 to 2 feet above the level of the water. Fish may escape from pens not properly embedded or that do not extend above the water sufficiently. Spawning pens do not have tops and bottoms. A spawning receptacle must be placed in each pen. The spawning receptacle should generally be anchored facing the center of the pond.

A pair of fish is placed in each pen just prior to the time of spawning. The male should be about the same size or slightly larger than the female. When the pen method of spawning is used, it is essential that one be able to reliably sex fish and identify the various species. The spawning receptacles should be checked

Figure 11-2. Spawning Pens with Receptacles Ready for Adding Water to the Pond. (Courtesy, Master Mix Feeds)

daily or at least on alternate days. If spawning has occurred, the female may be removed from the pen and returned to the broodfish pond. Either the male fish is left to hatch the eggs or the egg mass is collected and mechanically hatched. After being hatched by the male, the fry may swim out of the nest, through the mesh wire, and into the pond for rearing. A new pair of broodstock is then placed in the pen to spawn.

The number of pairs of broodfish that can be spawned per acre of water with pens varies with the method of hatching the eggs and rearing fry. If fry are hatched and remain in the pond, only about 20 pairs of fish should be allowed to spawn per acre. If the eggs are removed and mechanically hatched, 50 pairs may be spawned per acre.

Pen spawning is often preferred because it allows for some control over the spawning conditions. It is possible to delay spawning by keeping the males and females apart. Spawning can be more or less scheduled so that hatching facilities are not overloaded by all fish spawning at the same time. The pen method permits the pairing of broodfish so that only selected broodfish are spawned. This is one way of attempting to genetically improve fish stock. Pens protect spawning pairs of fish from other fish that might intrude in an open pond. Also, pens allow for the use of hormones to speed up or delay spawning.

Aquarium Spawning. The aquarium method of spawning is the least common of the spawning methods. The major advantage of this method is that the spawning process may be controlled. With this method, a pair of fish is placed in an aquarium which may have a water capacity ranging from 20 to 50 gallons. The aquarium must be designed so that water is constantly flowing through it rather than being bubbled, as in a pet fish aquarium. Only one pair of fish is put in each aquarium. Fish can be spawned at any season of the year by injecting the female with hormone substances obtained from the pituitary glands of other fish, or with human chorionic gonadotropin. This method of spawning is best suited to biologists or other persons with special interest and knowledge in aquarium spawning. It is used more by fishery biologists in research than by farmers for commercial catfish farming. Farmers considering using the aquarium method of spawning should consult a fishery biologist for more detailed information.

Control of Spawning

Sometimes it is desirable either to delay spawning or to encourage it at an earlier date. Several techniques may be used to manipulate the production of eggs, and hence fingerlings. These techniques are often used to insure that a supply of fingerlings is available when needed.

Encouraging Spawning. Catfish can be encouraged to spawn with several techniques. Some farmers, using small ponds of about $1/10$ acre in size, warm the water slightly. This technique can be used to induce fish to spawn two weeks earlier. Attempting to warm the water may be impractical with large ponds.

Spawning may be advanced by injecting brood females with human chorionic gonadotropin before placing them in spawning ponds. The range in amount of the injection is 300 to 1,000 International Units (IU) per pound of body weight, depending on the condition of the fish. One injection of about 800 IU per pound of body weight is usually sufficient to induce spawning in two days. Injections are usually made into the body cavity. Human chorionic gonadotropin is available at most drugstores.

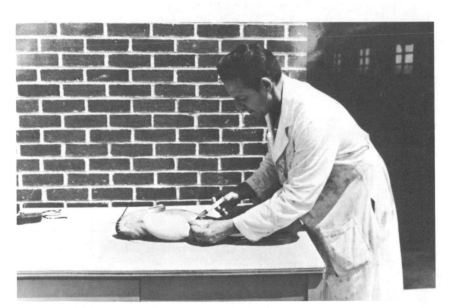

Figure 11-3. Injecting a Female Catfish with Hormones to Encourage Spawning. (Courtesy, Bureau of Sport Fisheries and Wildlife, U.S. Department of the Interior)

Sometimes it is possible to encourage spawning by raising the level of the water 1 to 2 inches at the time spawning is desired. Raising the water level has been found to be especially useful with the pen method when catfish spawn a few days and then, for some reason, stop.

Delaying Spawning. Spawning may be delayed indefinitely by separating male and female catfish prior to the spawning season. Holding broodfish in water with a temperature of 62 to 65°F in May, June, and July will also delay spawning. The length of time fish are held in the colder water will depend on how long spawning is to be delayed. Spawning normally occurs when water temperature is 70 to 85°F, with the optimum being about 80°F. Late spawns can also be obtained by capturing wild fish from streams in July and August and encouraging spawning. An injection of hormones to encourage spawning may be necessary. Of course, the use of wild fish may introduce diseases and parasites into a fish farm.

Handling Eggs

The eggs of catfish are susceptible to damage when handled. Most often, eggs are handled when removed from the spawning nest for mechanical hatching. This usually means that the eggs are transported only a short distance from pond to hatchery on a farm. Occasionally, eggs are shipped greater distances, meaning that special precautions are necessary. Damaged egg masses may have low rates of hatching or may result in deformed fry. Eggs which are allowed to remain in the pond to hatch are not handled; therefore, they are not damaged in this manner.

Damage to eggs may be brought about in several ways. One of the most important relates to sudden changes in the temperature of the water. Sudden changes in water temperature may reduce hatchability by as much as 50 percent and cause deformities in fry. If possible, the temperature of the water in which eggs are placed should be the same as that from which they were removed and should never vary more than 9°F. While in transit, the temperature of the water should remain relatively constant, never varying more than 9°F.

In handling, the exposure of eggs to direct sunlight should be avoided. It is possible that such exposure may reduce the hatchability of eggs.

During transit, the water in which eggs are placed should be well aerated. It should contain at least 3 ppm of dissolved oxygen. Sufficient aeration may be maintained by using mechanical aerators or injecting oxygen into the water.

The distance eggs are to be transported to some extent determines the precautions that should be followed. Eggs transported only a short distance from a pond to a hatching facility on a farm are often carried in a bucket or tub containing water from the pond. In this case, only a few minutes should be involved in moving. For intermediate distances requiring an hour or less, the eggs may be transported in shallow boxes (about 1 foot deep) equipped with aeration devices. The egg masses are usually placed in small screen baskets to prevent movement or breaking of the mass during shipment. For longer distances, eggs may be shipped in plastic bags. Sufficient water to cover the egg mass is needed. Oxygen is injected into the bag to fill space not occupied by the water. Eyed eggs (eggs that are near hatching) are less sensitive to damage in shipment. However, if they should begin to hatch while in shipment, considerable losses might occur. This is due to the accumulation of egg shells and wastes.

Hatching Eggs

Six to 10 days are required for catfish eggs to hatch. Water temperature for hatching should range from 70 to 85°F. Progress in the development of the embryo can be determined by observing the color of the eggs. Newly laid eggs are yellow. Fertile eggs in which the embryo is developing turn pale pink at first and then reddish when near hatching. Eggs which have not been fertilized turn white and increase slightly in size. The pink color in fertile, incubating eggs is caused by the development of a blood supply within the egg.

Two methods of hatching catfish eggs are commonly used: (1) leaving the eggs in the spawning receptacle for the male to hatch and (2) removing the egg masses from the spawning receptacle to hatch mechanically. Some farmers let the male fish hatch the eggs and remove the fry immediately after hatching. The fry are then reared in a mechanical facility or a rearing pond. Combined spawning and rearing ponds, meaning that the eggs and fry are not removed but remain in the pond, are sometimes used.

Artificially hatching eggs requires diligent labor, specialized

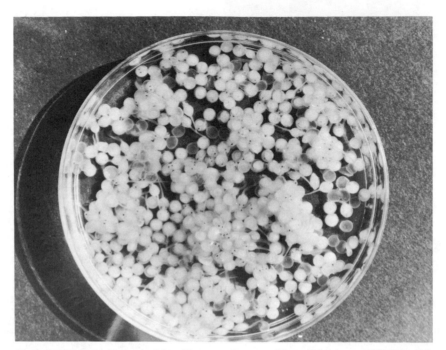

Figure 11-4. Recently Hatched Fry. (Courtesy, Bureau of Sport Fisheries and Wildlife, U.S. Department of the Interior)

equipment, and skill. The major advantage of removing the eggs and artificially hatching is that the spread of diseases and parasites from the adults to the young is minimized. Artificially hatching also reduces losses to predacious insects and other fish, including the female catfish. The female catfish may eat the eggs, if she remains near them, and if the male fish does not keep her away.

Several different mechanical arrangements have been used in artificially hatching eggs. Some of these include jars and troughs. The hatching trough is most commonly used. Hatching troughs are usually constructed of sheets of 14-gauge aluminum or stainless steel. A sheet that is 42 inches wide and 10 feet long will make a trough 20 inches wide and 10 inches deep. Partitions may be placed across the middle to strengthen the trough and to allow eggs of different ages to be separated. Each section must have a drain and an incoming water pipe. A ½-inch pipe is usually adequate for the incoming water, while a 1-inch pipe is used for the drain. A 1-inch pipe or rod extends the length of the trough in

Figure 11-5. Hatching Trough with Baskets.

the center. This pipe functions as a revolving shaft to which paddles are attached. It is mounted in bearings located at each end of
the trough and, possibly, at the partition. The paddles are made of
sheet metal and are spaced so that two or three baskets of eggs
may be accommodated in each end section of the trough.

The shaft to which the paddles are attached is made to turn at
a speed of 30 revolutions per minute (rpm) by an electric motor
using a series of pulleys. A ¼-horsepower motor (1,750 rpm) with
a combination of a 1½-inch pulley belted to a 10-inch pulley and a
1½-inch pulley belted to a 12-inch pulley will turn the shaft at 30
rpm.

The baskets containing the egg masses are often suspended
by a wire from the sides of the trough so that the waterline is just
below the top of the basket. Baskets are usually 3 inches deep and
partitioned into two compartments. They are constructed of
¼-inch mesh hardware cloth.

The paddles on the shaft should extend below the depth of
the baskets so that rotation will cause water movement on the eggs
similar to that made by the male fish when the eggs are being
hatched naturally. The whole mass should be moved by the water
but should not be washed out of the basket. Fresh oxygenated

water should continuously flow at a gravity rate into the trough from the ½-inch pipe. As the eggs hatch, the fry swim out of the baskets through the hardware cloth and into the trough. Hardware cloth with a mesh smaller than ¼-inch will not allow the fry to swim out, while a larger mesh may allow water action to cause the egg masses to drift apart.

One of the problems with artificial hatching is the tendency of fungi to accumulate in the trough. Fungi begin to grow on dead eggs (eggs in which an embryo is not developing) and will spread to eggs in which an embryo is developing. To combat the growth of fungi, troughs should be treated one or two times each day with malachite green at the rate of 2.0 ppm in the water. A flush treatment is recommended whereby the chemical remains in the trough only a short time and is washed away by the incoming water. This treatment should not be used when fry are present, or within 24 hours prior to hatching. Malachite green is highly toxic to fry.

It is important that sufficient agitation be provided to aerate the entire egg mass. Temperature of the water must be controlled so that it ranges from 70 to 85°F. Water that is too warm may cause the eggs to hatch faster than normal. Occasionally, eggs that hatch too quickly may produce fish without caudal fins and the last few vertebrae. Water must also contain sufficient oxygen. Well water may require oxygenation and heating. A dependable water source must be available so that the incoming water never ceases to flow. After being artificially hatched, the fry may be placed in rearing troughs or rearing ponds.

Rearing Fry

Two methods are commonly used to rear fry: trough and pond. These are closely related to the methods of hatching eggs. The trough method of rearing fry is most often used in association with the trough method of hatching eggs. However, some producers take newly hatched sac fry from pond-spawning receptacles and rear them in troughs. Sac fry tend to cluster together near the bottom of the spawning receptacle and are therefore easy to obtain. To obtain fry from a spawning receptacle, the male fish should be driven away and the receptacle tilted in an upright position. The top water in the receptacle should be poured off. The bottom water, containing the fry, should be poured into a wash tub which contains 1 or 2 inches of water. Fry hatched in a trough are removed by siphoning them out into a wash tub or pail. Fry, especially in the sac stage, are sensitive to shock and should be handled similarly to eggs.

Trough Rearing. Rearing fry in troughs is considered to be a good cultural practice, since greater control can be had over the fry. Susceptibility to predacious insects and other animals is reduced when fry are reared in troughs. Rearing troughs are usually 8 to 12 feet long, 12 to 15 inches wide, and 10 to 12 inches deep, and are constructed of wood, metal, plastic, or fiberglass. A standpipe 8 inches high is placed near one end of the trough for regulating water depth and overflow purposes. With an 8-inch standpipe, water depth is maintained at 8 inches. A screen should be placed over the standpipe to prevent the escape of fry. Fresh oxygenated water should flow into the trough at the end opposite the standpipe at the rate of 1 to 5 gallons per minute. Water temperature should range between 70 and 85°F. The water supply should be tested to determine if it can be used safely in rearing

Figure 11-6. Hatching Troughs Being Used for Rearing Fry. (Feed is being sifted into the trough with a tea strainer.)

troughs. Water should not contain less than 6 ppm of dissolved oxygen. A pH near 7.0 (neutral) is preferred. Harmful minerals, pesticide residues, and pathogenic organisms should not be present.

Meeting the nutritional requirements of fry is more critical in troughs than in ponds. It is possible for fry to obtain some of the needed food from water in a pond, but not in a trough. Fry do not need to be fed the first four to eight days after hatching, because they subsist on the egg sac. When the egg sac is absorbed and the fry swim up along the sides and surface of the trough searching for food, feed must be supplied. The rate of feeding is very light the first four or five days. Catfish fry will eat a variety of feeds. A floating-type commercial dry feed of small particle size is satisfactory. Sometimes a powdered, nonfloating feed is fed in a flat, open

Figure 11-7. Standpipe with Box Screen.

container. This is a good practice, because the feed that is not consumed can be removed. Such a container is placed on the bottom of the trough. All feed not consumed in two hours should be removed. The feed should be nutritionally complete; that is, it should contain the essential vitamins, proteins (28 to 32 percent), carbohydrates, and fats. Feeding should be routinized so that fry are fed at regular intervals five or six times each day. Some farmers feed fry every two hours. Fry are small and therefore do not consume much feed. Usually an amount equivalent to 4 or 5 percent of the weight of the fry is sufficient each day. The number of fry required to weigh 1 ounce varies from 750 to 1,800. Therefore, the amount of feed required for fry is very small.

Fry raised in troughs may need to be treated to prevent diseases. A common treatment is to place 5.0 ppm acriflavine in the trough for four hours twice each week.

Fry can be raised to the fingerling stage in troughs or moved to rearing ponds at any time. Some farmers prefer to grow fry in troughs until a length of ¾ inch has been reached, and then move them to rearing ponds. Others maintain the fry in troughs until a length of 1 to 2 inches has been reached.

Figure 11-8. Rearing Trough.

Pond Rearing. Three approaches may be used in rearing fry in ponds: (1) The fry may be hatched in spawning ponds and transferred to rearing ponds. (2) The spawning ponds may be used as rearing ponds, especially when pens are used in spawning. (This involves removing the adult fish from the pond when pens are used.) (3) The fry may be hatched in a trough and transferred to ponds for rearing.

The number of fry to stock per acre of rearing pond is determined by the size of fingerlings desired, number of days in the growing season, and quantity and quality of supplemental feed to be provided. Larger fingerlings are obtained by reducing the number of fry stocked per acre. Six- to 8-inch fingerlings can be produced in 120 days when fry are stocked at the rate of about 20,000 to 50,000 per acre. Rearing ponds are frequently about 1 acre in size; however, sizes may range from $^1/_{10}$ acre to 5 acres.

A major problem encountered with rearing fry in ponds is the presence of predatory insects and fish. Fry-eating insects can be controlled by applying to the surface of a pond a mixture of 1 quart of motor oil to 5 gallons of kerosene. This quantity will treat 3 acres. Twice a week applications should be made by pouring or spraying the mixture onto the water. It is preferable to make the applications on relatively calm days. This treatment should be continued until the fry are 2 inches long. It will assist in eliminating insects which must have air. Buildup of predacious insects and fish can be controlled by filling the rearing pond with water only a short time before stocking with fry. If water has been in the pond for awhile, it may be preferable to treat it with an insecticide two or three days before stocking. Predatory fish can be controlled by filling the pond with filtered water.

Fry are delicate and susceptible to changes in their environment. The procedure used to release fry into ponds may affect the rate of survival. Fry are sometimes released directly into a pond, but it is preferable that some way of gradually adjusting fry to pond conditions be used. Wooden frames with finely-screened bottoms or floating cages may be used. After a few days, the frames or cages are removed, and the fry have free access of the pond. This procedure also protects fry from predators. Frequently, fry are placed in partially filled ponds. Water is added as the fry grow.

The feeding of fry is important and should be initiated four to eight days after hatching. It is not so necessary for fry reared in ponds to receive the same complete feed as it is for those reared in troughs, but a complete feed is preferable. The pond water will provide a small amount of food for fry. Fry should be fed 1 pound of feed for each 2 acres of water to start them eating. The amount is gradually increased until it is equal to the amount that will be consumed in 20 to 30 minutes, or 4 to 5 percent of the body weight of fry. The feed should be in a meal or ground-mash form and may be changed to small pellets when the fish reach 1 inch in length. A good feed will contain 28 to 32 percent of protein, a minimum of 5 percent of fat, and 10 to 15 percent of fiber. A minimum of 8 percent of the ration should be fish meal. Cottonseed meal and other products containing pesticide residues should not be used in fish feed.

Classification of Fingerlings

A fingerling is a small catfish used for stocking growing ponds. Ponds are normally stocked with fingerlings that are 5 to 7 inches in length. The maximum length of a fingerling is 10 inches.

Figure 11-9. Fingerlings. (Courtesy, Master Mix Feeds)

Technically, the term *fingerling* is a classification based on length. The various sizes may be designated by numbers. For example, a No. 1 fingerling would range from 1.0 to 1.9 inches in length; a No. 2 would range from 2.0 to 2.9 inches; a No. 3 would range from 3.0 to 3.9 inches, and so on. Catfish less than 1 inch in length are known as fry. Those just over 10 inches long are stockers.

Identification of Stockers

A stocker catfish weighs less than the minimum weight for a food fish and is larger than the largest size of a fingerling. The minimum weight for a food fish is ¾ pound; therefore, a stocker fish weighs less than ¾ pound. Fingerlings for stocking growing ponds are seldom larger than 8 to 10 inches in length. Stockers are intermediate-sized fish; that is, they are neither fingerlings nor food fish. The length of a channel catfish stocker ranges from 10 to 14 inches. Stockers are sometimes known as yearling-size fish.

Stocker catfish should not be confused with fish for stocking purposes. Fry are used to stock rearing ponds, and fingerlings are used to stock growing ponds. Fry and fingerlings may sometimes

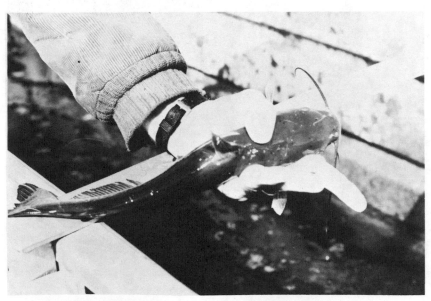

Figure 11-10. Stocker-Size Channel Catfish.

be referred to as stockers, but this size should not be confused with the stocker catfish.

Stocker catfish are preferred by some farmers, because only a short time is required for them to reach food fish size. Stockers will reach market size early in the growing season and may possibly be marketed when the volume of food fish available is low; thus a higher price may be received. It may also be possible for a grower to produce two crops of fish in a growing season by stocking ponds with the intermediate-sized stocker catfish in early spring.

Stocker fish production is a relatively new aspect of the catfish industry. If farmers find that using stocker catfish results in extra profit from food fish, the demand for 10- to 14-inch channel catfish may increase.

Rearing Fingerlings and Stockers

Rearing fingerlings and stockers is essentially a continuation of the practices followed with fry. As fish grow, the need for constant care may not be so critical but it is still important. Fingerlings and stockers are fed a complete feed at the rate of 3 to 4 percent of body weight each day. (Feeding is discussed in Chapter 7.)

An abundance of good water is essential. The number of fish in a pond should not be greater than the number that can be successfully grown to the desired size. Overstocking will result in slow growth and failure of the fish to reach the desired size. It may also result in oxygen problems and the loss of fish. Fingerlings are often grown in open ponds, but a few attempts have been made to grow them in cages.

Fish need to be checked regularly for disease. Evidence of diseases or parasites demands quick action. Periodic treatments may be needed to reduce disease and parasitic problems. The assistance of fish disease experts may be needed in diagnosing and treating problems.

Time Required to Produce Fingerlings and Stockers

Marketable fingerlings can usually be produced in four to eight months, or one growing season. This is about the amount of time between spawning in the late spring and early summer and stocking food fish production ponds in winter and early spring. Stocker catfish may require part or all of the growing season of a second year. The amount of time required to produce marketable, or stocking-size, fingerlings and stockers will depend upon the environmental conditions in which the fish are grown. Four inter-related factors are important: length of fingerling, feeding and management practices, length of growing season, and rate at which fry are stocked in rearing ponds.

Length of Fingerling. Generally, more time is required to produce a large fingerling than to produce a small fingerling; however, time alone is not the only factor. The rate of stocking and size attained are closely related. The management practices followed in rearing ponds are important.

Feeding and Management. Fry cannot be placed in a rearing pond and ignored. Fry that are not properly fed will not grow so fast as those receiving sufficient feed. The feed should be nutritionally complete and composed of particles of proper size for efficient consumption.

Length of Growing Season. Fish grow faster in warm weather. Geographic areas with long seasons of warm weather will produce fingerlings more rapidly than areas with short seasons of warm weather and long seasons of cold weather.

Rate of Stocking Fry. As a general rule, the larger the number of fry in a pond the slower the fingerlings will grow. Ponds stocked at the rate of 100,000 to 150,000 fry per acre will produce fingerlings that are 2 to 4 inches in length in 120 days. Most food fish producers prefer fingerlings slightly larger; therefore, the number of fry stocked per acre should be reduced. Six- to 8-inch fingerlings can be produced in 120 days when ponds are stocked with fry at the rate of 20,000 to 50,000 per acre. Some producers stock ponds at the heavy rate and selectively harvest a portion of the fingerlings at 2 to 4 inches, leaving others in the pond until a greater size is reached. Of course, with selective harvesting, more time will usually be required to produce the larger fingerlings because of the slower rate of growth in reaching the 2- to 4-inch size.

Number of Fingerlings and Stockers Produced per Acre

The number of fingerlings produced per acre of pond depends

upon the cultural practices followed and the size of fingerlings desired. Most fingerlings are grown in open rearing ponds that are ¹/₂ acre to 5 acres in size, but most are about 1 acre. A few fingerlings have been intensively produced in very small ponds of ¹/₁₀ acre or less. In the latter case, as many or more fingerlings may be produced on ¹/₁₀ acre as on 1 acre of regular rearing ponds.

Table 11-1

Number and Size of Fingerlings Produced
per Acre of Pond in 120 Days

Per Acre Rate of Stocking Fry	Size of Fingerling
	(inches)
10,000	8
30,000	7
53,000	6
73,000	5
95,000	4
116,000	3
138,000	2

Source: "Catfish Farming Profit Opportunities." Jackson: Mississippi Research and Development Center, 1967, p. 25.

In ordinary rearing ponds, it is possible to produce up to 150,000 fingerlings per acre. Most fingerling producers, however, prefer to reduce the number produced in order to increase size. A good yield to many producers of fingerlings is 50,000 per acre.

The number of stockers that can be produced per acre is less than the number of fingerlings that can be produced in the same amount of water. It is possible to harvest a portion of the fingerlings in a pond at the size of 6 to 8 inches, allowing those that remain to become stockers. A fish population of around 6,000 may be a good rate per acre for growing stockers.

Estimating Number of Fry, Fingerlings, and Stockers

It is frequently necessary to estimate the number of catfish in a pond or trough. Several techniques can be used. These do not give an exact count but are usually close enough for most cultural needs.

Volume. The volume, or space, occupied by fry can be determined. A small container, such as a graduated test tube or beaker, can be filled with fry, and the fry weighed or counted. Future estimates can be made by using the same container, once the number of fry the container will hold has been established. Of course, the number of fry held by a container will vary with the size of the fry. Estimates of fry numbers can also be made by siphoning the fry into a screenwire container (such as a small tea strainer). A container with a volume of 1 cubic inch is preferred. One cubic inch will hold about 500 sac fry.

Weight of Broodfish. A female catfish will produce 2,000 to 4,000 eggs per pound of body weight. By knowing the weight of the female, it is possible to estimate the number of fry hatched. This technique of estimating fry numbers lacks exactness but is more easily used than the other techniques if the weight of the female broodfish is known.

Weight of Fry. Channel catfish fry less than seven days of age usually number about 1,000 per ounce, but may range between 750 and 1,800. By dipping the fry from the water and quickly weighing them, it is possible to determine the number of ounces and thus estimate the number of fry. Some growers harvest as many as 1,000 fingerlings for each ounce of fry placed in rearing ponds.

The number of fingerlings or stockers can be determined by weighing the fish and referring to a length-weight chart.

Use of Length-Weight Charts. Studies have been made to determine the length-weight relationship in fish. This can be used in several ways. A sample of fingerlings or stockers can be taken with a seine or dip net, perhaps at the time of feeding. The sample should be weighed and counted. The weight of each fish is determined by dividing the weight of the sample by the number in the sample. Total poundage in a pond is estimated by multiplying the average weight per fish by the number of fry or fingerlings stocked in the pond. It is also possible to estimate the weight by finding the average length of the fish in the pond and referring to a chart to determine the average weight of fingerlings by length. If the average length is known, it is possible to obtain the average weight of each fingerling and multiply by the number of fingerlings stocked in the pond, yielding the total weight of fish. For example, if the average length of fingerlings is 6 inches, the aver-

Figure 11-11. A Sample of Fingerlings Being Used to Estimate Weight with a Length-Weight Chart.

age weight of each fingerling is .0588 pounds. If an estimated 20,000 fingerlings are present, the total weight of the fish is 20,000 multiplied by .0588, yielding 1176.0 pounds of fingerlings. (Appendix A contains a length-weight chart for channel catfish.)

Questions and Problems for Discussion

1. What is spawning? What are the roles of male and female fish in spawning?
2. Describe the natural spawning process of catfish.
3. What are the three most common methods of spawning used by fish farmers? Describe each.
4. What are the advantages of pen spawning over pond spawning?
5. What precautions should be followed in handling egg masses?
6. Describe color changes which occur in catfish eggs.
7. Describe the two common methods used to hatch catfish eggs.
8. What are the methods used to rear fry? Describe each.
9. Distinguish between a fingerling and a stocker.
10. Why are stocker-size catfish preferred by some farmers?
11. What determines the number of fingerlings that can be produced per acre of pond?

12. What factors affect the amount of time required to grow fingerlings and stockers?
13. Describe one method of estimating the number of fry in a rearing pond.
14. What is a length-weight chart? How is it used?

12

Growing Food Catfish

Catfish used for human food are known as "food fish." The size of each catfish that is grown commercially for food ranges from ¾ pound upward. Pond-raised food catfish usually weigh from 1 to 3 pounds, with many being harvested around the weight of 1 to 1¼ pounds. When dressed, a catfish this size is suitable for cooking whole and makes one serving. Larger food fish (3 pounds or more) are cut into fillets, steaks, or other various-sized portions. Sometimes fillets are removed from one side of smaller food fish, with both pieces being desirable.

Efficient food fish production requires good management. The most suitable cultural system must be used. The general principles of culture remain the same with each system, but the specific techniques vary.

This chapter presents information on the following:

> Production systems
> Time required to produce food catfish
> Selection of fingerlings
> Size of fingerlings
> Open-pond production
> Cage production
> Raceway production
> Tank production

Production Systems

Several production systems are used in growing food catfish. "System" primarily refers to the kind of water facilities that are used. The most popular system is the pond. Other systems include cages, raceways, and tanks. The number of catfish stocked in a given volume of water is usually smaller in ponds than in the other systems. The need for good management increases with the other more intensive systems.

Regardless of the system used, there are several limiting factors. These include the oxygen-carrying capacity of the water and the removal of wastes from the water. Some of the systems involve flowing water. Others reuse water after it has been filtered or treated in some way.

Time Required to Produce Food Catfish

Catfish of suitable size for use as food fish can usually be grown in a little less than two years following spawning. The first growing season involves hatching eggs and raising fingerlings to suitable size for stocking in growing facilities. The second season involves stocking the fingerlings in growing facilities and raising them until the end of the growing season, which is October or November. Normally, with pond culture, a 6-inch fingerling stocked in the spring will be food fish size in approximately 210 days. Systems of production utilizing heated water and other con-

Figure 12-1. Linear (Rectangular) Tanks in Food Fish Culture.

ditions which vary from the normal climates may be able to alter the time requirements by obtaining year-round growth.

Selection of Fingerlings

The quality of food fish is related to the fingerlings used. Fingerlings that are of uniform size and species and in good health should be stocked in growing ponds. If fingerlings are purchased, it is a good idea to know the reputation of the producer. Fingerlings should be purchased only from producers who have established good reputations for the quality of fish sold.

Uniformity of Size. Fingerlings should be graded so that uniform sizes are stocked together. Variable fingerling size will result in size variations at the time of harvest. Even with fingerlings that are of uniform size there may be considerable variation in the size of the food fish produced. Lack of uniform size of food fish is a current problem of the catfish industry.

Uniformity of Species. Mixed species of fingerlings are not usually desirable. Also, fingerlings should be free of trash fish, such as the "walking catfish," bullheads (mudcats), and scale fish. Undesirable fish must be sorted out at the time of harvest.

Health Conditions. Fingerlings should be free of diseases and parasites. It is a good procedure to use prophylactic treatments with fingerlings before placing them in growing ponds. This is easily done in tanks while hauling.

Size of Fingerlings

The size of fingerlings used in stocking ponds may range from 2 to 10 inches in length. Most growers prefer 6-inch fingerlings. Six-inch fingerlings stocked in March should weigh a pound or more in 210 days, or by October or November. Larger fingerlings of about 8 inches in length are preferred by some growers, but the cost of fingerlings increases with the larger sizes. Fingerlings under 4 inches should not be used.

Open-Pond Production

Open ponds are the most common facilities used in commercial catfish farming. The cost of ponds in proportion to the volume of fish produced is less than with other facilities. With open ponds, catfish have free access to all parts of the pond and are not restricted by cages or pens.

Two cropping patterns are used with ponds: clean cropping and multiple cropping.

Clean Cropping. Clean cropping involves placing fingerlings in a pond and growing them until all of the catfish are of average acceptable food fish size. At this point, all of the catfish are harvested. Water level in the pond may be lowered or the pond may be drained and prepared for another batch of catfish. With clean cropping, ponds are typically stocked in the spring and harvested in the fall.

Multiple Cropping. Multiple cropping (also known as topping) involves stocking a pond with fingerlings and selectively harvesting them when about one-third of them are food fish size. Shortly after this partial harvest, a number of fingerlings are added to the pond to equal the number of catfish that were removed. The pond is again partially harvested when one-third of the fish are of food fish size and the pond is again restocked with an equal number of fingerlings. This procedure is currently being repeated indefinitely. The long-term effects of multiple cropping are unknown but are currently being researched. (Note: With multiple cropping, a seine with a 1⅜- to 1⅝-inch mesh is used for the partial harvests. This seine will allow catfish weighing less than ¾ pound to pass through and remain in the pond.) A typical schedule for multiple cropping follows:

March or April	Initially stock pond with 3,000 fingerlings.
July or August	Selectively harvest when one-third are food fish size. A few days later, restock with the number of fingerlings equal to (or slightly more than) the number of food fish removed.
October or November	Selectively harvest and restock with the number of fingerlings equal to the number of food fish removed.
March or April	Selectively harvest and restock with the number of fingerlings equal to the number of food fish

harvested. (Theoretically at this point, all of the originally stocked fish have been removed.)

Repeat the process indefinitely, using the previous time schedule.

Time of Stocking. Growing ponds are often stocked when they are ready to receive fish, regardless of the time of year. The spring months of March and April are best for stocking growing ponds, while December and January are the poorest months, except in the extreme southern parts of the United States. The cold winter months are least preferable for stocking because the water temperature is low and the activity of catfish is at a minimum. Catfish do not seek out food as they do in warmer water; therefore, stocking fingerlings in the winter may result in a problem of getting them started on feed. Getting fingerlings started on feed immediately after stocking is of primary importance.

Fingerlings should be handled in cool weather. The fall and spring months are preferred for seining, grading, hauling, and placing in growing ponds. In the summer, fingerlings should be handled in the early morning hours when it is cool.

Preparation for Stocking. Prior to stocking, growing ponds should be prepared for the production of food fish. Wild fish should be destroyed when present in the water. Rotenone applied at the rate of 0.5 to 2.0 ppm will rid ponds of most wild fish. Treatment should be made several weeks prior to stocking with fingerlings. Rotenone may remain toxic for two weeks in warm water and longer in cold water. The bottoms of ponds that have been drained between fish crops should be disked and smoothed. After filling with water it may be a good idea to fertilize ponds, especially new ponds, with 16-20-4 or 16-20-0 fertilizer, or equivalent, at the rate of 50 pounds per acre.

Rate of Stocking. The rate at which ponds are stocked varies with the size of fish desired and the cultural practices to be followed. Stocking capacity is also limited by the available oxygen and by competition of other plants and animals. A rate of 750 to 1,000 fish per surface acre is used in ponds that depend on runoff water where there are no aerators or pumps being used. In ponds with a dependable water supply, and where aerators are used if

Figure 12-2. Growing Pond with a Smooth Bottom Ready for Water and Stocking.

needed, 3,000 to 4,000 fingerlings may be stocked per surface acre.

Experiments have been conducted with stocking rates of 8,000 to 10,000 fingerlings per acre. The total number of pounds of fish harvested at the end of the growing season is closely related to managerial and cultural practices. The size of individual fish varies according to the number of fish stocked and to the feeding practices of the farmer. At a rate of 3,000 per acre the fish will weigh about 1 pound after a growing season (210 days). At a rate of 1,500 per acre the fish will weigh 1¼ to 1½ pounds at harvest. Seldom should fingerlings be stocked at a greater rate than 4,000 per acre. The rate of 3,000 may give the best growth and most efficient use of feed. This is especially true for a beginning farmer. As the rate of stocking increases, the rate of growth of the fish decreases. Fish will reach an average weight of 1 pound each in a shorter time when stocked at the rate of 1,500 than when stocked at the rate of 3,000 per acre but the total number of pounds produced will be less.

It is possible to place fingerlings in a partially filled pond and add water as the fish grow. For example, 20,000 small fingerlings can subsist when stocked on 1 acre, but 6 to 7 acres of growing pond will be needed for this number to reach food fish size. The fingerlings can be stocked in a pond with a capacity of 6 to 7 acres containing 1 surface acre of water. As the fingerlings grow, more water should be added until the full 6 to 7 acres are available. The water level for which a pond is stocked must be maintained. Ponds have a tendency to lose water by evaporation in the summer, thus reducing the surface acreage. If water cannot be added to maintain a given level, it is suggested that ponds be stocked at the rate for the pond at the lowest surface area expected during dry periods.

Food fish weighing an average of 3 pounds each can be produced by growing a third year. A stocking rate of 800 to 1,000 per acre is recommended for this purpose. Growers producing the larger fish may stock ponds at the rate of 2,000 fingerlings and partially harvest at the end of the second growing season. The partial harvest should yield about 50 percent of the fish so that 1,000 remain for the third year.

Quality of Water. The quality of the water has much to do with the well-being of fish. A low oxygen level in the water of growing ponds is a serious problem with which farmers must cope. A lack of sufficient oxygen will cause the death of fish. Oxygen deficiencies most often occur in the early morning just before sunrise. Oxygen depletion may be evident by the apparent desperate attempts of fish to secure oxygen from the air. The fish come to the surface and leap a few inches into the air. Overfeeding will contribute to oxygen deficiency. The death of "plankton bloom," or tiny plants and animals in the water, will tie up oxygen in the decomposition process. Oxygen problems may be in the making if foul odors are emitted from the water or if dark streaks caused by the decay of organic matter are present.

Several techniques of coping with oxygen depletion problems may be used. These include: draining water from the bottom and adding fresh water (a double-sleeve turn-down pipe is useful), spraying water into the air to absorb oxygen, placing aerators in the pond, and using certain chemicals, such as potassium permanganate. (Maintaining the quality of water is more fully discussed in Chapter 6.)

Feeding. The amount of feed consumed by fish varies with temperature and other climatic conditions. Catfish consume the most feed and grow the best when the water temperature is 70 to

90°F. Fish should not be fed more than the amount eaten in 10 to 15 minutes. Overfeeding is said to cause more trouble than any other single practice in open ponds. Catfish are ordinarily fed at the rate of about 3 percent of the weight of the fish at each feeding. Some growers feed every day, whereas other growers omit feeding one day each week. (Feeding is discussed in Chapter 7.)

Figure 12-3. Food Fish Are Usually Fed Pelleted Feed. (The rounded pellets on the right float.)

Cage Production

Growing catfish in cages is simply confining fish by means of a cage to a small portion of a pond or stream. Cages are often used in water areas that are not readily seined. A distinction should be made between the cages used in food fish production and the pens used in spawning. A cage has a bottom and, usually, a top in addition to the four sides. It is designed to float in the water so that the top extends 3 or 4 inches above the water level. One foot or more of water should be between the bottom of the cage and the bottom of the pond. Spawning pens do not have tops or bottoms and are placed in realtively shallow water so that the bottom rests firmly

Figure 12-4. Catfish Cage. (Courtesy, BGK Industries)

on the floor of the pond. The tops of spawning pens extend above the water level several inches.

A small percentage of the commercially grown catfish are produced in cages. The use of cages in catfish farming has been compared to the use of cages in the poultry industry for producing broilers and eggs. Additional research is needed before cage culture is adopted on a wide scale in fish farming. Some fish farmers are using cages on a limited scale in catfish production. It is suggested that persons contemplating using cages should gradually make the change to cages. Large fish farming operations should be converted to cages only after small-scale experimentation with cages has been made on the farm and found to be successful.

Advantages and Disadvantages of Cages. Several advantages have been given for using cages. These should be analyzed in terms of the disadvantages. Table 12-1 presents a summary of the advantages and disadvantages of cages.

Design of Cages. Cages have been constructed in many different shapes and sizes and of a variety of materials. Most cages

Table 12-1

Summary of Advantages and Disadvantages of Cages in Catfish Farming

Advantages	Disadvantages
1. Water areas containing trees, stumps, and other obstacles that make seining impossible can be used for cage production. Cages are suited for use in gravel pits, strip-land mines, streams, large lakes, reservoirs, and irrigation canals. Sometimes cages are placed in regular growing ponds. Also, cages permit catfish to be raised in water containing wild fish.	1. The possibility of problems with oxygen depletion may be increased when cages are used in ponds. Wild fish with free access of the pond compete with the caged fish for oxygen. When the oxygen becomes low, fish in cages may be lost before those having free access to the pond. The problem of oxygen depletion is reduced when cages are placed in flowing streams.
2. Aeration of water in the immediate vicinity of the fish may be simplified. It is possible to place a small aerator in a cage if a power source to operate the aerator is available.	2. The materials of which the cages are constructed may fail, allowing the catfish to escape. Materials used in making cages should be durable and resistant to decay.
3. Harvesting is simplified and can be completely mechanized. It is possible to mechanically lift entire cages from the water for emptying. Also, cages make it possible to harvest a portion of the fish crop at a time without seining or draining an entire pond.	3. Catfish may damage each other by fighting. Fighting is reduced when fish are stocked at high densities of 150 or more fish per cubic yard. Damage by fighting is said to be reduced by placing cages in deeper water. This apparently works, because the smaller fish are better able to escape the larger, more aggressive fish. Catfish, like other animals, establish a "peck order." However, some persons who use cages indicate that damage from fighting is not a problem.
4. Losses to predation can be eliminated. Cages with tops keep out water snakes and similar aquatic animals.	4. Considerable difference may exist in rate of growth even though the cages were stocked with fish of uniform size. The less aggressive or smaller fish may be forced to the bottom of a cage at feeding time. The larger, aggressive fish consume a greater proportion of the feed and consequently grow at a faster rate.
5. Observation of the growth, feeding, and health of the fish is simplified. Samples of fish can be taken easily.	
6. Treatments for diseases and parasites are simplified. It is possible to slip a large polyethylene (plastic) bag over a cage as it floats and treat only the water held in the bag and cage. Another method of treatment is to quickly lift the cage and place it in a dipping vat. Fish in cages do not come into contact with the bottom mud of a pond which may be a holding place for parasites or diseases.	5. Caged fish require feed that is more nutritionally complete and that has a higher percentage of protein. Confining catfish to cages prevents them from obtaining the supplemental feed that may be present in streams and ponds.
	6. Fish are easily stolen.

are designed so as to have a capacity of 1 cubic yard or slightly more. Cage dimensions of 3 feet deep by 3 feet wide by 4 feet long, or 1.33 cubic yards capacity, have been used. Recent research has found larger cages, 4 feet deep by 4 feet wide by 10 or 15 feet long, to be better than smaller cages.

Cages are constructed of wooden, plastic, or metal frames covered with a meshed material such as aluminum wire, nylon netting, or polypropylene. Some cages are constructed of galvanized welded wire with a ½- by 1-inch mesh. A 16-gauge wire is most common. It is a good idea to treat zinc-coated wire with tar or asphalt to prevent zinc poisoning and decay. Mesh sizes for other materials vary from ⅛ to ½ inch, with the latter most popular. The tops of cages may be constructed of nonmeshed materials, such as wood or fine netting. Cages constructed of wooden frames may have tops of marine plywood hinged to the frame of the cage. Construction design should facilitate easy entry of the cages. Cages with tops that lock may be preferred to prevent theft and unwanted disturbance of the fish. Cage facilities may be constructed so that several are connected by means of a floating platform or connecting bars. Floating platforms are preferred by some farmers. Floating platforms of sufficient size will usually support one or two men, thus facilitating feeding and observation.

Feed rings should be constructed around the tops of cages to prevent the loss of feed. Water movement tends to cause feed to drift out of cages. A feed ring may be made of wood, fine screen, or other material. Some cages are made so that a fine screen or ⅛-inch hardware cloth extends several inches down the sides from the top. This screen will hold feed in the cage.

Cages should be constructed of materials that are sturdy, relatively light in weight, rust and corrosion resistant, and slow to decay in water. Some type of floating material to keep the cage afloat must be used. Common float materials include expanded urethane foam, expanded polystyrene, and styrofoam. These materials are dissolved by oil or gasoline and, therefore, should be coated with fiberglass if there is a possibility of contact with liquid petroleum products. Some commercial cages are constructed for easy disassembly. This feature facilitates storage and transportation.

Rate of Stocking. Factors relating to the stocking of cages are rate per acre and rate per cage. The total poundage of fish produced per acre in ponds is no greater with cages than it is in open-pond production. The limiting factor is the amount of dissolved oxygen in the water. A stocking rate designed to produce 1,500 to 2,000 pounds of food fish is suggested. Frequently, 175 to 250 catfish are stocked per cubic yard, or 8 to 9 fish per cubic foot. Cages may be stocked with either fingerlings or stockers. A minimum fingerling length of 5 to 7 inches is preferred. Stocker catfish are also commonly used for cage culture. Catfish can be stocked in cages in the early spring or in the fall with the fish permitted to overwinter in the cage. It is best that fish not be handled in the warm summer months. Channel catfish are often recommended for cage culture.

Feeding. Catfish grown in cages depend almost entirely upon feed supplied by the farmer. The supplemental feed normally available to catfish in ponds and streams is not available in cages. Floating feed that is nutritionally complete is preferred for feeding fish in cages.

The rate of feeding in cages varies. Frequently, the rate is reduced as the fish grow. A rate of 4 to 5 percent per day of fish weight is often fed when fish are first placed in cages. Gradually this may be reduced to about 2 percent or slightly less, depending on how much the fish actually consume. If all feed is eaten in less than 10 minutes, the rate of feeding should be increased slightly.

Fish in cages will gain at a slightly more rapid rate if they are fed twice daily than if they are fed once each day, but the difference in rate of gain is not considered to be sufficient to justify the twice-daily feeding. Late afternoon is the best time to feed. Feed should be placed inside the cages. Catfish should be fed no more than they will consume in 30 minutes. Pelleted feed is recommended for fish in cages. Catfish may not consume feed when the water temperature is below 60°F or shortly after a major weather change has occurred.

Raceway Production

The cultural practices used with catfish in raceways vary according to whether a true raceway or a semi-raceway system is used. True raceways are usually relatively small, frequently $1/50$ to $1/10$ acre, with flowing water. The water should be exchanged twice each hour. The poundage of fish that can be produced in a raceway is much greater than in a pond of similar size. The water in raceways flows much more rapidly and is exchanged more often than in semi-raceways. Semi-raceways are usually larger and do not produce as many fish per acre as do raceways.

Growing catfish in raceways is still in the experimental stage and should be considered with caution. The trend of a few years ago toward using both raceway and semi-raceway systems has about ended. Semi-raceway systems involving a series of small ponds located on a hillside so that water flows from one pond to another are being used in some areas.

Rate of Stocking. The rate of stocking in raceways is based on the size of fish desired at marketing and on the rate of flow of water. A common rate is based on $1/2$ pound of fish per cubic foot of water volume held by a raceway. For example, a raceway with a volume of 4,000 cubic feet can be stocked with 2,000 fingerlings. With proper feeding and exchange of water, 2,000 pounds of fish can be produced in 180 to 210 days. Another rate of stocking is 50,000 to 60,000 per acre. Most individual raceways are less than 1 acre; therefore, it is necessary to determine the acreage and calculate the number of fingerlings to stock accordingly.

The rate of stocking fingerlings in semi-raceways is considerably less than that in raceways. It is difficult to state a suggested stocking rate unless the rate of water flow and other conditions are known. In long semi-raceways, or semi-raceway systems, in which water flows at the rate of 150 gallons per minute, 3,500 to 5,000 fingerlings may be stocked per surface acre. Raceways as well as ponds are usually stocked in spring and early summer. Raceways are often stocked with 6-inch fingerlings.

Feeding. Catfish grown in raceways require feed that is more nutritionally complete than do those grown in ponds. The density of fish population in raceways is much greater, and the water does not contain zooplankton. Many raceway producers of catfish feed pelleted trout feed. Trout have been grown in raceways for a number of years.

The rate of feeding is usually 4 to 5 percent of fish weight for 60 days after stocking. Afterward, the rate is gradually reduced to about 3 percent. In terms of amount, no more than 1 pound of feed per 100 cubic feet of water should be fed a day in raceways. Of course, fish should never be fed more than they will consume.

Fish in raceways may be fed twice each day. Approximately one-third of the daily amount should be fed in the early morning and two-thirds of the daily amount should be fed in late afternoon. Floating feed is preferred.

Tank Production

The use of tanks in growing catfish is an interesting system of culture. A very small proportion of the commercially grown fish are reared in tanks. Even though tanks have not been widely used,

Figure 12-5. Linear Tank Equipped with Floating Aerators.

many farmers who have used them have been pleased with results. A round tank 20 feet in diameter and 2 feet deep is considered by some producers to be equivalent to a 1½-acre pond. Tanks are also widely used in fish research work.

Rate of Stocking. The rate of stocking in tanks may range from 5 to 15 fish per cubic foot of water. Research has not yet determined the best rate of stocking, but it is related to the rate of water flow and aeration. As the number of fish stocked per cubic foot increases, the total production increases; but the rate of growth per fish declines. Larger fish are produced in the same length of time at 5 per cubic foot as they are at 15 per cubic foot. When all factors are considered, the best rate of stocking may be 5 to 10 fish per cubic foot when a size of 1¼ to 1½ pounds each is desired. Fingerlings are usually 6 to 8 inches long when placed in growing tanks.

Feeding. Floating feed is often used in tank culture. The feed should be nutritionally complete and should contain increased amounts of vitamins over feed for pond systems. Rate of feeding is gauged by the amount of feed consumed. A daily level of around 3 percent of fish weight is used. Fish in tanks are often fed by hand two or three times per day. Overfeeding should be avoided as it will contribute to a buildup of wastes and increase the effort required in waste removal. Some producers have found that efficiency of production is increased significantly when the tanks are protected from bright light. This protection may be provided by covering the tanks or enclosing them in a building.

Questions and Problems for Discussion

1. What is a food fish? What is the best size for food catfish?
2. What is a production system?
3. How long does it take to produce a food fish?
4. What size of fingerlings is preferred?
5. What cropping patterns are used with ponds?
6. How are ponds prepared for initial stocking?
7. What factors determine the rate of stocking to use with ponds? What stocking rates are used?
8. Describe a typical multiple cropping schedule.
9. How does a cage differ from a pen?
10. Why is the number of pounds of fish produced per acre in cages no greater than that in open ponds?
11. What are the advantages and disadvantages of cages?

12. Describe how cages should be designed.
13. How often is the water in a raceway exchanged?
14. What rate of stocking is used with raceways?
15. What is the relationship between stocking density and production with tanks?

13

Harvesting, Holding, Grading, and Hauling Catfish

Catfish have to be harvested as do other agricultural products. The procedures used in harvesting are critical in delivering a quality product. As a part of harvesting, catfish are also stored (or held), graded, and hauled. Each of these activities places the catfish in conditions which cause stress. Rough procedures with any of these activities can cause injuries to the fish.

This chapter presents information on the following areas:

The meaning of harvesting
Types of harvests
Precautions in harvesting
Methods of harvesting
Hooking
Draining
Seining
Trapping
Procedures in harvesting fingerlings and stockers
When to harvest food fish
Lifting fish
Holding fish
Grading fish
Hauling fish

The Meaning of Harvesting

Harvesting involves gathering in catfish. Another way of describing catfish harvesting is to say that the fish are "captured."

In practice, catfish may be harvested two or three times. First, fingerlings may be harvested by a fingerling farmer when they are 6 to 8 inches long. Secondly, catfish may be harvested by a stocker producer when they are 12 inches long. Thirdly, food fish may be harvested when they weigh 1 pound or more. In some cases, the second harvesting may be omitted on farms which go directly from fingerlings to food fish.

Figure 13-1. Catfish Being Unloaded into a Holding Facility.

In many situations, harvesting is associated with marketing. Usually the ownership of the fish changes. With food fish, processing occurs. Regardless of the nature of the harvesting operation, catfish should never be harvested until they can be moved to market. Live catfish can be stored (held) for a while, but this creates the possibility of losing fish. For the large farmer, considerable investment in vats would be required if many fish were to be held.

Closely associated with harvesting are grading and hauling. Grading may occur either during the harvesting process or later. In effect, grading occurs when seines are used which allow the smaller fish to pass through the seine and remain in the water.

Some lifting and hauling are required to get fish where they are needed—either to the processor or to another pond or raceway.

Catfish in tanks or vats are easier to harvest than those in ponds. The catfish may be lifted out of tanks with a dip net. Seines and traps are used to harvest catfish in ponds. The seine is by far the most popular way of harvesting large quantities of catfish.

Types of Harvests

With food fish production, two types of harvest may be used, partial or complete. Partial harvesting involves capturing a portion of the catfish in a pond or other facility. For example, a partial harvest has been made if 10,000 pounds are harvested from a pond containing 20,000 pounds of fish. Partial harvests are used if the market does not demand a full number of fish in a pond or if it is desired to remove a portion of the fish in a pond and allow those remaining to grow to a larger size. Partial harvesting is used with multiple cropping.

Complete harvesting involves capturing all of the fish in a pond. It may be used to remove the remaining fish following a partial harvest or to remove all of the fish at one time without a prior partial harvest. Clean cropping involves making a complete harvest.

Precautions in Harvesting

The possibility of losses occurring in harvesting catfish is fairly great. The likelihood of such losses is reduced if several precautions are observed:

1. Before beginning harvesting operations, a check should be made for undesirable flavor by cooking several fish. If vats are available, fish with off-flavors may be harvested and held for several days. Otherwise, fish with off-flavors should not be harvested. Steps should be taken to correct the conditions causing the off-flavor problem. Feed known not to cause off-flavors should be fed during the holding period.
2. Before harvesting is begun, steps should be taken to insure that adequate handling, hauling, and holding facilities are

available. Likewise a market for the fish should be available.

3. Harvesting procedures should be followed that minimize muddying the water. Fish are sometimes in ponds for several days after harvesting has begun, especially when ponds are drained. Muddy water may create conditions which cause off-flavors.

Figure 13-2. Harvesting Food Fish. (Courtesy, National Marine Fisheries Service)

4. Harvesting and holding procedures should be followed that minimize the possibility of oxygen depletion. In draining methods, oxygen deficiencies may result if bottom water low in oxygen remains when the top water is removed.

5. Feeding fish just prior to harvest should be avoided. When handled, catfish tend to disgorge any feed recently consumed. The expelled feed may contribute to oxygen problems.

6. Procedures and equipment should be used which will cause a minimum of physical damage to the fish. Rough handling in seining, lifting, sorting, and hauling may injure fish. Fish may become hung in the seine and receive abrasions or broken spines.

Methods of Harvesting

Most catfish are harvested in four ways: (1) by hooking, (2) by draining, (3) by seining, and (4) by trapping. With food fish, the first three are the most widely used, while the fourth is still in the experimental stage for large-scale use. Fingerlings are primarily harvested by seining. Sometimes various combinations of these methods are used. Other methods involving chemicals, sound waves, and electrical shock have been used experimentally.

Hooking

The hook and line method is used for obtaining partial harvests. It is primarily used by sport fishermen and involves the use of an ordinary fish hook on a pole, trotline, or spinning rod. Persons operating catch-out ponds need to be able to advise sport fishermen on the "how" of catching fish. Much of the know-how will be learned through experience.

A common cane pole equipped with a strong line (18-pound test) and a number 2/0 to 4/0 hook is used by many sport fishermen for catching catfish. Catfish will bite a variety of baits. Commonly used baits include minnows, crayfish or shrimp, chicken entrails, and others, especially those which are foul-smelling. Some fishermen use a dough mixture made of equal parts of cottonseed meal and ordinary flour. This mixture is made into small wads by adding sufficient water to cause the mixture to hold together. Various commercially made doughs are also available.

Hooking involves knowing the habits of catfish. During the day catfish seek refuge in protected places, such as brush piles and deep holes, and move into fairly shallow water at night. Usually catfish are caught on hooks more easily in the summer than in the winter, because they do not feed during low water temperatures.

Draining

Draining usually results in a complete harvest. It involves draining the water from a pond so that the catfish are concentrated in a small area. It has been a widely used method of harvesting but is declining as other better methods are developed. Refilling large ponds can become expensive. In addition, the great volume of water required when secured from wells will contribute to a reduction of the water level in the ground.

Many ponds are constructed with a harvest or catch basin to facilitate the use of the draining method. The fish are concentrated in a small portion of the harvest basin with a seine and are removed with dip nets and placed in nearby transport tanks. Usually 3 feet of seine for each 2 feet of harvest basin width are required.

The draining method of harvesting is best suited for use in ponds that are small or that cannot be seined. Ponds should be constructed so that the harvest basin is smooth and free of stumps and other obstacles that would interfere with using a seine. The bottom of a pond should slope toward the water outlet and should be free of low spots that might hold water and trap fish.

One of the major disadvantages of draining is that water is usually wasted. Before another fish crop can be grown, the pond must be filled. Pumping costs for water may run as high as $25 per acre-foot. A 10-acre pond with an average depth of 4 feet will require 40 acre-feet of water. The cost for refilling the pond will range from $250 to $1,000. An advantage to completely draining the pond is that the pond bottom can be dried, disked, and smoothed for the next growing season.

Concentrating catfish into a small area, as in draining, increases the danger of oxygen depletion, especially during the warm summer months. The risk of losing fish in cooler weather is not so great. The draining method should be avoided in the summer.

Several hours, or even days, may be required for a pond to be drained. It is not always possible to predict the actual time drainage will be completed. Fish haulers usually have a full schedule of hauling and, therefore, do not have the time to wait for water drawdown to be accomplished.

Draining usually produces a high percentage of fish. Other methods of harvesting are less efficient in terms of total fish harvest. However, the cost of labor per pound of fish with the drainage method is usually greater than other methods, especially if certain machinery is not used.

Seining

Seining permits the harvesting of entire ponds without water drawdown. Power equipment is used, thus reducing the amount of hand labor required. This method may be used to harvest large ponds of up to 100 acres or more and requires a greater investment in equipment than does the drainage method.

Use of Seining. The seining method has several advantages. Labor requirements are usually less. Four to six men can efficiently harvest fairly large ponds with mechanized seining equipment. Since there is no water drawdown, it is possible to harvest in the summer without the danger of oxygen depletion that occurs with draining. Water is conserved, and time is saved because there is no waiting for the water to drain. Powered booms can be used to eliminate the backbreaking work of lifting and carrying tubs of fish.

Figure 13-3. Seining Operations in Harvesting. (Courtesy, Louisiana Wildlife and Fisheries Commission)

Limitations to the seining method of harvesting do exist, however. It is essential that pond bottoms be smooth and free of obstructions. Not all fish are captured by seining—15 to 30 percent may escape. Full harvest can be achieved only by draining the pond. The cost of mechanized harvesting equipment may run into thousands of dollars. It is possible that some of the equipment on hand on a farm can be adapted for use in seining.

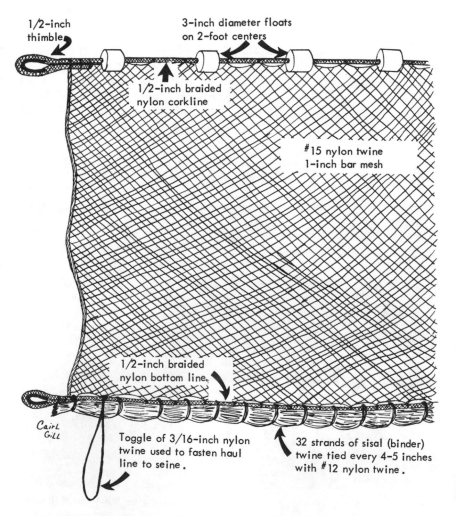

1/2-inch thimble

3-inch diameter floats on 2-foot centers

1/2-inch braided nylon corkline

#15 nylon twine 1-inch bar mesh

1/2-inch braided nylon bottom line

Carl Gill

Toggle of 3/16-inch nylon twine used to fasten haul line to seine.

32 strands of sisal (binder) twine tied every 4-5 inches with #12 nylon twine.

Figure 13-4. Specifications of Seine. (Courtesy, National Marine Fisheries Service)

Seine Construction. Seines are often made of number 15 nylon twine with a 1-inch mesh. Floats are located at the top and weights are at the bottom to keep the seine upright and to prevent folding, which would allow fish to escape. The bottom may have a mudline of 32 strands of sisal twine which serves as a weight and reduces cutting into the mud. Seines for normal catfish ponds should be 10 feet wide (deep) and in sections so that the length

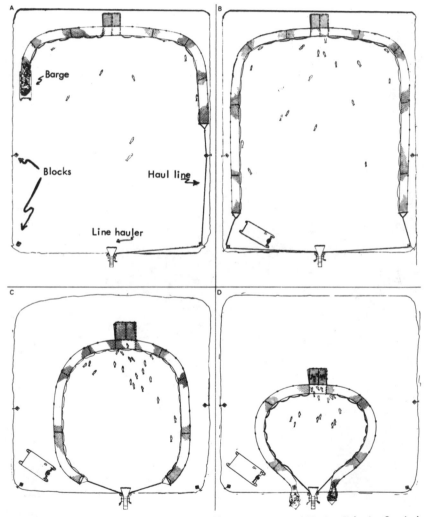

Figure 13-5. Procedure for Setting a Seine. (Courtesy, National Marine Fisheries Service)

may be varied to suit a particular-sized pond. Sections are normally 200 feet long. It is generally agreed that 3 feet of seine are required for each 2 feet of pond width.

Procedures in Seining. A commonly used procedure involves setting the seine around the outer perimeter of a pond on the levee opposite the landing site. With large ponds, a barge or boat is used in setting the seines. Haul, or pull, lines are attached for easy detachment along the seine and are led through snatch blocks on the sides of the pond. The function of the snatch blocks is to keep the net ends spread apart and close to the shoreline. The haul lines pass through a powered line hauler. The line hauler pulls the ropes and, hence, the seine so that the seine ends are drawn along near the bank to the landing site. As the end of the seine approaches the landing site, it is detached from the haul lines and stacked on the edge of the pond.

Figure 13-6. Tractor-Mounted Power Seine Hauler in Operation. (Courtesy, National Marine Fisheries Service)

Hauling in a seine is usually stopped while the bag section of the seine is still well out in the pond in order to avoid overcrowding the fish in shallow water. With large catches, and especially in warm weather, a smaller seine may be used inside the larger seine to concentrate a ton or so of fish. The smaller seines used for this purpose are usually about 50 feet long and 4 feet wide. Small ponds may be manually harvested by placing the seine around the pond and hauling by hand.

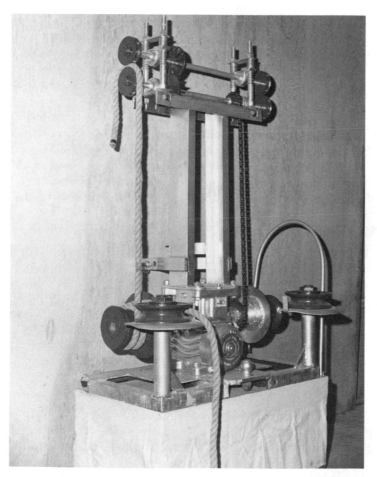

Figure 13-7. A Seine Hauler Designed for Mounting on a Farm Tractor. (Courtesy, National Marine Fisheries Service)

Trapping

Traps have been widely used to harvest wild catfish. Results with traps in cultured fish ponds have not been so successful. When traps are used, only a partial harvest is obtained. Very few catfish are currently harvested with traps, but interest in trapping continues.

Three kinds of traps have been used: cylindrical, box, and double funnel. Traps are usually constructed of ½-inch hardware cloth or 1-inch poultry netting with wood or steel reinforcement materials. Baits of soybean cake, cottonseed cake, and other fish attractors have been used. The bait may be placed in a cloth bag and suspended inside the traps. Some traps have been designed so that a self-feeder that dispenses feed is located inside the trap. Traps should be checked daily for fish and turtles. Turtles enter traps to feed on the captured fish.

Additional research in the use of traps is needed. Research at the Fish Farming Development Center in Rohwer, Arkansas, revealed that some of the practices used in trapping fish were not very efficient. Small wire traps placed near feeders were not very successful. Tests with trapping enclosures showed that drop-seines and panel traps were practical only for partial fish harvests.

Procedures in Harvesting Fingerlings and Stockers

The harvesting of fingerlings is usually not so difficult as the harvesting of food fish, because rearing ponds are often considerably smaller than growing ponds. Most rearing ponds are 1 acre or less and rarely more than 5 acres in size. The problem of harvesting is virtually eliminated with trough-reared fingerlings.

The procedures used in harvesting fingerlings should insure good-quality fingerlings and minimize injury. Fingerlings should not be held out of water for more than a few seconds. Fingerlings which "slip their slime," or become dry, are very susceptible to disease and parasites even if they are returned to water before they die. The seines and equipment used in harvesting should be constructed to minimize bruises and abrasions. Harvesting procedures should include a prophylactic treatment to aid in disease prevention. It is preferable to harvest fingerlings in the early morning while the water and air are relatively cool. Persons involved in harvesting should avoid muddying the water excessively.

Most pond-reared fingerlings are harvested by seining. Rearing ponds are usually relatively shallow, thus making it possible for a person at each end of the seine to wade out into the water to pull the seine. The size of the mesh in the seine should prevent

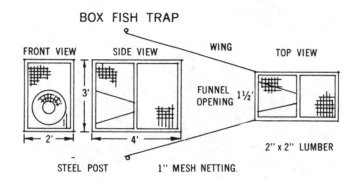

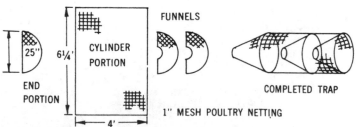

Figure 13-8. Fish Traps: Cylindrical, Box, and Double Funnel. (Courtesy, Illinois Division of Fisheries, Department of Conservation)

the escape of fingerlings through the mesh. Common mesh sizes for harvesting fingerlings are ¼ to ½ inch. The width of the seine should be sufficient to prevent the escape of fingerlings under the bottom. Seines for harvesting fingerlings may be constructed of lighter materials than those for harvesting food fish. It is fre-

Figure 13-9. Seine for Harvesting Fingerlings.

quently a good idea to seine around the feed-areas to partially harvest the fingerlings. After being concentrated into a small area, the fingerlings are dipped out with dip nets or other devices. The harvested fingerlings should be placed immediately in holding or hauling facilities which have adequate aeration.

Fingerlings may be completely harvested by draining. It is suggested that partial harvests be made before lowering the water level. Seining around feeding areas may yield 75 percent of a fingerling crop.

When to Harvest Food Fish

Catfish should be harvested when market size is reached and a demand exists. Market size is considered to be ¾ pound or larger. Fish should not be harvested until a market outlet has been secured. Arrangements should be made with the processor or other market outlet specifying the day and time at which delivery is to occur. Farmers and processors are obligated to deliver and accept fish as scheduled.

Some catfish farmers have buyers who regularly purchase fish each week throughout the year. With this marketing arrangement, partial harvests are made weekly by seining a portion of the pond. A partial harvest in the feeding area will usually yield sufficient fish for small orders. This may work only once or twice, however, as the fish may become wary.

Various factors related to fishery biology and marketing economics should be considered in determining when to harvest. It is best to harvest large volumes of catfish during cool weather. Fish survive better and there is less chance of oxygen depletion if the water temperature is 55°F or lower. Fingerlings stocked in the early spring will usually be ready to harvest when the weather begins to cool in the fall. This is a busy time of the year for processors; therefore, it may be best to delay harvesting until the rush season is over. Feed consumption declines as the weather cools so that profits may not be reduced by delaying harvest, especially if price increases occur.

Lifting Fish

In harvesting, fish are often concentrated into a small area by draining or seining. From here they must be lifted for grading and hauling. Various kinds of bags, baskets, pumps, vacuum tanks, and conveyor belts are used.

A common procedure is to scoop the fish in the concentrated area into a brailing bag, or brailer, and lift with a powered boom to the hauling tanks. Booms may be mounted on farm tractors or on

Figure 13-10. Brailing Bag for Lifting Fish. (Courtesy, Bureau of Sport Fisheries and Wildlife, U.S. Department of the Interior)

Figure 13-11. Truck-Mounted Powered Boom Used for Lifting Fish. (Courtesy, Bureau of Sport Fisheries and Wildlife, U.S. Department of the Interior)

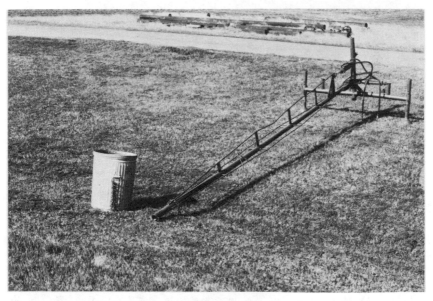

Figure 13-12. A Farm-Constructed Boom for Mounting on a Tractor.

trucks. Various kinds of brailing bags, or baskets, are used. Some have a trap door in the bottom which is opened to empty the fish into the transport tank. Brailing baskets may hold 250 pounds or more of catfish. Scales may be placed above the baskets so that weight records may be easily obtained.

Large fish-handling pumps have been developed which will pump catfish out of the concentrated area in a pond and into transport tanks. Catfish up to 19 inches long have been success-fully lifted with 6-inch pumps. One hundred pounds of fish may be pumped per minute. Injuries to the fish may occur but are usu-ally of minor consequence if the fish are processed within a few hours. This method of lifting is not widely used.

Conveyors similar to those used on many farms to move hay into barns have also been used to lift catfish. The lower end of the conveyor is stationed near the water, and the fish are hand-dipped onto it. The upper end empties the fish directly into the transport tank. Positioning conveyors is difficult because of the variability of the slopes and the construction of ponds.

Some transport trucks are equipped with special vacuum

Figure 13-13. Hand Lifting Fish. (Courtesy, Bureau of Sport Fisheries and Wildlife, U.S. Department of the Interior)

tanks. A compressor removes air from the tanks, and catfish and water are lifted through a 6-inch intake hose. Catfish can be lifted up to 18 feet by using the vacuum technique—a method of lifting rarely used.

On small farms lacking mechanical lifting methods, the fish may be hand-carried in wash tubs from the pond to the hauling tank. This method requires a considerable amount of strenuous labor.

Holding Fish

It is sometimes necessary to hold harvested catfish for several days before marketing. The facilities which may be used for holding include vats, tanks, and small ponds. A major consideration in holding is the maintenance of fish in good condition. This includes insuring that an adequate supply of oxygenated water is available. Concentrating fish in holding facilities increases the demand for oxygen. Feeding, which is discontinued 24 to 36 hours prior to hauling, may not be needed if the fish are held for only a short while. Fish held for several days will need to be fed, but the amount should never be more than what is consumed in a few minutes. Facilities for holding fish should be designed to minimize injury and disease problems. During holding, prophylactic treatments may be administered to the fish that are not to be used for food.

Use of "Live Car." Large ponds may yield many tons of fish. Handling large quantities may present a problem that is not easily overcome. Some growers are using fish holding bags, commonly referred to as "live cars." A "live car" is a rectangular box of netting (much like a seine) with floats on the top line. A framed opening, or coupling, at one end is designed to join through a funnel section with a similarly shaped opening in the seine. The "live car" is constructed so that it may be opened or closed by means of a drawstring.

In harvesting, the fish are guided through the funnel into the "live car." The "live car" may be closed off with a drawstring to prevent fish from escaping back into the area in front of the seine; then the "live car" is detached from the seine. Fish may be held for several days in "live cars." Fish cannot be lifted in a "live car" for loading, because the materials used in the construction are not

Figure 13-14. Two "Live Car" Fish-Holding Bags Attached in Tandem to Seine. (Courtesy, National Marine Fisheries Service)

strong enough to lift 15,000 to 20,000 pounds. "Live cars" are constructed of 2-inch mesh nylon webbing and are buoyed by a series of 3- by 3-inch sponge floats spaced 1 foot apart. When closed, the "live car" is usually about 75 feet long and 20 feet in circumference.

Weight Loss. Catfish lose weight during holding. The amount of weight they lose depends upon the conditions under which they are held and upon the length of time they are held. Research by the National Marine Fisheries Service on holding catfish for 7 days revealed that most of the weight loss occurred during the first 48 hours. Further, catfish held in vats with agitators lost slightly less weight than those held in vats with compressed air. However, mortality was somewhat greater with the agitators.

The best water temperature for holding catfish at a processing plant is 48 to 59°F. Mortality and weight loss are lower at this temperature.

Additional research on weight loss is underway. How holding influences dressing percentage is not known. Also, the density of the fish in vats is being studied.

Grading Fish

Harvesting usually includes grading, both with fingerlings and with food fish. Grading is done to insure uniformity of size in processing food fish. With fingerlings, it is done to provide fish of uniform size for stocking growing ponds. Grading into lots of uniform sizes also simplifies the estimation of numbers.

Figure 13-15. Fingerling Grader.

Various kinds of grading devices are used. Food fish are graded in different ways, often by passing through a flat box with a slatted bottom. Spacing between bars retains fish larger than a certain size and permits smaller fish to pass through. Such graders must be calibrated to sort out the fish according to desired sizes. Fingerlings may be graded in slightly different ways. The grader sizes for channel catfish fingerlings are shown in Table 13-1.

Table 13-1

Grader Sizes for Channel Catfish Fingerlings

Distance Between Grader Bars	Average Size of Fingerlings Retained
(inches)	*(inches)*
27/64	3
1/2	4
40/64	5
3/4	6
56/64	7
1	8

Figure 13-16. Bar-Type Fish Grader.

Hauling Fish

Catfish may be hauled in tanks or bags. Tanks are most commonly used and are constructed of wood, fiberglass, or aluminum. Most tanks are partitioned into compartments, thus making it possible to haul different sizes and species of catfish. As a general rule, a maximum of 3 pounds of fish may be hauled per gallon of water. The water in haul tanks should be changed every 24 hours if fish are in it that long.

Devices for aerating the water must be installed in each compartment of a haul tank. Agitators which stir the surface of the water are adequate for most fish loads, provided the water is not more than 2 feet deep below the agitator. Depths more than 2 feet require aeration by introducing air or oxygen into the water at the bottom of the tank.

The amount of fish that can be hauled in a tank depends on water chemistry, water temperature, and amount of agitation and on the size, condition, and species of fish. Sixty channel catfish weighing 1 pound each can be held for 24 hours in 4 cubic feet of water, provided the water is not more than 1 foot deep or warmer than 65°F. An agitator must introduce 1 cubic foot of air per minute at the bottom of the tank. Agitators which operate off the electrical system of a truck are available; otherwise, a small auxiliary gas engine may be used to aerate the water.

Large polyethylene bags may be used for transporting fish. Bags for hauling fish should be at least 4 millimeters thick. The fish are added to a bag that is one-quarter full of water. After the water and fish are in place, air or oxygen is pumped under pressure into the remainder of the bag. Catfish may puncture bags unless their spines have been removed. Filled bags should not be placed directly on ice for hauling. Fish bags should be handled carefully to prevent their bursting.

Catfish should not be fed immediately prior to hauling. Fish that have been fed should not be hauled until their stomachs are empty. A waiting period of up to 36 hours may be required. Feeding fish before hauling will cause a buildup of fecal material and disgorged feed in the water.

Catfish should be conditioned before hauling and unloading if differences exist in water chemistry or temperature. Water in haul tanks should be free of harmful impurities and pollution. It is preferable to use water of high hardness and alkalinity in hauling. The temperature of the water in haul tanks should not vary more than 5 degrees from the temperature of the water from which the fish were removed or in which they are to be placed. However, it is preferable to haul fish in water that has a temperature of 50 to 60°F. Some haul tanks are equipped with refrigeration coils to keep the water cool on long hauls. Catfish can be conditioned by gradually introducing different water to them.

Figure 13-17. Haul Truck Equipped with Oxygen Cylinders.

Figure 13-18. Haul Truck Equipped with Electrical Generator and Aerators.

Fish are subject to slight injuries, such as abrasions, torn fins, and scratches, each time they are handled. Acriflavine at the rate of 2 ppm is usually added to the hauling water to prevent bacterial growth and to aid in preventing diseases among stocker fish. Other medications may be used if needed. Food fish should not be treated.

Questions and Problems for Discussion

1. What is harvesting?
2. Why should catfish be harvested only after a market has been found?
3. What are two types of harvests?
4. What precautions should be followed in harvesting?
5. What are the four methods of harvesting? Describe each.
6. How are seines for harvesting food fish constructed?
7. What happens when fish "slip their slime"?
8. When should catfish be harvested?
9. How are fish lifted from ponds?
10. What is a "live car" and how is it used?
11. Why is grading important?
12. How are fish hauled?
13. Why should catfish not be fed just before hauling?
14. Describe the water that should be used in haul tanks.

14

Marketing Catfish

Marketing is a final and important part of catfish farming. It is the link between farmers and consumers. Growing operations should be based on the available marketing arrangements. A market for catfish should be secured before a fish farm is established. The profitability of catfish farming is influenced by the marketing alternatives that are available. There are several ways of marketing catfish, and farmers need to determine which are best suited to their farms.

In the early days of the catfish industry, there were no coordinated marketing efforts. There were no processors of any size to buy the fish from farmers, to process them, or to sell them to restaurants, food stores, and other outlets. Not only did the early farmers raise the catfish but also they processed and distributed them. Some farmers had roadside fish stores, others operated small specialty restaurants, and still others sold their catfish to local restaurants. The nature of the marketing process has changed considerably. Today there are large processors with reliable outlets for the processed fish.

This chapter contains information on the following areas:

> Meaning of marketing
> Processes and functions in marketing
> Available markets for food fish
> Problems in marketing catfish
> Selecting a market
> Costs in marketing
> Market promotion

Meaning of Marketing

Marketing involves getting catfish from the grower to the consumer. It includes a number of processes, functions, and services in preparation for consumption. Many farmers view marketing as simply finding a buyer for the fish that are produced, but it is much more than this. The roles of farmers in marketing catfish vary. Some (those owning processing plants or retail markets) may be concerned with the entire process of marketing. Others may end their involvement at one of several steps along the way.

Processes and Functions in Marketing

The processes and functions in marketing involve preparing catfish for consumption. The manner in which these are performed relate to the quality and desirability of catfish as food. Some of the major steps (processes and functions) in marketing are discussed here.

Assembling. Catfish are concentrated into small areas of water and are lifted and loaded into tanks for hauling to a market outlet. Sometimes several small growers may combine their harvests of

Figure 14-1. Assembling Fish of Uniform Size Is an Important Role of the Producer in Marketing. (Courtesy, Master Mix Feeds)

catfish for hauling. An additional part of the assembling operation includes grading, which is often included as a separate step in marketing.

Grading. Grading is done to insure uniformity of size and species. Considerable variation may exist in the size of fish obtained from a pond. Processors usually want fish in lots of uniform sizes. Normally, a range of acceptable size is established, such as a range of 1 to 2 pounds. A few processors are able to handle all sizes of fish and do not emphasize grading. Grading also involves removing trash fish, turtles, and other undesirable catch from the harvested catfish.

Hauling. After fish have been harvested, graded, and loaded, they are hauled to a market outlet, such as a processing plant. The fish may change ownership at this point, and the farmer's role may end. However, as a part of getting fish to the consumer, the fish may be hauled several more times, such as from the processor to the distributor and from the distributor to the retailer.

Changing Ownership. The fish may be sold by the farmer at one of several steps in the marketing process, often upon arrival at a processing plant. Change of ownership also includes the establishment of a price. Prices may vary from day to day and are determined when buyers and sellers agree on a common evaluation.

Processing. Most catfish are processed in some way before reaching the consumer. This includes dressing and other steps necessary for catfish entering retail trade. (Processing is discussed in the next chapter.)

Packaging. Packaging is one of the final steps in processing. The purpose is to place the fish in a convenient container for shipping, storing, and selling in retail markets. It serves to protect the fish and to make them attractive and appealing to consumers. The attractiveness and convenience of the packaging materials are influential in selling the dressed fish, especially in supermarkets. Neat and appealing containers increase the sales of fish in retail markets.

Storing. It may be necessary to hold (store) catfish for a short time before processing. After processing, catfish may be stored unfrozen for a short period of time and for longer periods if they are frozen or preserved in some other way.

Wholesaling. This involves the selling of fish by processors to jobbers and by jobbers to retail outlets. Jobbers are known as middlemen. Some processors sell directly to retailers and omit the jobber.

Retailing. Retail outlets for catfish include restaurants, supermarkets, and fish markets. A few farmers operate retail outlets for dressed or live fish, either on the farm or in a separate facility.

Advertising. The awareness and use of products by consumers is often related to advertising and promotional efforts. This is especially true in the case of catfish in some areas of the United States. The desirability of catfish as food is often stressed in promotional campaigns. Advertising may be conducted by a single producer or retail outlet or by an association of producers.

Available Markets for Food Fish

More than half of the catfish produced are marketed through processed food markets. Other markets available to growers include recreational markets, retail roadside markets on the farm, retail markets in cities, and farmer-owned restaurants, including catfish specialty houses. Some growers have utilized all of these markets in disposing of their catfish.

Processed Food Markets. The processed food markets are concerned with preparing catfish for use as food. The fish may be prepared for cooking and then frozen or sold as fresh fish to various retail outlets. Fish farmers are usually more concerned with finding a sale for the fish produced rather than with how consumption ultimately occurs, but a farmer who produces quality fish will be interested in the consumer's being satisfied with the product.

Processors of catfish may enter into contractual agreements with growers. Such an agreement is called "contract farming." Producing catfish under contract has advantages to both growers and processors. One of the most attractive advantages to the grower is that, by entering into a contract, a sale for the fish to be produced is virtually assured when market size has been reached. The problem of finding a buyer for fish at the time of marketing is eliminated. Contract growing also offers advantages to the processor. One advantage is that the processor is assured of a uniform

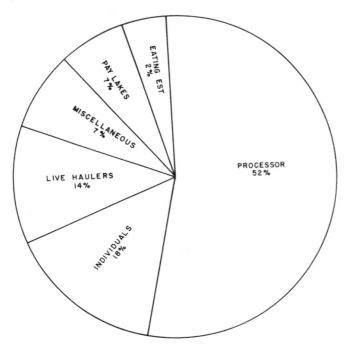

Figure 14-2. Sales Outlets for Farm-Reared Catfish. (Courtesy, W. R. Morrison, University
of Arkansas)

supply of catfish when needed, thus keeping the processing
equipment in operation.

Processing plants for catfish are located throughout the southeastern part of the United States, especially in areas along the
Mississippi River. The trend in recent years has been for the establishment of plants further from this region. In other words, the
catfish industry is spreading and moving into new areas. Processing plants may be cooperatively owned and operated by fish farmers or owned and operated by large corporations.

Recreational Markets. The recreational market outlets are
second to the processed food markets in terms of volume of catfish
handled. Catfish marketed in this manner are primarily for sport
fishing purposes. There are two main ways in which the recreational markets use fish: (1) Farmers may open "fee-lakes" stocked
with catfish to the public for sport fishing. Income is from fees
which are charged persons who fish in the ponds. (2) Farmers may

Figure 14-3. Modern Processing Plants Use Attractive Packaging Materials.

sell catfish to live fish haulers who haul to fee-lakes located in other areas. These fee-lakes are often located near large cities and are open to fishing by the public.

Retail Markets. Some fish farmers operate retail markets to sell live or dressed fish. These markets may be located on the farm or in a nearby town. The volume of fish sold through these markets in terms of the total volume produced by the industry is small. However, a few enterprising farmers have found these markets to be highly profitable and capable of handling a sizeable quantity of fish.

Restaurants. A few fish farmers operate restaurants in which they market some or all of the catfish produced. Often, these restaurants specialize in catfish. The operation of a restaurant adds another aspect of management and one which many farmers do not particularly like.

Problems in Marketing Catfish

Practically all facets of the catfish industry may experience problems in marketing. Generally, the major problems are associated with the grower and his getting fish of high quality to consumers. Some problems are industry-wide, while others may be more or less isolated to individual growers.

Industry-Wide Problems. The greatest problems of the catfish industry are related to quality control and attracting consumers. Producers can assist the industry by growing a quality product and marketing in lots of uniform sizes. Processors can assist by checking the fish before delivery to the plant. Fish which have off-flavors or which are of undesirable size should be rejected. Processors are aware that a uniform, palatable product that will compete with other meat products is a must. Farm-raised catfish must be superior in quality to imported catfish and should be clearly labeled to avoid confusion. Consumers frequently feel that the quality of the imported fish is inferior to that of farm-raised fish. If the two products are confused, the consumer may avoid future purchases of catfish because of dissatisfaction with quality.

Another industry problem involves the preparation of the fish in restaurants. Cooked fish must be attractive and appetizing so that restaurant patrons will repeatedly request catfish. Increased consumption will be possible only by offering a good product and by conducting carefully planned promotional campaigns.

Grower Problems. The problems faced by growers in marketing catfish have not been so great as they may be in the future. This is due to the demand for catfish exceeding the supply. Rapid increases in production may result in the supply more nearly meeting the demand. When supply and demand begin to be similar or when the supply is greater than demand, the less efficient producers may find catfish culture to be unprofitable. Growers who stay in catfish farming will need to study the market, analyze marketing alternatives, and make decisions accordingly.

The growth and harvest of fish should be timed to coincide with maximum prices. The best time for harvesting is November through February, but this may not be the time when prices are highest. Producers growing catfish under contract do not have the problems of locating markets and uncertain prices, but must harvest the fish on schedule.

Producing catfish of uniform size and within an acceptable weight range is a problem to many growers. The size preferred by most processors ranges from ¾ pound to 1½ pounds live weight. This size is usually processed whole.

It is preferable to stop feeding one to two days before harvesting and marketing. This improves the flavor and tends to eliminate the danger of oxygen depletion during harvesting.

Diseased or injured fish should not be hauled to market. Processors will reject such fish and thus create problems of what to do with those that are rejected. Medications should not be given food fish on the way to market.

Selecting a Market

Selecting a market involves determining which outlets will result in the greatest profit and which are accessible to the fish farmers. Some of the markets in which fish sell for the most per pound may require specialized equipment and know-how.

It is impossible to state that one method of marketing is more profitable than another. Fish growers must analyze the marketing alternatives that are available and make their selection on the basis of potential profit. Some producers may choose to use more

Figure 14-4. A Roadside Retail Marketing Facility Showing Holding Vats.

than one market as protection against the loss of a single market. Persons raising catfish need to keep aware of changes so that the most favorable markets can be used.

The price received by the farmer per pound for catfish is usually greater when the fish are sold through fee-lakes. Fish sold for processing usually bring a lower price per pound, but the volume that can be marketed in this manner is usually greater than with fee-lakes. Also, returns from a fee-lake are dependent on sport fishermen being attracted to a particular fish farm or pond. Some growers find that the greatest returns from catfish are received through small fish markets and restaurants. Returns from retail markets may vary considerably depending upon location of the market and quality of the fish. The profitability of different market outlets may vary from year to year.

Costs in Marketing

Costs are involved in all of the steps in marketing. These costs add to the retail price but are usually necessary and make catfish attractive to consumers. Many of these steps also reduce preparation efforts and time and costs in the kitchen. Since catfish as harvested are not ready to cook, many of these costs are essential.

The main costs in marketing catfish are for labor, transportation, packaging, loss incurred when head and viscera are removed, advertising, rent, interest, and taxes. The amount for labor is often considerable in processing because of inefficiency and lack of mechanical advances to replace the demand for hand labor. Packaging costs have increased but attractive packaging is usually beneficial in promoting consumption.

The share of the retail price that goes to the farmer varies considerably with the market outlet. With processed fish sold in supermarkets, the farmer's share may be only 20 to 40 percent of the retail price. On-the-farm sales result in the farmer's receiving 100 percent of the price, but this does not mean a high profit. The quantity sold and cost of selling must be considered.

Market Promotion

Several associations have been formed to promote catfish. Some of these are concerned with specialized aspects of the catfish industry, but most are concerned with one particular phase, namely, marketing. Organized marketing is the key to success in catfish farming, especially for growers with small acreages.

A major effort in promoting and improving catfish marketing has been undertaken by the American Catfish Marketing Association (ACMA). Membership in this organization is limited to processors of farm-raised catfish with annual sales of $250,000 or more. The purposes of the ACMA include promoting and developing markets for farm-raised catfish, improving and developing new techniques in processing, and working with growers to improve the supply and quality of catfish. The ACMA was formed in 1971.

An organization concerned with the total industry is the Catfish Farmers of America (CFA). Founded in 1968, it serves to speak for the entire industry of catfish farming. As a national organization, it has members in nearly all states. Several states, including Arkansas, California, Georgia, Louisiana, Mississippi, North Carolina, and Texas, have established affiliated state associations. Headquarters for the CFA is located in Little Rock, Arkansas.

Assistance in marketing catfish is also provided by various state and Federal government agencies. In the 1970's, the National Marketing Service Office of the National Marine Fisheries Service probably had the most impact on consumption. This agency developed various promotional materials on preparing and serving catfish, but this service is no longer available in catfish marketing.

The U.S. Department of Agriculture has been assuming an increasingly important role in the catfish industry. Areas of activity include research, extension-education programs, disease laboratories, pamphlets to promote catfish culture, and other areas.

Market-promotion activities are also carried out by feed companies, equipment manufacturers, catfish processing companies, and other businesses associated with catfish farming. A good example is Welfed Catfish, Inc., of Belzoni, Mississippi. This company publishes attractive promotional literature, recipe pamphlets, and other materials.

Questions and Problems for Discussion

1. What is marketing?
2. How has catfish marketing changed?
3. What are the steps (processes and functions) in marketing catfish?

4. What are the available markets for catfish?
5. What are the major problems facing the catfish industry?
6. How does the price received for catfish vary with the different methods of marketing?
7. What are the costs in marketing catfish?
8. What associations are active in market promotion for catfish?

15

Processing Catfish

The most important step in getting catfish ready for consumption is that of processing. This involves preparing fish for purchase by retail outlets or by consumers. It usually does not include cooking, but it may in the case of canned catfish and frozen partially or fully cooked convenience foods. Processing is sometimes referred to as "dressing"; but, in commercial catfish farming, processing is actually more than dressing. When fish are dressed, the head, internal organs (known as viscera), and skin are removed. Processing includes other activities, such as packaging and storing, and is used to provide a product that is attractive and appetizing.

This chapter presents information in the following areas:

> The processing industry
> Processing procedures
> Forms of fish preparation
> Dressing percentage
> How the farmer is a part of processing

The Processing Industry

Catfish are processed in a variety of situations. These range from small farmer-operated facilities located on farms to large plants using the latest in technological advancements. Most large processing plants use an automated assembly line procedure and are designed to handle large volumes of fish. The labor requirements are often large because of the newness of the catfish industry and the lack of sophisticated equipment. The procedures used by some plants are crude compared to those in other processing industries, such as livestock slaughtering plants. Equipment to completely mechanize every phase of fish processing is not yet

Figure 15-1. Processing Plant Scene. (Courtesy, Ralston Purina Company)

available. In addition to the necessary equipment for dressing fish, most plants also have packaging and storing facilities.

A steady supply of fish is required to keep a plant operating. To prevent periodic shortages of fish, some of the larger processors have harvesting equipment. This equipment and a small work crew to operate it are available to farmers. Charges for such harvesting are made on an hourly, daily, or weight-of-fish basis.

Small fish markets, such as those operated on the farm by fish farmers, do not handle large volumes of fish. Most of the work is done by hand because of the expense involved in obtaining equipment. The cost of dressing fish varies with labor cost and the time required to complete cleaning. An experienced workman can dress a fish weighing 1 pound in one minute.

Facilities required for dressing fish in small fish markets include running water, receptacles for water, skinning hook, knife, skinning pliers, and draining board. Holding vats for live fish and refrigerators for dressed fish may be needed. Many small markets sell both dressed fish and live fish.

Catfish processing plants must conform to health and safety regulations. Health departments inspect and certify facilities before, during, and after construction. Some of the features needed in processing plants include concrete floors, floor drains, walls which can be washed (usually made of tile), stainless steel work benches (tables), and waste-disposal facilities. Sanitary toilets and wash areas must be provided for employees. The Occupational Safety and Health Administration has regulations applicable to maintaining healthful and safe working environments for employees.

Processing Procedures

The procedures, or steps, used by large-scale processing plants in processing catfish are essentially the same. Most differences can be attributed to the extent of mechanization and the arrangement of the equipment.

After delivery to the plant, the fish may be held several hours or days, depending upon the backlog of fish and the weather. Catfish should be processed as quickly as possible after delivery— within 24 hours in warm weather. During hauling, fish may re-

Figure 15-2. Receiving Area at a Catfish Processing Plant. (The catfish are unloaded into holding vats under the shed.)

ceive minor abrasions and damage. If the fish are held several days, the minor injuries may develop into more serious problems.

The steps in processing may include the following: checking for off-flavor, grading, stunning, beheading, skinning, eviscerating, washing, cutting, packaging, storing, and transporting.

Checking for Off-Flavor. This is preferably done at the farm before harvesting. Most processors check fish for off-flavor when the fish arrive at the plant. Fish with off-flavors are rejected.

Grading. Catfish are graded to insure that fish of uniform size are processed together. This simplifies processing and packaging. Grading may be done on the farm, at the processing plant, or both. Some processors have not been concerned with strict uniformity of fish but the trend is toward greater uniformity.

Stunning. Many processing plants use a procedure of paralyzing catfish by means of an electric shock. Large tubs or tanks of fish are shocked at a time. This procedure makes fish lifeless but keeps them alive. Dead fish deteriorate very quickly; therefore, fish are kept alive as long as possible.

Figure 15-3. Catfish Being Prepared for Stunning with an Electrical Shock Prior to Being Processed.

Beheading. Heads are removed with a fish head saw or band saw. Fish are kept alive until the head is removed so that a minimum of deterioration occurs.

Skinning. The skin may be removed by manual, mechanical, or other methods. The manual method is similar to that used by most sport fishermen. It is used by smaller plants and fish markets.

Figure 15-4. Using a Band Saw to Remove Catfish Heads.

Figure 15-5. Fish Head Saw Used for Beheading. (Courtesy, D and D Manufacturing Company, Inc.)

The fish are hung by their heads on large hooks. The dorsal and pectoral fins are snipped off, and the skin is cut through all around the fish just behind the operculum. Pliers are used to grasp the edges of the cut skin which is stripped off in a tailward direction. The dorsal fin is cut out as the back strip of skin is removed. The ventral side is left until last and, as it is pulled, the belly is slit open and the viscera are removed along with the anal fin.

Several methods of mechanical skinning are available. With mechanical methods, the head and viscera may be removed before skinning. One method involves pushing the fish over the skinner much as a joiner is used in a woodworking shop. The machine must be adjusted for proper clearance between the blade and toothroll so that a minimum of flesh is removed with the skin. Three passes over the machine are usually required to remove the skin from a catfish. A disadvantage that is sometimes given for this method is that it removes a thin, white membrane which lies between the skin and the flesh. This membrane protects the flesh

Figure 15-6. Mechanical Fish Skinner. (Courtesy, Townsend Engineering Company)

and keeps it moist. When it is removed, the quality of the fish declines more rapidly.

Another mechanical method involves a combination of rubber and stainless steel rollers. The steel roller has thousands of tiny teeth which grip the skin and peel it from the flesh. This method leaves the thin protective membrane on the flesh.

Other methods make use of high-pressure water systems. These do not completely remove the skin but do remove the outer portion of it when used on smaller fish. Research has been made to determine the feasibility of removing skin by dipping the fish into chemical solutions.

Eviscerating. This step is involved with all methods of dressing fish. With manual methods, the viscera are removed as part of skinning. With mechanical methods, including the vacuum system, it is a separate step. Usually, the entire length of the belly is slit when the viscera are removed.

Washing. A final check is made of each fish after skinning, beheading, and eviscerating. This step involves washing and re-

Figure 15-7. Eviscerating Line in a Processing Plant.

moving any skin, viscera, or fins which were not previously removed. The tail fin usually remains on dressed fish.

Cutting. This step is used with the larger fish that are suitable for making steaks and fillets. When fish are small enough to be cooked whole, this step is omitted. Cutting often involves preparing portions of prescribed sizes and weights for restaurant and institutional use.

Figure 15-8. Processed Catfish Packaged in Wholesale Boxes for Shipment.

Packaging. The fish are packaged for quick-freezing or marketing fresh. Most fish are individually wrapped in polyethylene film or small bags. Labels may be added to give information about the fish and to make the package more attractive.

Storing. Storing is a step in most processing operations. Wrapped fish are frozen or refrigerated until entering retail trade. Frozen fish are stored at 0 to 5°F. Fish deteriorate very rapidly when improperly stored.

Transporting. Processed catfish are transported in modern refrigerated trucks. The truck may be loaded by using a fork lift to raise boxes of fish stacked on pallets.

Figure 15-9. A Refrigerated Tractor-Trailer Truck for Transporting Frozen Catfish.

Forms of Fish Preparation

In processing, catfish may be prepared in several different forms. The forms are based on the extent to which the fish have been readied for consumption. The size of the fish may dictate the form of preparation required; that is, large fish are usually cut into

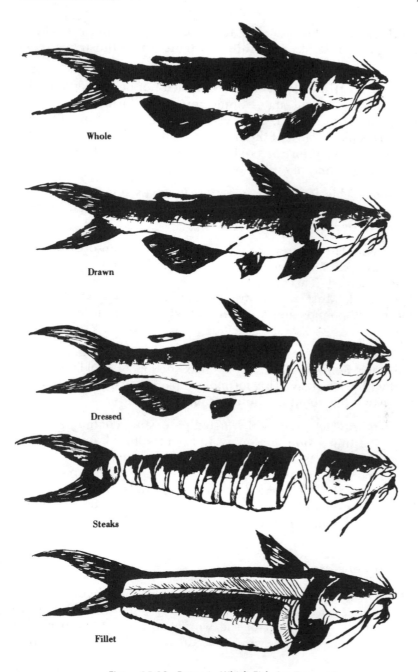

Whole

Drawn

Dressed

Steaks

Fillet

Figure 15-10. Forms in Which Fish Are Prepared.

several pieces. The common forms of preparation are whole, drawn, dressed, steaks, and fillets. (Figure 15-10 illustrates these forms.)

Whole. Catfish sold as whole fish have not been dressed. The fish is in the natural state. Sometimes this form is known as "round" or "in the round." The viscera should be removed before the fish is cooked. Most of the time the skin, head, and some of the fins are removed prior to cooking. A fish weighing 1 pound will yield ⅓ to ½ pound of edible portion.

Drawn. This form of preparation involves removing the viscera and leaving the head and skin on the fish. Catfish are seldom prepared in drawn form.

Dressed. The dressed form is also known as pan-dressed. The viscera and skin are removed. The head and some of the fins are usually removed. This is the most popular form in which catfish are prepared. Most catfish are marketed at a live weight of 1 pound to 1½ pounds and are well suited to this form of preparation.

Steaks. Steaks are made by cutting crosswise slices ¾- to 1-inch thick from dressed fish. A cross-section of backbone is included with each steak. This form of preparation is used with large catfish weighing about 2 pounds or more.

Fillets. A fillet, a cut which usually does not contain bones, is made by cutting a side section away from the backbone. The skin is removed. This is a form of preparation which yields a low-dressing percentage unless some use is made of the remaining parts, such as the backbone. Occasionally, fillets may be cut from only one side of fish, leaving the backbone intact on the other. Fillets may be made from either large or small fish.

Dressing Percentage

Catfish usually yield 55 to 60 percent of their live weight in dressed form. This means that the head, viscera, and skin are equal to 40 to 45 percent of the weight of a whole catfish. The exact dressing percentage varies and depends on the form of preparation.

How the Farmer Is a Part of Processing

Some processors will accept only those fish that have been graded into lots of uniform quality, size, and species. The ideal size of catfish for the retail market is a live weight of 1 pound to 1¼ pounds each so that the dressed fish will weigh from 8 to 10 ounces. Some processing plants have technicians check conditions at the pond sites during harvest. These technicians will cull fish weighing ¾ pound or less, and they will reject the fish if they detect any off-flavors.

The farmer's part in processing is to meet the processor's requirements. Harvesting and hauling procedures that will not damage the fish should be used. Fish should be graded before being loaded. It may be necessary to sort out the undesirable fish, turtles, and snakes which have managed to get into the ponds. If any off-flavors are detected, the steps necessary to eliminate them should be taken before loading. By following good management, a catfish farmer should be able to furnish the processor, at the scheduled time, with a supply of fish that is uniform in quality, size, and species.

Questions and Problems for Discussion

1. What is meant by "processing" in the catfish industry?
2. What is the current status of processing in the catfish industry?
3. What are the common steps in processing catfish?
4. What methods of skinning are used?
5. What are the common forms of fish preparation? Describe each.
6. What is the dressing percentage with catfish?
7. How is the farmer a part of processing?

16

Operating Recreational Fishing Facilities

Recreational fishing facilities are very popular for sport fishing and can produce attractive economic returns in some locations. It is based on the notion that people are willing to pay to fish. Recreational fishing farms (also known as fee-lakes) require special management. A successful operation must be attractive to people who sport fish. A number of "extras," such as catfish cleaning services and facilities and food and beverage services, will add to the desirability of a fee-lake operation.

This chapter presents information on the following areas:

> Kinds of recreational fishing farms
> Planning recreational fishing ponds
> Stocking recreational ponds
> Setting fees
> Assisting people who sport fish
> Providing for safety
> Handling liability
> Promoting recreational fishing
> Determining the desirable characteristics of a
>   recreational catfish farm

Kinds of Recreational Fishing Farms

Types of recreational catfish facilities operated are catch-out ponds and put-and-take ponds. The management required for these operations is similar in most respects, yet there is considerable difference.

A catch-out type of recreational facility involves raising the catfish in the ponds where the fishing occurs. The amount of management required varies from very little to a program of stocking, fertilizing, feeding, and other activities. Good management practices are needed if consistently good catches are to be obtained. People who sport fish will not likely return to catfish ponds where the fishing is poor. Catch-out ponds are said to be "extensive" in that the operator must be able to perform a variety of activities. The rate of stocking for catch-out ponds is about the same as for food fish lakes.

A put-and-take recreational facility involves keeping the ponds stocked with catchable-sized catfish. The catfish are raised somewhere else and placed in the put-and-take pond. In some cases, the owner may raise the catfish. In other cases, the catfish are purchased from other catfish farmers. Put-and-take ponds are said to be intensive in that the manager must concentrate on one size of catfish and on one type of operation. The ponds are designed more with recreational aspects in mind than with what is needed for catfish farming. The rate of stocking may range from 6,000 to 20,000 pounds per acre. Careful water management is required, especially at the higher stocking rates.

Planning Recreational Fishing Ponds

Good fee-lakes do not just happen—they are planned. The same kind of detailed attention to planning is needed for fee-lakes as is used with food fish growing ponds. The arrangement and construction features of ponds used for fee-lakes may determine the success of such an operation.

Determining the Facilities Needed. One of the first steps in planning a fee-lake operation is to make an informal community study. This involves developing an overall description of the community. The nature of the population should be investigated to determine age trends, interest in fishing, and income level. An inventory of similar recreational facilities in the community should be made. This procedure will aid in determining if a fee-lake would be patronized and in preventing the establishment of such facilities when they are not needed. Also, any deficiencies in the present operations should be noted so that the same mistakes would not be repeated. Of course, the kinds of facilities that may be established are often somewhat limited by the site that is available.

Developing a Plan. In developing a plan, it may be a good idea to prepare it in two parts. One part would be concerned with short-range plans that could be implemented fairly soon. Another part would consist of long-range plans that might require 5 to 10 years, or more, for implementation. Developing a plan may involve making detailed drawings of the area to be developed, including both present features and features to be constructed. Such plans may be prepared to reflect step-by-step implementation.

Location and Size of Ponds. Fee-lake operations should be located near areas of concentrated population so that they can be easily reached by automobile. Locations near intersections of

Figure 16-1. A Nice Stringer of Catfish. (Courtesy, Master Mix Feeds)

major highways are desirable. It is preferable to have several ponds available for fishing. The ponds may be stocked with different species and sizes of fish. Ponds that are 3 acres or larger are preferred, but smaller ponds may be very successful. Some fee-lake operators have been more successful with long, narrow ponds than with ponds of other shapes. This is because fishermen are able to cast to the middle of the pond and catch fish which flee the shore area as a result of disturbances caused by fishermen. Ponds should not be too long, however, as long ponds may require fishermen to walk considerable distances.

Convenience Facilities. Sport fishermen are attracted by the facilities that accompany a fee-lake. Facilities that may be provided include concession stands or vending machines for food, drinks, tackle, baits, and boat rental; shade; picnicking and camping areas; fishing piers and platforms; parking areas; fish cleaning tables; restrooms; and freezing lockers. Not only do these facilities attract fishermen but also they provide additional income.

Stocking Recreational Ponds

Most fee-lakes are stocked with channel catfish, including albino channel catfish. The albino channel catfish (not a separate species) is an attractive novelty for sport fishermen. Some fee-lake operators give prizes to persons who catch albino fish. The blue and white species of catfish are also used in stocking fee-lakes. In fact, the white catfish may be preferred, since it is more active in extreme cold and hot weather than the other species. A few fee-lakes are stocked with a mixture of scale fish and catfish.

The rate of stocking in a fee-lake should insure a good catch by sport fishermen. A rate of 4,000 to 10,000 pounds may be stocked per acre, depending on how well the water is managed. A few highly intensive fee-lakes have been stocked at the rate of 50,000 pounds per acre. The rate of stocking depends on the volume of fish caught by fishermen each day and on the use of aeration devices. A supply of catchable-sized fish should be available for restocking.

Setting Fees

Fees for fishing are assessed in four ways:

1. Privilege or annual fees.—Some fee-lakes are operated on the basis of annual fees or dues. Persons paying the privilege fee are allowed to fish as often as they like over a period of time, usually a year. Associations may be formed to which membership dues are paid.
2. Daily fee.—A flat rate, usually ranging from 50 cents to $3 per day, is charged with no guarantee of any fish being caught. A disadvantage of this method is that fishermen may catch a large volume of catfish and soon deplete the supply in the pond.
3. Weight of fish fee.—Fishermen pay only for the pounds of fish caught. The rate ranges from 50 cents to $1 per pound. This is a commonly used method.
4. Combination of daily fee and weight-of-fish fee.— Fishermen pay a fee to fish each day and also a fee for each pound of fish caught.

Someone must always be on duty around fee-lakes to weigh fish and collect fees. It is common for fee-lakes to be open only during certain hours and on certain days of the week. This makes attending fee-lakes less demanding.

Figure 16-2. Some Farmers Have Combination Fee-Lake and Food Fish Operations.

Assisting People Who Sport Fish

Fee-lake operators often assist persons who visit their ponds in selecting tackle and with techniques of fishing. The success of a fee-lake may be related to the kind of assistance offered and how it is given. Assistance should be given when it is needed and then *only* when the sport fisherman desires it. Most persons visit fee-lakes for the pleasure of fishing. Nothing detracts from the fisherman's pleasure more than having someone constantly telling him how to do it or what he did wrong when the big one got away.

Catching Catfish. Wild catfish in natural waters are often caught on the bottom of the stream or lake. In culture, the habits of catfish are somewhat changed. The best fishing is near where the fish are fed and that may not be on the bottom, especially if floating feed is used. Fishing can be stimulated by throwing a handful of floating feed on the water and then fishing near the surface where the feed has been thrown. The best time for fishing may be in the late afternoon or at night.

Bait Selection. Catfish feed by scent. Baits which have foul odors usually produce best results. Stink baits are available commercially or they may be homemade. Baits of cheese, dried blood, and spoiled chicken entrails are favorites of catfish. Dough baits made of a variety of ingredients are available and are used by placing a small wad on the hook. Worms, minnows, small chunks of liver, shrimp, crayfish, and other common baits may be used.

Various artificial baits also may be used. These include spoons, jigs, imitation worms, and spinner flies.

Tackle selection. A wide range of tackle may be used by sport fishermen to catch catfish. Many fishermen have distinct preferences. Generally, all tackle has the same major parts: hook, sinker, line, float, and rod, or pole. Trot lines are sometimes used and consist of a long heavy line to which several shorter lines with hooks are attached. The heavy line is stretched across the water, and the shorter lines with baited hooks hang down into the water.

The most common tackle used with catfish involves a cane pole and line. A cane pole is a stalk of bamboo ranging from 8 to 15 feet long. A line with a float, sinker, and hook is attached. Most sport fishermen use 18-pound test lines with 4/0 hooks. Lines are usually nylon and are made of one filament, or strand, known as monofilament.

A wide assortment of fly and spinning tackle may be used. These permit reaching further out into the water than do regular poles. Artificial, natural, or a combination of baits may be used with fly and spinning rods. Often, certain techniques and equipment become preferred in local areas. A certain amount of practice may be needed before the use of this equipment is mastered. Some of this equipment may be rather expensive to purchase.

Sport fishermen may use many accessories in fishing. These include bait containers, tackle boxes, creels and stringers, landing nets, special clothing, and tools.

Providing for Safety

All recreational areas near the water should be equipped for safety. The following precautions should be observed by operators of fee-lakes:

1. Lifesaving equipment should be placed near ponds. A rope that is 100 feet long with a life ring attached is considered essential.
2. Warning signs should be placed near danger areas and deep-water areas. Some operators put up signs warning fishermen that they fish at their own risk.
3. Boats used in the pond should be in good condition and should never become overloaded. Many fee-lake operators do not permit the use of boats.
4. Swimming areas should be marked off if swimming is permitted. Most fee-lake operators do not permit swimming.
5. Fences should be placed around ponds to keep children and persons not fishing away from the danger of the water.

Handling Liability

There is more to operating a fee-lake than merely erecting a sign opening it to the public. Fee-lake operators may be held liable for accidents resulting in injury to fishermen. Even though liability suits may be involved with any property, the owner is generally more vulnerable when a fee is charged to others for the use of the property and facilities.

The essential element which must be proved before a person can be held legally liable for unintentional injury to others is negligence. Generally negligence is the failure of an individual to do something a "reasonable person" would do under similar circumstances. Dangers which can be foreseen but are not corrected may be sufficient for charges of negligence in case of injury.

The operator of fee-lakes should have insurance protecting against liability claims. Such insurance should provide legal aid in the event of a law suit and should pay claims or awards as awarded by court action. Most insurance policies have limits on the amount that can be awarded per claim.

Promoting Recreational Fishing

Before a pond will be patronized, the fishing public must be aware that it is open. Advertising—in newspapers, with signs, and on the radio—is helpful in attracting sport fishermen. Roadside signs giving directions to fee-lakes are frequently necessary. Some operators release tagged fish into fee-lakes and award prizes to fishermen who catch fish with tags.

Figure 16-3. Attractive Signs Are Helpful in Promoting Fee-Lakes.

Determining the Desirable Characteristics of a Recreational Catfish Farm

The desired characteristics of a recreational catfish farm are those which will attract customers. Without customers who are willing to pay to fish, a fee-lake operation will not be successful. Several characteristics which contribute to success are:

- Convenient location.—Fee-lakes must be located near centers of population and must be easily reached.
- Comfortable facilities.—The ponds and other facilities must be arranged and constructed in a manner that is comfortable to patrons.
- Good fishing.—Customers must be able to catch healthy fish of satisfactory size.
- Fair fees.—The fees that are charged must be in line with those in other recreational areas.
- Aesthetic qualities.—The surroundings must be attractive to encourage patronage and to make fishing more pleasant.

Questions and Problems for Discussion

1. What are the two kinds of recreational catfish farms? Distinguish between the two.
2. Why is it necessary to plan a fee-lake operation?
3. How does one determine the kind of fee-lake facilities that may be needed?
4. What factors should be considered in determining the location and size of ponds?
5. What species of fish and stocking rates are used with fee-lakes?
6. How are fees for fishing determined?
7. What safety provisions are needed?
8. How is negligence related to liability in the operation of a fee-lake?
9. How are recreational catfish farms promoted?
10. What are the characteristics of an ideal recreational catfish farm?

APPENDIX A

Length-Weight Chart for
Channel Catfish

Length	Average Weight per Thousand Fish	Number of Fish per Pound	Average Weight of Each Fish
(inches)	(pounds)		(pounds)
1	1.3	767.7	.0013
2	3.5	285.7	.0035
3	10.0	100.0	.0100
4	20.0	50.0	.0200
5	32.0	31.1	.0321
6	60.0	17.0	.0588
7	93.0	10.8	.0926
8	112.0	9.0	.1111
9	180.0	5.5	.1818
10	328.0	3.1	.3280
11	395.0	2.5	.3950
12	509.0	1.9	.5090
13	656.0	1.5	.6560
14	850.0	1.1	.8500
15	1,090.0	0.92	1.0900
16	1,290.0	0.82	1.2900
17	1,432.0	0.69	1.4320
18	1,750.0	0.57	1.7500
19	2,200.0	0.45	2.2000

APPENDIX B

Table of Equivalents

1 acre-foot
= 1 acre of surface area covered by 1 foot of water
= 43,560 cubic feet
= 2,718,144 pounds of water
= 325,851 gallons of water (326,000 is often used in computations.)

1 cubic foot
= 7.481 gallons
= 62.4 pounds of water
= 28,354.6 grams of water

1 gallon
= 8.34 pounds of water
= 3,800 cubic centimeters
= 3,800 grams of water

1 quart
= 950 cubic centimeters
= 950 grams of water

1 pound
= 453.6 grams (454)
= 16 ounces

1 ounce
= 28.35 grams

1 ppm requires:
2.7 pounds per acre-foot
0.0038 grams per gallon
0.0283 grams per cubic foot
0.0000623 pounds per cubic foot

APPENDIX C

Recipes for Preparing Catfish

FAMOUS "BAG-SHOOK" CATFISH FILLETS

This is a favorite catfish recipe for at-home entertainment and is especially well suited for backyard cooking. (Some cooks prefer a deep cast-iron container on a camp stove or other heat source. It is important to have the oil hot—rolling in the container! Hot oil is dangerous, and care should be taken in cooking and handling so that no one is burned and that no fire is started.)

Fresh or frozen catfish fillets (½ to ¾ pound per serving)
Salt
Black pepper (if desired)

1 or more cups cornmeal (depending on number of servings needed) placed in a clean, medium-to-large-sized paper or plastic bag

Thaw frozen fillets. Wash and dry fillets. Sprinkle lightly with salt and pepper. Place seasoned fillets (no more than 10 at a time) into the bag of cornmeal, close the top, and shake the bag until the fillets are coated with the cornmeal. Fry in deep fat, 375 to 400°F, for about 7 minutes or until brown. (Fillets will rise to the top of the oil when done.) Drain on absorbent paper. Serve immediately, or keep hot until served.

CATFISH GUMBO*

1 pound skinned catfish fillets or other fillets, fresh or frozen
½ cup chopped celery
½ cup chopped green pepper
½ cup chopped onion
1 clove garlic, finely chopped
¼ cup melted fat or oil
2 beef bouillon cubes
2 cups boiling water

1 can (1 pound) tomatoes
1 package (10 ounces) frozen okra, sliced
2 teaspoons salt
¼ teaspoon pepper
¼ teaspoon thyme
1 whole bay leaf
Dash liquid hot pepper sauce
1½ cups hot cooked rice

*Recipes courtesy of Mississippi Department of Agriculture and Commerce.

Thaw frozen fillets. Cut into 1-inch pieces. Cook celery, green pepper, onion, and garlic in fat until tender. Dissolve bouillon cubes in water. Add bouillon, tomatoes, okra, and seasonings. Cover and simmer for 30 minutes. Add fish. Cover and simmer for 15 minutes longer or until fish flakes easily when tested with a fork. Remove bay leaf. Place ¼ cup rice in each of 6 soup bowls. Fill with gumbo. Serves 6.

CONTINENTAL CATFISH*

6 skinned, pan-dressed catfish or other fish, fresh or frozen
1 teaspoon salt
Dash pepper
1 cup chopped parsley
¼ cup butter or margarine, softened
1 egg, beaten
¼ cup milk
1 teaspoon salt
¾ cup dry bread crumbs
½ cup grated Swiss cheese
3 tablespoons melted fat or oil

Thaw frozen fish. Clean, wash, and dry fish. Sprinkle inside and out with salt and pepper. Add parsley to butter and mix thoroughly. Spread inside of each fish with approximately one tablespoon parsley butter. Combine egg, milk, and salt. Combine crumbs and cheese. Dip fish in egg mixture and roll in crumb mixture. Place on a well-greased cooky sheet, 15½ × 12 inches. Sprinkle remaining crumb mixture over top of fish. Drizzle with fat. Bake in an extremely hot oven, 500°F, for 15 to 20 minutes or until fish flakes easily when tested with a fork. Serves 6.

BAYOU CATFISH*

6 skinned, pan-dressed catfish or other fish, fresh or frozen
1 cup dry white wine
½ cup melted fat or oil
1 can (4 ounces) mushroom stems and pieces, drained
¼ cup chopped green onions
2 tablespoons lemon juice
2 tablespoons chopped parsley
2 teaspoons salt
¼ teaspoon crushed bay leaves
¼ teaspoon pepper
¼ teaspoon thyme

Thaw frozen fish. Clean, wash, and dry fish. Cut 6 squares of heavy-duty aluminum foil, 18 inches each. Grease lightly. Place each fish on one-half of each square of foil. Combine remaining ingredients. Pour sauce over fish, using approximately ⅓ cup sauce for each fish. Fold other half of foil over fish and seal edges by making double folds in the foil. Place packages of fish on a barbecue grill about 6 inches from moderately hot coals. Cook for 20 to 25 minutes or until fish flakes easily when tested with a fork. To serve, cut a big crisscross in the top of each package and fold the foil back. Serves 6.

*Recipes courtesy of Mississippi Department of Agriculture and Commerce.

COUNTRY-FRIED CATFISH*

Portion: 5¼ ounces

Ingredients	25 Portions	50 Portions	100 Portions
Pan-dressed catfish (fresh or frozen)	25 (6 oz. each)	50 (6 oz. each)	100 (6 oz. each)
Eggs, beaten	3½ oz. (2 large)	7 oz. (4 large)	14 oz. (8 large)
Milk	¼ cup	½ cup	1 cup
Salt	1½ tsp.	½ oz. (1 tbsp.)	1 oz. (2 tbsp.)
Pepper	¼ tsp.	½ tsp.	1 tsp.
All-purpose flour	8 oz. (2 cups)	1 lb. (1 qt.)	2 lb. (2 qt.)
Dry bread crumbs	7½ oz. (2 cups)	15 oz. (1 qt.)	1 lb. 14 oz. (2 qt.)

Thaw frozen fish. Combine eggs, milk, salt, and pepper. Combine flour and crumbs. Dip fish in egg mixture and roll in flour mixture. Fry in deep fat, 350°F, for 3 to 5 minutes or until fish flakes easily when tested with a fork. Drain on absorbent paper. Serve with hush puppies and tartar sauce.

HUSH PUPPIES*
(To go with country-fried catfish)

Portion: 2 hush puppies (1¾ oz.)

Ingredients	25 Portions	50 Portions	100 Portions
White cornmeal	15 oz. (3⅓ cups)	1 lb. 14 oz. (1 qt. 2⅔ cups)	3 lb. 12 oz. (3 qt. 1⅓ cups)
All-purpose flour	5 oz. (1¼ cups)	10 oz. (2½ cups)	1 lb. 4 oz. (1¼ qt.)
Baking powder	¾ oz. (2 tbsp.)	1½ oz. (¼ cup)	3 oz. (½ cup)
Salt	2 tsp.	¾ oz. (1½ tbsp.)	1½ oz. (3 tbsp.)
Pepper	¾ tsp.	1½ tsp.	1 tbsp.
Eggs, beaten	5¼ oz. (3 large)	10½ oz. (6 large)	1 lb. 5 oz. (12 large)
Milk	1¼ cups	2½ cups	1¼ qt.
Onions, finely chopped	4 oz. (⅔ cup)	8 oz. (1⅓ cups)	1 lb. (2⅔ cups)
Oil or fat, melted	4 oz. (½ cup)	8 oz. (1 cup)	1 lb. (2 cups)

*Recipes courtesy of Mississippi Department of Agriculture and Commerce.

Sift dry ingredients together. Combine eggs, milk, onions, and fat. Add to dry ingredients and stir only until blended. Portion with a No. 40 scoop (1³/₅ tbsp.) onto trays. Fry in deep fat, 350°F, for 3 to 4 minutes or until brown. Drain on absorbent paper.

APPENDIX D

Sources of Assistance with Catfish
Diseases and Cultural Information*

ALABAMA: Farm Fresh Catfish Co., P.O. Box 188, Greensboro, Alabama 36744 (205-624-3064). Southeastern Cooperative Fish Disease Laboratory, Dept. of Fisheries and Allied Aquacultures, Auburn University, Auburn, Alabama 36830 (205-826-4786).

ARIZONA: Hatchery Biologist, U.S. Fish and Wildlife Service, P.O. Box 398, Whiteriver, Arizona 85941 (602-338-4765).

ARKANSAS: Hatchery Biologist, Greers Ferry National Fish Hatchery, Rt. 4, Box 296, Heber Springs, Arkansas 72543 (501-362-6038). Fishery Biologist, Arkansas Game and Fish Commission, P.O. Box 178, Lonoke, Arkansas 72086 (501-676-7963). U.S. Fish and Wildlife Service, Fish Farming Experiment Station, Stuttgart, Arkansas 72160 (501-673-8761).

CALIFORNIA: Monterey Bay Research Institute, 2700 Chanteleer Ave., Santa Cruz, California 95065 (408-476-9497). School of Natural Resources, Dept. of Fisheries, Humboldt State University, Arcata, California 95521 (707-826-3954). Fish Disease Laboratory, California Dept. of Fish and Game, 407 W. Line St., Bishop, California 93514 (714-872-2791). Fish Disease Unit, California Dept. of Fish and Game, Mojave River Hatchery, P.O. Box 938, Victorville, California 92392 (714-245-9981). Fish Disease Laboratory, California Dept. of Fish and Game, 2111 Nimbus Rd., Rancho Cordova, California 95670 (916-355-0809).

COLORADO: Fish Disease Control Center, U.S. Fish and Wildlife Service, P.O. Box 917, Fort Morgan, Colorado 80701 (301-867-9497). Fisheries Research Center, P.O. Box 2287, Fort Collins, Colorado 80522 (303-484-2836). Colorado State University, Diagnostic Laboratory, Fort Collins, Colorado 80523 (303-491-6128).

---

*"Principal Diseases of Farm-Raised Catfish," Bulletin 225. Auburn, Alabama: Agricultural Experiment Station, 1979.

DISTRICT OF COLUMBIA: Fishery Biologist, National Aquarium, Commerce Bldg., U.S. Dept. of the Interior, U.S. Fish and Wildlife Service, Washington, D.C. 20230 (202-967-2826).

FLORIDA: Fish Doctor Laboratory, Inc., 9225 Bay Plaza Blvd., Suite 408, Tampa, Florida 33619 (812-626-1805).

GEORGIA: North Georgia Diagnostic Assistance Laboratory, College of Veterinary Medicine, University of Georgia, Athens, Georgia 30602.

IDAHO: Rangen Research Hatchery, Fish Pathologist Laboratory, Rt. 1, Hagerman, Idaho 83332 (208-837-4464). Fisheries Resources, College of Fisheries, Forestry, Wildlife and Range Sciences, University of Idaho, Moscow, Idaho 83843 (208-885-6336). Dwarshak National Fish Hatchery, Box 251, Ahsahka, Idaho 83520 (208-476-4591). Idaho Dept. of Fish and Game, Fish Disease Laboratory, Hagerman State Hatchery, Hagerman, Idaho 83332 (208-837-6672).

ILLINOIS: Fisheries Research Laboratory, Southern Illinois University, Carbondale, Illinois 62901 (618-536-7761).

IOWA: State Conservation Commission, Big Spring Hatchery, Elkader, Iowa 52043.

KANSAS: H-D Fish Farm, Rt. 1, Box 71A, Cheney, Kansas 67025 (316-542-3686).

LOUISIANA: Fisheries Biologist, Louisiana Wildlife and Fisheries Commission, P.O. Box 4004, District II, Monroe, Louisiana 71203 (318-343-4044).

MICHIGAN: Fish Pathologist, Wolf Lake State Fish Hatchery, R.R. No. 1, Mattawn, Michigan 49071 (616-668-2132).

MINNESOTA: Fish and Wildlife Pathologist, Dept. of Natural Resources, 390 Continental Office Bldg., St. Paul, Minnesota 55155 (612-296-3043).

MISSISSIPPI: Area Extension Wildlife and Fisheries Specialist, Stoneville, Mississippi 38776 (601-686-9311). Fishery Biologist, U.S. Fish and Wildlife Service, P.O. Box 4389, 2531 N. West Street, Jackson, Mississippi 39216 (601-354-6089). Leader, Extension Wildlife and Fisheries, P.O. Box 5405, Mississippi State, Mississippi 39762 (601-325-3174).

MISSOURI: Missouri Department of Conservation, 666 Primrose Lane, Springfield, Missouri 65807 (417-883-6677). Missouri Dept. of Conservation, Blind Pony Hatchery, Rt. 2, Sweet Springs, Missouri 65351 (816-335-4531). U.S. Fish and Wildlife Service, Fish Pesticide Research Laboratory, Rt. 1, Columbia, Missouri 65201 (314-442-2271).

NEW MEXICO: Pathologist, Rainbow Acres Trout Farm, P.O. Box 29, McIntosh, New Mexico 87032 (505-384-2944).

NORTH CAROLINA: Fish Hatchery Biologist, P.O. Box 158, Pisgah Forest, North Carolina 28768 (704-877-3122).

OHIO: Biologist, 6354 Low Rd., Lisbon, Ohio 44432 (216-227-3242). Ohio Cooperative Fish Unit, 1735 Neil Ave., Columbus, Ohio 43210.

OKLAHOMA: Warm Water Hatchery Biologist Center, National Fish Hatchery, Tishomingo, Oklahoma 73460 (405-384-5463).

OREGON: Chief Pathologist, Oregon Dept. of Fish and Wildlife, 17330 S.E. Evelyn St., Clackamas, Oregon 97015. Dept. of Microbiology, Nash Hall, Oregon State University, Corvallis, Oregon 97331 (503-754-4441).

PENNSYLVANIA: Fisheries Biologist, 850 E. Schuy Kill Rd., EC2, Pottstown, Pennsylvania 19464 (215-327-2631).

SOUTH DAKOTA: Fisheries Management Specialist, 3305 W. South St., Rapid City, South Dakota 57701 (605-394-2391).

TEXAS: Veterinary Pathologist, Texas Veterinary Medical Diagnostic Laboratory, Drawer 3040, College Station, Texas 77840 (713-845-3414). Extension Fish Disease Specialist, Dept. of Wildlife and Fisheries, Room 202, Nagle Hall, Texas A&M University, College Station, Texas 77843 (713-845-7471). Dept. of Veterinary Microbiology, College of Veterinary Medicine, Texas A&M University, College Station, Texas 77843 (713-845-5941). U.S. Fish and Wildlife Service, Fish Cultural Development Center, P.O. Box 786, San Marcos, Texas 78666 (512-392-0983).

UTAH: 153 WIDB, Zoology Dept., Brigham Young University, Provo, Utah 84602 (801-374-1211).

WISCONSIN: Dept. of Natural Resources, Technical Investigation Section, 3911 Fish Hatchery Rd., Madison, Wisconsin 55711 (608-266-0816). Fish Hatchery Biologist Laboratory, U.S. Fish and Wildlife Service, P.O. Box 252, Genoa, Wisconsin 54632 (608-689-2730).

WYOMING: Wyoming Game and Fish Laboratory, University of Wyoming, P.O. Box 3312, Laramie, Wyoming 82071 (307-745-5865).

Selected Bibliography

Allain, Robert E., and W. R. Morrison. "Costs and Returns for Producing Catfish Fingerlings." Fayetteville, Arkansas: Agricultural Experiment Station, Bulletin 831, November 1978.

Avault, James W. "Channel Catfish Feeding." Baton Rouge: Louisiana State University, 1967.

Avault, James W. "Oxygen Depletion in Channel Catfish Ponds." Baton Rouge: Louisiana State University, 1968.

"A Basic Guide to Buying Fish." Memphis: Dixie Mills Company (n.d.).

Boussu, Marvin F. "New 'Live Car' Improves Catfish Harvesting and Handling." Washington: U.S. Department of the Interior, December 1967.

Boyd, Claude E., and Frank Lichtkoppler. "Water Quality Management in Pond Fish Culture." Auburn, Alabama: International Center for Aquaculture, Research and Development Series No. 22, 1979.

Brown, E. Evan, and John B. Gratzek. *Fish Farming Handbook*. Westport, Connecticut, Avi Publishing Company, Inc., 1980.

Brown, E. Evan, M. G. La Plante, and L. H. Covey. "A Synopsis of Catfish Farming." Athens: University of Georgia, Bulletin 69, 1969.

Burke, Robert L., and John E. Waldrop. "An Economic Analysis of Producing Pond-Raised Catfish for Food in Mississippi." Mississippi State, Mississippi: Agricultural and Forestry Experiment Station, 1978.

"Catfish Processing . . . A Rising Southern Industry." Washington: U.S. Department of Agriculture, Agricultural Economic Report No. 224, 1972.

"Commercial Fish Farming Conference." Stillwater: Oklahoma State University, 1968.

"Controlling Plant and Animal Pests in Farm Ponds with Copper Sulfate." New York: Phelps Dodge Refining Corporation (n.d.).

Crawford, Kenneth W., and E. W. McCoy. "Budgeting for Selected Aquacultural Enterprises." Auburn, Alabama: Agricultural Experiment Station, Bulletin 495, October 1977.

Davis, James T., and Janice S. Hughes. "Channel Catfish Farming in Louisiana." Baton Rouge: Louisiana Wildlife and Fisheries Commission, Wildlife Education Bulletin No. 98, 1970.

Fichter, George S., and Phil Francis. *Guide to Fresh- and Salt-Water Fishing.* New York: Western Publishing Company, Inc., 1965.

"Fish Farming: A Commercial Realty." Portland, Oregon: U.S. Department of Agriculture, Soil Conservation Service, 1969.

Gray, D. Leroy. "The Biology of Channel Catfish Production." Fayetteville: Arkansas Agricultural Extension Service, Circular No. 535, May 1969.

Greenfield, J. E. "Economic and Business Dimensions of the Catfish Farming Industry." Ann Arbor, Michigan: Bureau of Commercial Fisheries, January 1970.

Greenfield, J. E. "Some Economic Characteristics of Pond-Raised Catfish Enterprises." Ann Arbor, Michigan: Bureau of Commercial Fisheries, June 1969.

Grizzel, Roy A., Olan W. Dillon, and Edward G. Sullivan. "Catfish Farming: A New Farm Crop." Washington: U.S. Department of Agriculture, Farmers' Bulletin No. 2244, November 1969.

Grizzle, John M., and Wilmer A. Rogers. "Anatomy and Histology of the Channel Catfish." Auburn, Alabama: Agricultural Experiment Station, 1976.

Harris, Wayne. "Channel Catfish Farming in Arkansas." Unpublished Thesis, Southern Methodist University, July 1968.

Kennamer, Earl Franklin. "Catfish for Fun and Cash." Auburn: Alabama Cooperative Extension Service, Circular 528, 1959.

Lagler, Karl F. *Freshwater Fishery Biology.* Dubuque, Iowa: William C. Brown Company, Publishers, 1956.

Lagler, Karl F., John E. Bardach, and Robert R. Miller. *Ichthyology.* New York: John Wiley & Sons, Inc., 1962.

Lee, Jasper S. *Catfish Farming . . . A Reference Unit.* State College: Mississippi State University, Curriculum Coordinating Unit, 1971.

Lopinot, A. C. "Pond Fish and Fishing in Illinois." Springfield: Illinois Department of Conservation (n.d.).

Lopinot, Al, and Ray Fisher. "Potentials of Catfish Farming in Illinois." Springfield: Illinois Department of Conservation (n.d.).

Mack, Jerry. *Catfish Farming Handbook.* San Angelo, Texas: Educator Books, Inc., 1971.

Madewell, Carl E., and Billy B. Carroll. "Intensive Catfish Production and Marketing." Muscle Shoals, Alabama: Tennessee Valley Authority, 1969.

Maloy, Charles R., and Harvey Willoughby. "Rearing Marketable Channel Catfish in Ponds." Washington: U.S. Department of the Interior, RP-31, January 1967.

McCoy, E. W., and J. L. Boutwell. "Preparation of Financial Budget for Fish Production." Auburn, Alabama: Agricultural Experiment Station, Circular 233, March 1977.

Meyer, Fred P. "Parasites of Freshwater Fishes." Washington: U.S. Department of the Interior, FDL-2, February 1966.

Meyer, Fred P. "Parasites of Freshwater Fishes." Washington: U.S. Department of the Interior, FDL-5, 1966.

Meyer, Fred P. "A Review of the Parasites and Diseases of Fishes in Warm-Water Ponds in North America." Rome, Italy: FAO World Symposium on Warm-Water Pond Fish Culture, 1966.

Meyer, Fred P. "Treatment Tips." Stuttgart, Arkansas: Fish Farming Experimental Station, RP-66, June 1968.

"Mississippi Wildlife Conservation Manual." Jackson: Mississippi Game and Fish Commission, 1967.

Murray, Roger D., and Louis F. Twardzik. "Planning Community-Wide Recreation." East Lansing: Michigan State University, Cooperative Extension Service, Extension Bulletin E–684, 1970.

Mustin, Walter Gilbert. "An Integrated Approach to Small Scale Harvesting, Processing, and Marketing Channel Catfish," Master of Science Thesis. Auburn, Alabama: Auburn University, 1979.

"Parasites and Diseases of Warm-Water Fishes." Stuttgart, Arkansas: Fish Farming Experimental Station, May 1969.

Plemmons, Bryan, and James W. Avault, Jr. "Six Tons of Catfish per Acre with Constant Aeration," *Louisiana Agriculture.* Baton Rouge, Louisiana, 1980.

"Proceedings Commercial Fish Farming Conference." Athens: University of Georgia, 1969.

"Proceedings First Annual Kerr Foundation Fish Farming Conference." Poteau, Oklahoma: Kerr Foundation, Inc., 1971.

"Proceedings 1971 Fish Farming Conference and First Annual Convention of Catfish Farmers of Texas." College Station: Texas A&M University, 1971.

"Proceedings of the 1978 Fish Farming Conference." College Station, Texas: Agricultural Extension Service, 1978.

"Proceedings of the 1979 Fish Farming Conference." College Station, Texas: Agricultural Extension Service, 1979.

Plumb, John A., ed. "Principal Diseases of Farm-Raised Catfish." Auburn, Alabama: Agricultural Experiment Station, 1979.

Producing and Marketing Catfish in the Tennessee Valley. Muscle Shoals, Alabama: Tennessee Valley Authority, Bulletin Y-38, 1971.

"Report to the Fish Farmers." Washington: U.S. Department of the Interior, Bureau of Sport Fisheries and Wildlife, February 1970.

Rogers, Bruce D., and Carl E. Madewell, *Catfish Farming—Cost of Producing in the Tennessee Valley.* Muscle Shoals, Alabama: Tennessee Valley Authority, Circular Z-22, 1971.

Schmittou, H. R. "Developments in the Culture of Channel Catfish, *Ictalurus punctatus,* in Cages Suspended in Ponds." Auburn, Alabama: Auburn University, Agricultural Experiment Station, 1969.

Simco, Bill A., and Frank B. Cross. "Factors Affecting Growth and Production of Channel Catfish, *Ictalurus punctatus.*" Lawrence: University of Kansas, 1966.

Smitherman, R. O., Hussein El-Ibiary, and R. E. Reagan. "Genetics and Breeding of Channel Catfish." Auburn, Alabama: Agricultural Experiment Station, Southern Cooperative Series Bulletin 223, October 1978.

Spotte, Stephen H. *Fish and Invertebrate Culture.* New York: John Wiley & Sons, Inc., 1970.

Stickney, R. R., and R. T. Lovell, eds., "Nutrition and Feeding of Channel Catfish." Auburn, Alabama: Agricultural Experiment Station, 1977.

Sullivan, E. G. "Technical Notes—Catfish Production." Jackson, Mississippi: U.S. Department of Agriculture, Soil Conservation Service, 1967.

Twardzik, Louis F., and Richard E. Cary. "Liability Protection and Insurance in Rural Recreation Enterprises." East Lansing: Michigan State University, Cooperative Extension Service, Extension Bulletin 580, 1969.

Wellborn, Thomas L. "Aquatic Weed Identification and Control." Mississippi State, Mississippi: Cooperative Extension Service, 1979.

Wellborn, Thomas L., N. N. Fijan, and J. P. Naftel. "Channel Catfish Virus Disease." Washington: U.S. Department of the Interior, FDL–18, August 1969.

Index